ENGLISH TEACHER'S GREAT BOOKS ACTIVITIES KIT

60 Ready-to-Use Activity Packets Featuring Classic, Popular & Current Literature

GARY ROBERT MUSCHLA

THE CENTER FOR APPLIED RESEARCH IN EDUCATION
West Nyack, New York 10995

10 9 8 7 6 5 4 3 2 1

Library of Congress Cataloging-in-Publication Data

Muschla, Gary Robert.
    English teacher's great books activities kit : 60 ready-to-use
activity packets featuring classic, popular, and current literature
/ Gary Robert Muschla.
        p.   cm.
    ISBN 0–87628–854–9
    1. English literature—Study and teaching—Aids and devices.
2. Literature—Study and teaching—Aids and devices.   3. Activity
programs in education.   I. Title
PR35.M87   1994
820'.71'273—dc20   93–44779
                                                                    CIP

ISBN 0-87628-854-9

**THE CENTER FOR APPLIED
RESEARCH IN EDUCATION**
Business Information & Publishing Division
West Nyack, New York 10995
Simon & Schuster, A Paramount Communications Company

Printed in the United States of America

❈ *Dedication* ❈

As always, for Judy and Erin.

❦ *About the Author* ❦

Gary Robert Muschla received his B.A. and M.A.T. degrees from Trenton State College in New Jersey. He teaches at Appleby School in Spotswood, New Jersey, where he has specialized in the teaching of reading and writing, conducted writing workshops for teachers and students, and edited magazines of students' writing.

In addition to his 19 years as a classroom teacher, Mr. Muschla has been a successful freelance writer, editor, and ghostwriter. He is a member of the Authors Guild, the Authors League of America, the National Writers Club, and the Associated Business Writers of America.

Mr. Muschla has also authored three other resources for teachers: the *Writing Workshop Activities Kit: Ready-to-Use Worksheets and Enrichment Lessons for Grades 4-9* (The Center for Applied Research in Education, 1989), *The Writing Teacher's Book of Lists* (Prentice Hall, 1991), and the *Writing Workshop Survival Kit* (The Center for Applied Research in Education, 1993).

❉ *Acknowledgments* ❉

I'd like to thank John C. Orlick, my principal, for the support he has always given me. My appreciation also to Julia Rhodes, our district's language arts supervisor, and my colleagues, for their encouragement and help.

Special thanks go to my wife Judy for her work in choosing and arranging the artwork throughout this book.

I'd also like to thank Brian Blatz for his help in research, and for sharing his understanding and insight of literature.

My thanks to Donna Cooper, my typist, who somehow managed to keep the manuscript updated despite all the little (but nagging) revisions that I always seem to make right up until production.

I greatly appreciate the work and suggestions of Susan Kolwicz, my editor, who helped me to fashion this book into what I hope will be a useful resource for teachers. Thanks also to Zsuzsa Neff, my production editor, and Dee Coroneos my desktop editor, whose efforts resulted in a book design that is attractive and easy to use.

And finally, I'd like to thank my students whose enthusiasm, curiosity, and friendship over the years have been a wonderful source of inspiration.

❧ *About English Instruction* ❧

I like to argue that learning English is crucial to the overall success of any student. When a student understands the skills vital to reading and writing in the English language, he or she has acquired the ability to communicate—to express, share, and discuss ideas. Effective communication is essential to every other discipline.

While there are many ways to teach English, probably the best is through a linkage of reading and writing. The research clearly indicates that students who read well also write well, and students who enjoy writing usually are good readers. Reading and writing are the foundation of effective English instruction.

The research also indicates that students learn the skills of language best when the skills are taught in relationship and context. Literature, therefore, is an excellent tool for teaching English, because students learn the skills for language in their relationship to an entire story rather than in isolation on a drill sheet where there is little or no contextual meaning. Moreover, when you use literature to teach English, you are opening the world to your students, giving them the chance to glimpse new places, contemplate fresh ideas, and imagine things of which they had no previous inkling.

This resource provides you with the opportunity to teach English skills through exciting literature that covers various genres, themes, and cultures. Not only will you be teaching the skills for effective reading and writing, but you will be helping your students to experience the world. My best wishes to you as you begin.

❧ *How to Use This Resource* ❧

The *English Teacher's Great Books Activities Kit* is divided into two major parts. Part I offers classroom management strategies for the teaching of reading and writing that can help you make your teaching efficient and effective. Part II contains teaching suggestions and reading and writing activities for 60 novels (and plays), selected especially for their relevance and use in middle and high school English classes.

Part I contains Sections 1 through 3, and provides detailed information on topics such as management, setting up your classroom, organizing your reading and writing instruction for the whole class, groups, or individuals, building a classroom library, the writing process, and evaluation and grading. There is also information on whole language for teachers who are using this approach. These sections contain various reproducibles for both students and teachers. (You may prefer to make transparencies of some and use them on overhead projectors.) I suggest that you read through Part I first, and use the materials that best suit your needs and program.

Part II, Sections 4 through 6, contains materials for 60 novels (and plays), organized into three groups: grades 7-8, 9-10, and 11-12. Based on the specific needs and abilities of your students, however, the grade level designations may vary. The material for each novel includes information and teaching suggestions for you, a reproducible writing assignment, and reproducibles for questions, projects and activities for the students. There are also questions that extend into other subject areas.

You have several options for teaching the novels. The material for each novel is suitable for whole-class, group, or individual learning. All of the materials for students are reproducible. You may assign all of the questions or just some; you may form groups and assign each a different project. You may even work with another teacher. For example, as you teach the novel, students may work on the "Curriculum Connections" with a teacher from another discipline. If you select some of the novels for whole-class reading, you might provide students with a list of the remaining books and encourage them to read these titles individually. You can then make packets of the reproducibles available to your students to work on as they go along.

The more than 180 reproducibles throughout this resource contain numerous activities and projects. They will provide your students with a variety of interesting and challenging assignments for a broad range of literature, which will help make your teaching easier and more effective.

❀ Contents ❀

PART II. READY-TO-USE ACTIVITIES

❀ *Chart for Interdisciplinary Activities* ❀

While many of the activities in Part II touch upon other subject areas, the questions for each book appearing under "Curriculum Connections" are designed for interdisciplinary development. The following chart identifies specific questions for each book that can be easily used in other subject areas. In many cases, there is more than one question for each category marked.

Key: SS - Social Studies, Sci - Science, M - Math, A - the Arts, including music, dance, and artwork.

		SS	Sci	M	A
1.	*Homecoming*	x	x		
2.	*One Fat Summer*	x	x		x
3.	*Call It Courage*	x	x		x
4.	*The Outsiders*	x			
5.	*A Wizard of Earthsea*	x			x
6.	*Roll of Thunder, Hear My Cry*	x			x
7.	*The Chocolate War*	x			x
8.	*The Slave Dancer*	x			x
9.	*The Princess Bride*	x			x
10.	*Julie of the Wolves*	x	x		x
11.	*The Contender*	x			x
12.	*The Sword in the Stone*	x			x
13.	*The Upstairs Room*	x			x
14.	*The Pigman*		x	x	x
15.	*Sing Down the Moon*	x	x		x
16.	*I Will Call It Georgie's Blues*	x			x
17.	*Durango Street*	x			x
18.	*House of Stairs*		x		x
19.	*Home Before Dark*	x			
20.	*Farewell to Manzanar*		x		
21.	*A Separate Peace*	x			x
22.	*To Kill a Mockingbird*	x	x		
23.	*Animal Farm*	x			x
24.	*A Tale of Two Cities*	x			
25.	*Of Mice and Men*	x			x

		SS	Sci	M	A
26.	*I Know Why the Caged Bird Sings*	x			x
27.	*After the First Death*	x			x
28.	*Dicey's Song*	x		x	x
29.	*I Never Promised You a Rose Garden*		x		x
30.	*Flowers for Algernon*		x		x
31.	*Hiroshima*	x			x
32.	*The Miracle Worker* (play)		x		x
33.	*Dragonwings*	x	x		x
34.	*Running Loose*	x			x
35.	*Flowers in the Attic*	x	x	x	x
36.	*The Adventures of Huckleberry Finn*	x			x
37.	*Something Wicked This Way Comes*	x	x		x
38.	*The Pearl*	x	x		x
39.	*The Hitchhiker's Guide to the Galaxy*	x	x		x
40.	*Night*	x			x
41.	*Lord of the Flies*	x	x		
42.	*The Scarlet Letter*	x			x
43.	*All Quiet on the Western Front*	x			x
44.	*Wuthering Heights*	x			x
45.	*Brave New World*	x	x		x
46.	*Fahrenheit 451*	x			x
47.	*A Raisin in the Sun* (play)	x			x
48.	*Watership Down*		x		x
49.	*A Little Love*	x			x
50.	*Dune*		Sci	x	x
51.	*Gone with the Wind*	x			x
52.	*Native Son*	x			x
53.	*Jane Eyre*	x			x
54.	*Dinner at the Homesick Restaurant*	x	x		
55.	*Slaughterhouse-Five*	x	x		x
56.	*One Flew Over the Cuckoo's Nest*	x	x		
57.	*The House on Mango Street*	x			x
58.	*Fallen Angels*	x			x
59.	*Hamlet* (play)	x			
60.	*Memory*	x	x		x

PART I

MANAGING YOUR ENGLISH CLASSES

❧ 1 ❧

An Overview

There are many kinds of English classes. Whether it is called a traditional class, literature-based program, or whole language, each one reflects the philosophy and personality of its teacher. You should develop your classes in a way that meets your needs and the needs of your students. While individual English classes may differ, all share many common components. See the "Elements of Effective English Classes," which follows.

In a well-run English class, students use language even as they learn language. In the typical class, reading is taught through the use of various types of literature. Writing is done for meaningful purposes, frequently on self-selected topics. The connection between reading and writing is a strong one and becomes one of the interweaving threads of the class.

Effective English classes are filled with activity. There is much cooperation, collaboration, and sharing. Students learn language by observing others using it well, and also by using it themselves. The classes are busy places where students work alone, interact with each other, and confer individually and in groups with the teacher. An entire class may listen to you present a mini-lesson, and then break into groups to discuss a novel that the students are reading. Depending on how you organize your classes, all students may be reading the same novel or they may be reading different novels. Small groups of students may be reading a particular novel. In writing, students may be working on a variety of different topics. Some of these topics may grow out of their reading, while others may be separate topics that the students want to write about. Some students may be writing material for a class publication. Successful English classes offer almost limitless possibilities for learning.

Of course, classroom rules, routines, and standards of behavior must be set and maintained. Methods of evaluation must be determined to insure that course requirements are met. You must decide on how you will run your classes, based on district guidelines and your objectives and expectations.

As their teacher, you will provide the environment where your students can become immersed in all aspects of language. Through the effective management of your classroom, you will offer your students the wonder and power of language in context and meaning.

ELEMENTS OF EFFECTIVE ENGLISH CLASSES

Although English classes may differ because of the personality of the teacher and the particular needs of students, all effective English classes share many of the following:

* Language is respected and celebrated.
* Language skills are taught in context.
* Literature is used meaningfully.
* A variety of reading materials is available.
* Various types of reading and writing are studied.
* Students have some choice in what they read.
* Students are encouraged to generate their own topics for writing.
* Writing is purposeful and on meaningful topics.
* Writing is treated as a process of stages—prewriting, drafting, revising, editing, and publishing (sharing).
* Students assume responsibility for their learning.
* Cooperation and collaboration are encouraged.
* Language is used as a tool for learning even as it is being learned.
* Students and teachers become partners in learning.
* Students understand how they will be evaluated.
* Evaluation is consistent.
* Goals and objectives are made clear to students.
* Sufficient time is allotted for learning.
* Striving toward excellence is required.

The Whole Language Class

No definition can accurately describe whole language. Nor is there a specific program or step-by-step methodology that can be labeled whole language. Rather, whole language is an approach to instruction that focuses on the teaching of language skills *in context*. Instead of breaking language learning down into isolated skills that fit neatly into a day's lesson, the whole language teacher presents language "whole" in real and relevant relationships. Most good English teachers do that no matter what type of program they teach.

At the core of the whole language movement is the belief, based on research and observation, that language is learned more effectively when it is meaningful and functional. Quite simply, students learn to read best by reading, and they learn to write best by writing. Few English teachers would disagree.

Because the whole language class is nontraditional in its structure, should you decide to teach in this manner, you will assume new roles. See "The Role of the Whole Language Teacher." No longer will you be a mere provider of information who lectures, leads discussions, and assigns homework on isolated skills in English texts or workbooks, but instead you'll be the manager of learning in your classroom. Much of your teaching will be via mini-lessons. You will work with the whole class, small groups, and individuals. The greatest amount of class time will be spent on reading and writing. You will model many of the skills your students will encounter.

As a whole language teacher, you will become a facilitator and resource. Instead of "spoon-feeding" facts in small, bite-sized pieces, you will guide your students as they discover language for themselves. By presenting students with a setting in which they find meaningful uses for language, you will be offering them the opportunity for learning.

During the class you circulate, meet with students, and maintain an orderly environment. Your tasks will be many and varied. Based on how you structure your class, you might speak with individuals about the novels they are reading, or meet with small groups. You might ask probing questions of a student to help him see the author's purpose in a story, or you might listen to a student share her ideas for a piece of writing. From there you might sit in on a literature response group and model the appropriate behavior. For many teachers, their whole language classes become workshops for students in which the opportunities for learning and individual growth are boundless.

Using Mini-Lessons in Your Classes

An effective way to teach concepts and skills in any English class is to use mini-lessons. Since the major portion of class time should be spent allowing students to read, write, and confer, mini-lessons offer an efficient way of teaching specific language skills, techniques, and strategies. They provide a time at the beginning of the period when the class comes together as an entire group.

Mini-lessons also can be used with small groups. If you find that some students in your class are having trouble with a particular skill—for instance, an author's choice of point of view in a novel—you might offer a mini-lesson to just these students. It makes no sense to spend the valuable class time of other students on a skill they have already mastered.

THE ROLE OF THE WHOLE LANGUAGE TEACHER

The role of the whole language teacher is a varied one. Each day you may do any or all of the following:

* Guide a literature response group.
* Affirm students' efforts in identifying a story's theme.
* Help a student select a book to read.
* Encourage a reluctant reader to read.
* Share your impressions of a good book with students.
* Answer students' questions.
* Ask students questions.
* Help a student find a topic for writing.
* Remind students of class rules and routines.
* Maintain an orderly learning environment.
* Plan with students the publication of a class magazine.
* Help a student writing on a word processor.
* Help a student create an idea cluster for writing.
* Train parent volunteers to help maintain book inventories.
* Confer with students about writing.
* Offer revision strategies to a student.
* Order books to build a class library.
* Meet with peer groups to confer about writing.
* Help students focus topics for research papers.
* Teach a mini-lesson on a specific writing skill.
* Teach a mini-lesson on a reading strategy.
* Read a favorite piece of poetry to the class.
* Read a passage of a favorite book to the class.
* Read a piece of your own writing to the class.
* Listen to a student explain how he or she will open a story.
* Plan an interdisciplinary thematic unit with other teachers.

The typical mini-lesson takes less than ten minutes, and should focus on one skill. A mini-lesson might share a reading strategy, point out the use of imagery in novels, discuss a particular genre, or demonstrate a specific writing skill. As you get to know your students and come to see their strengths and weaknesses, you will likely design mini-lessons for their needs.

While the information shared through some mini-lessons will be used right away, for example, the theme of a particular novel, others, like how to use italics in writing, may not be used until students need that specific skill. You will find that once a mini-lesson is presented, you will refer to it as necessary when you confer with students. As the year progresses, the information shared through mini-lessons will build an impressive wealth of knowledge about language.

The best English classes are those built on the way people actually learn language. When a young child first begins to talk, he or she uses language to communicate. The child doesn't acquire the skills of language in isolated parts, but rather in the context of communication in order to express needs. The use and learning of language is meaningful. Effective English teachers recognize that natural process and seek to continue it in the classroom.

2

Managing Your English Classes

Effective management in any English class begins with a basic understanding of how language is learned. Language is learned best through reading, writing, speaking, and listening. Even as the need for language increases, learning and language development is individual. Everyone learns the skills and use of English in his or her own time. All babies don't utter "da-da" when they're the same age; but all babies eventually learn to talk. (By two or three most exasperated parents feel their kids talk too much.) Focus your program on the individual as much as possible. Allow each of your students to start at his or her own level and progress from there.

A successful English class is a place of vigorous ideas. As you develop your routines and methods, work hard to make your classes forums where students feel comfortable and confident to express their thoughts. Insure that opinions are respected and valued, and efforts toward excellence are supported and applauded by all.

Since the purpose of language is communication, which transcends all fields of learning, always be ready to bring other subjects and disciplines into your classes. Look to link up with math teachers, the arts, sciences and social studies. Working with teachers across the curriculum on interdisciplinary projects enhances the importance of language in the eyes of students and shows them that language is vital to communication and understanding.

Developing Your Curriculum

In today's English classes teachers and students often have the chance to make decisions about and plan their curriculums. The degree to which you do this, of course, depends on your personal tastes as well as the requirements of your department. When it comes to determining what kinds of topics to study, consider seeking the input of your students. The advantage of this is clear. When students help select topics for study, they gain a measure of ownership in the learning process. They will likely be more interested in studying topics they suggested, and this makes your classroom management easier.

There are several ways to obtain student suggestions for topics. Probably the most direct is to brainstorm ideas with the class. At the beginning of the school year, explain to your students that you would like their suggestions for topics to study. As they offer ideas, write them on an overhead projector or the board. A class of 25 can quickly generate several possible topics. After compiling the topics, eliminate those that you feel could not be developed into solid units, and allow students to vote from among the rest. You might want to let them vote the next day, for this will give you some time to reflect on the topics.

Another method of gathering students' ideas for topics is to ask students for their input by way of a questionnaire. See "A Questionnaire of Student Interests," which is included in this section. Distribute copies of the questionnaire and ask students to complete it. Afterward, as you review the information, look for some common interests or trends. (It's not necessary to tabulate the responses for each question.) As trends emerge—for example, the same books or movies keep coming up—note them. This will give you clues to the interests of your students. If you have several classes, note the trends and interests for each, and then compare them. You can then write a list of several possible topics. You might distribute this list to students and let them pick their top three choices. From that list you should be able to identify good topics. To reduce the workload, have students compile the information. You might even work with the math teacher on this and have students graph the results. Using computers for the graphics is a way to include yet another discipline.

In addition to having students select topics, gather topics from teachers of other content areas. You can do this at department meetings, informally in the teacher's room, or leave a brief note in teachers' mail boxes. Obtaining topic suggestions from teachers of other subjects will help you to develop a list of interdisciplinary selections.

The key to selecting any topic is that it provides a rich language experience. Topics may be developed into units that run two to three weeks; thus you will cover several topics throughout the year. See "Possible Topics for a Core Curriculum," which is included here. The list of topics provided offers opportunities to study various human conditions, issues and genres. If you were studying science fiction, for example, you might have your class read *Dune* by Herbert, and then have students select another science fiction book to read individually. A writing activity could be class book reviews. If you were doing a unit on plays, you might have students read Shakespeare's *Romeo and Juliet* or perhaps a modern play. A culminating activity might be to encourage students to form groups and write and perform their own plays. If you were doing a theme-based unit on minority authors, you might assign *Native Son* by Wright and then have students research the racial problems that affect the United States. You could organize debate teams and examine the causes of our problems and their possible solutions. Such units are a marvelous way for students to learn language even as they are using it.

Building a Positive Climate

A successful English class is distinctive in its emphasis on language learning. The physical arrangement of the classroom and the atmosphere within it help to create a positive climate. Although secondary teachers often are not able to control much about their classroom setting—especially if they have a different room for each section—there is much they can do about the atmosphere of their classes. See "Promoting a Positive Atmosphere," which follows.

Before students can be expected to do well in any class, they must clearly understand its goals and objectives. The tone you establish on the first day of school can do much to set the climate of your classes. Try to handle all the preliminaries as soon as possible and get your students into routines.

A QUESTIONNAIRE OF STUDENT INTERESTS

To help me make this class meaningful to you, I'd like to know some of your interests, especially in reading and writing. Please answer the following questions.

1. What is your favorite book? _____

2. What are your favorite types of books? _____

_____

3. What is your favorite TV show? _____

_____

4. What is your favorite movie? _____

_____

5. Do you like to write? _____ If yes, what types of writing do you like to do (stories, articles, poems, etc.)? _____

_____

_____

6. Name three things you like to do. _____

_____

7. Name three things you dislike doing. _____

_____

8. Name three things you would like to find out more about. ___

_____

9. Name three things you worry about. _____

_____

POSSIBLE TOPICS FOR A CORE CURRICULUM

— *UNIT THEMES* —

Relationships
Nature
Struggle for Life
Poetry
   Types
   Individual Authors
Challenges
True Stories
The Newspaper
The Environment
Minority Authors
Survival
Competition
Modern Essays
Breaking Away
Winning/Losing

Growing Up/Coming of Age
War
Strivings of Minorities
Strange and True
Values
Change
Heroes/Heroines
Sports
Short Stories
The Future
Women Authors
Conflict
Beyond Reality
The Classics
Exploring
Dilemmas

— *GENRES* —

Mystery, Suspense,
Detective
Romance
Realistic Fiction
Biographies
Autobiographies
Comedy, Humor
Historical

Adventure
Westerns
Science Fiction and Fantasy
Mythology, Folklore
Plays
Horror
Screenplays

11

PROMOTING A POSITIVE ATMOSPHERE

There are many things you can do to promote a positive atmosphere in your classes. Here are just a few:

- Encourage the use of language by providing a variety of purposeful language experiences. Remember that language is best learned by using language.

- Encourage independence. Encourage students to "do" for themselves—choose books to read, find writing topics, revise and edit their own writing, learn the new skills necessary to get through difficult material.

- Establish and maintain effective routines.

- Create a class which is an open forum for sharing ideas.

- Set standards for completing work. Make sure that students clearly understand course requirements.

- Set clear standards for behavior.

- Encourage cooperation and sharing.

- Maintain a belief that all students in your class can learn. Express this belief to students frequently through your words and actions.

- Encourage students to assume responsibility for their learning.

- Model the behaviors you want your students to adopt. Read, draft, write, and edit yourself in class, and show students how you use language in your professional life.

- Accept that learning is individual. Students will arrive in your class with different skills and will progress at different rates.

- Adopt teaching methods whereby you build on the strengths of a student even while correcting weaknesses.

First, explain to your students that they will be taking part in an English class in which they will learn reading and writing in meaningful ways. You should also discuss how the class will be organized, for example, how much class time will be spent on reading, on writing, whether students will work individually, in groups, or a combination of both. You might also wish to discuss class rules and behavior. If you find it helpful, distribute copies of or project "Student Responsibilities," which follows. After that describe your schedule—for example, which days you will be meeting for reading and writing—and also explain your grading system and course requirements. (See "Evaluation" later in this section for information on grading and evaluating reading and writing.)

The first day is the time to start building a positive atmosphere. Remember that even after having established routines, you'll need to remind students of procedures and appropriate behavior. Effective modeling is essential. You should frequently model suitable behavior in various activities, for example, by sitting in and sharing with groups. Students take cues from their teachers, and your modeling can make it easier for them to understand the behaviors you expect. The time period for students to become familiar and comfortable with the class might take a week or two to several weeks.

Once you have established effective routines, remain consistent. It is in classes with predictable, steady patterns that learning flourishes.

Setting Up the Room

If you are one of those fortunate secondary teachers who has his or her own room throughout the day, you can do wonderful things to make it a learning center. Even if you must share a room, or travel throughout the day, you still can do some of the suggestions that follow.

No matter what type of room you have, it should be set up so that students can read, write, confer, and work cooperatively. You might arrange one corner for partner conferences, and another as a reference section, or set up a part of the room to house writer's supplies. If you have computers or word processors, you might set them against the back or side wall, leaving the rest of the room for whole-class, group, and individual work. If your classroom is very small, or you can't section it off, you might have students confer in the hallway, just outside the door. (Before doing this, however, check with your principal about your school's policy and regulations. Some districts, for example, require that students always be supervised by a teacher when in class. A hallway, even if it is just beyond the door, might not be acceptable.)

Ideally, you should replace desks with tables, which are more conducive to group activities; however, it's easy to cluster four desks to make a table. For large group activities, have your students form their chairs and desks into a U-shape or semi-circle. Such arrangements break down barriers and promote a sense of belonging.

Any English class needs language materials. Try to fill your classes with as many books, magazines, newspapers, posters, and examples of print as possible. Utilize bulletin boards to highlight items about language, as well as to display the work of your students. In particular, highlight things like the "Book of the Week," and the "Author of the Week" (which might be a professional or a student). If you run out of space in the room, use hallway displays.

STUDENT RESPONSIBILITIES

You can help make this English class a successful and exciting learning environment by assuming the following responsibilities and attitudes:

* Recognize the importance of learning language; respect and celebrate language.

* Use language even as you learn language.

* Understand that language is our means of communication, and is important to every class, not just this one.

* Come to class each day ready to read and write.

* Accept the responsibility of choosing books to read.

* Accept the responsibility of selecting meaningful topics to write about.

* Do your best to learn the skills of language.

* Accept the responsibility of completing work on time.

* Support your peers in the learning process, just as they support you.

* Work with your peers in the learning of reading and writing skills and strategies.

* Try new techniques, methods, and strategies in the learning of reading and writing skills.

* Behave appropriately.

* Take pride in your work and produce the best you can.

* Grow as a reader, writer, and individual.

To reduce your workload, encourage students to be responsible for bulletin boards and

displays. Not only does this give you more time to work directly with students on language skills, but it gives students a sense of ownership and commitment to the class. You can assign volunteers or appoint committees of students to organize bulletin board ideas such as "Top Science Fiction Authors," "Novel of the Week," and "Favorite Books."

While some environments are more easily changed than others, virtually any physical plan can be made to work. It is your outlook, attitude, and efforts that create a climate for learning.

Organizing Your Day

Planning and scheduling are crucial to smooth-running English classes. Unlike many elementary schools where teachers are self-contained or team teach in blocks, either of which offers great flexibility, the set time frames of most of the upper grades present restrictions. However, careful planning can overcome most obstacles.

First, it might be possible to schedule English classes in longer time periods. In many middle schools, for example, reading and English are taught in separate classes. Scheduling such classes back-to-back, or even setting up an environment where the reading and English teachers team teach, can result in tremendous flexibility.

If your classes are set in chunks of 45 to 50 minutes, you can still teach reading and writing effectively. You might, for example, alternate reading and writing workshops in two-week time frames. For two weeks, schedule reading, and then for two weeks do writing. You can easily carry over many of the ideas and concepts covered in reading to the writing that follows it. For example, if you have just covered plays in reading, students could write plays during writing. You will find, however, that many students will naturally write even as they read.

Another method is to do writing three days a week—Monday, Tuesday, and Thursday—and reading on Wednesday and Friday. At less than three meetings per week, it will be hard to sustain interest in writing except for the most motivated students. Moreover, most students find it easier to read a novel at home than it is to write. I prefer this schedule because it offers the advantage of easily linking reading and writing. See "A Sample Schedule" and "A Sample Lesson Plan," both of which follow.

If you prefer more individualization, you can do both reading and writing daily. At any given time, some students will be reading and some will be writing. Students work on their own projects and progress at their own paces.

Providing a Supply of Reading Materials

Essential to any successful English class are reading materials. You might utilize your school library, a classroom library, a public library, or all three. Students need to be able to choose from a variety of fiction and nonfiction books, magazines and newspapers. Various genres and subjects should be included.

A SAMPLE SCHEDULE

Writing:
(Based on a workshop model. Total time, 50 minutes.)

Students enter class and pick up writing folders. (2 minutes to get settled)

Mini-lesson. (8 minutes)

Students write in journals or continue writing works-in-progress, confer with other students or teacher, generate ideas, revise, edit. (25 minutes)

Peer response groups. Students break into prearranged groups, share works-in-progress, and respond to each other's writing. Or a few students share their work with the entire class. (15 minutes)

Students deposit writing folders and leave.

Reading:
(Class is literature-based. Total time, 50 minutes.)

Students enter class and get settled. (2 minutes)

Teacher shares a passage taken from the last assignment and notes the powerful imagery. (10 minutes)

Students break into groups to share journal responses on their last reading, compare and discuss ideas. (15 minutes)

Students read individually, write answers to specific questions in their reading journals, or confer with teacher about their reading. (20 minutes)

Teacher gives the next assignment, including additional questions to be answered in reading journals. (3 minutes)

Students leave.

<u>Note</u>: Times are estimates and can be changed to fit various plans.

A SAMPLE LESSON PLAN

The following lesson plan is based on a schedule in which writing workshop meets three times per week, and reading meets twice. (Note—the reading assignments used for this sample can be found on Activity Packet 2-5 in Part II of this book.)

Monday: Writing Workshop

Mini-lesson: Writing leads. Discussion of the importance of leads. Sharing of examples of leads.

Procedure: Students write in journals and on works-in-progress.

Closure: Peer response groups.

Tuesday: Writing Workshop

Mini-lesson: Writing conclusions for nonfiction. Discussion of the elements of conclusions. Share two examples.

Procedure: Students write in journals and on works-in-progress.

Closure: Peer response groups.

Wednesday: Reading

Mini-lesson: The characterization of George and Lennie in *Of Mice and Men*.

Procedure: Students meet to share and discuss answers in their reading journals. Students will then continue reading novels.

Closure: Assignment, read chapters 1 and 2, and answer questions 1 and 2 on Activity Packet.

Thursday: Writing Workshop

Mini-lesson: Cutting clutter; listing of several "cluttered" phrases on overhead projector.

Procedure: Students write in journals and on works-in-progress.

Closure: Two volunteers read a script for a radio commercial they co-authored.

Friday: Reading

Mini-lesson: Steinbeck's use of foreshadowing.

Procedure: Students meet to share and discuss answers in their reading journals. Students then continue reading novels.

Closure: Assignment, read chapters 3 and 4, and answer questions 3 and 4 on Activity Packet.

Along with providing access to plenty of reading materials for your students, encourage them to borrow books from public libraries and buy their own from local bookstores. Also suggest that they build their own libraries at home. I still have books I read in junior high in my home library. A good book remains a good book.

Utilizing Your School Library

Most middle and high school libraries can service the requirements of English classes, if the librarians know what you need. You should discuss with your librarian how you would like to utilize the school library.

Ideally, the library will be available when you have your classes. To allow students access, you might arrange to send five or six at a time at the beginning of the period to select books. To reduce confusion of who goes when, assign five or six students to go each Monday, an equal number on Tuesday, Wednesday, and so on. A class of 25 to 30 students can easily be serviced in this way. Since students know when they go, they can plan on it. You can give the librarian a list so that she knows who to expect. If your librarian requires passes, let students sign up at the beginning of the period as they walk in. If the library is not open every day during your classes, you might send larger groups and encourage students to go on their free periods or after school.

Insist that students always come to class with at least one book to read. Even if they are reading a novel with the whole class, I require students to have an extra book in case they have free time and want a change of pace.

When I discuss the use of the library with students, I remind them that they are going there to find books, not to gossip or kill time. Browsing for books is fine, but wasting time is not. If I find students spending too much time, I set time limits of 10 to 15 minutes for them to return. You might also enlist the librarian's help in this. Anyone wasting time gets sent back. The message will get across.

Rather than sending students to the library in groups, you might conduct class in the library once every two weeks (of course this depends on the media director's schedule). Meeting in the library will give students ample time to select, return, renew books, and browse. An advantage to this option is that you will be there to help them.

Working closely with the librarian will help her to obtain books to support your teaching. When your students are reading science fiction, for example, your librarian might be able to reserve various appropriate titles. Most librarians will do this if you give them advance notice. To help your librarian help you, explain the needs of your classes, share book lists with her, and inform her of the kinds of books your students prefer. Most librarians are happy to order materials that they know will be used.

Utilizing Public Libraries

If your school library is small or you have only limited access to it, encourage your students to use public libraries. Contact the librarian and let him know that your students will be using the public library to support their studies. You might also tell the librarian what types of books your students like and will be using. Try to work with the head librarian, or at least a person who has the authority to handle your requests. After you establish contact with such a person, continue to work with him or her. This will prevent your requests from becoming lost in channels.

When suggesting to students that they use the public libraries, emphasize the importance of library courtesy. Students should obtain their own library cards. They should treat books with care and return them on time. When in the library, students should be quiet and not disturb others.

Many public libraries will permit you to sign out multiple copies of books for your program if you check with them first. Explain that you are teaching a literature-based English program. Some librarians will be happy to work with you and stock multiple copies of many paperback books you'll be using. When you talk with the librarian, be sure to have a list of book suggestions. If the librarian is unfamiliar with your program, explain the underlying principles and how the library can support your teaching efforts.

Building Your Own Library

Because the use of books is so important to students in English classes, it is helpful to have a classroom library. If you have your own classroom, or share a room with another teacher, you can easily build a classroom library. Even if you don't have your own room, you might be able to build a small library in a spare room, or add your books to the school's library, perhaps stocking them in a separate section.

There are many ways to obtain books. First, try to have the administration provide money to purchase books for your library. If you can't build a classroom library, suggest (and push) to have money allocated to the school librarian so that he or she can purchase the books you'll need.

To raise additional funds, consider organizing bake sales, car washes, and other promotions. Have your students write the advertisements and promotional flyers.

The local PTA can also be a source of funds. Many PTAs give grants to school programs for the purchase of supplies and materials. Few things are as worthy as the purchase of books.

Mail-order book clubs are another avenue through which you can obtain books. Many of these companies offer bonus points, based on the amount of books students buy. The bonus points can frequently be cashed in to obtain books for the class.

If you like to browse through garage sales, rummage sales, used book shops and similar places, you will often find books that are in surprisingly good condition. You might have to plop down your own money, but many schools have petty cash accounts from which teachers are reimbursed for personal purchases of classroom materials. Before buying like this, however, check with your principal to make sure your school has petty cash available and that you will be reimbursed. If you are not reimbursed, but still want to buy books, save any receipts and record the purchases on your income taxes. They're deductible.

Parents, private citizens, and community organizations can be additional sources of used reading materials. Don't hesitate to ask parents and district residents to donate old books. Sometimes doctors and dentists will provide old magazines. Advertise for old books and magazines in school publications, PTA newsletters, and flyers to parents. Encourage students to write the material. Talk up your need for books every chance you get, mentioning it at back-to-school night and parent-teacher conferences. You'll be surprised at how many people will help.

Despite your best efforts at obtaining books, seldom will there be enough money to buy all that you want. If budgets are tight—which they usually are—buy single copies of many books rather than many copies of a few books. Quality and variety should be your objectives in the building of a classroom library.

Choosing Books

Since the funds for book purchases are probably as scarce in your school as they are in mine, you must select your books carefully. Before buying any books, make a list of some that you feel are especially appropriate to your classes. Check with colleagues, language arts supervisors, and librarians. Consult book lists and identify books you feel should be purchased. Aim for books that will satisfy a variety of interests and abilities. For further suggestions on choosing books, consult the "Book Buying Checklist," which follows.

Maintaining the Inventory of Your Books

If you have your own classroom, or share a room with another teacher, it's relatively easy to house a classroom library. It becomes more complicated with several people sharing a room, especially if all are not English teachers. If you travel among many rooms, you'll need to rely on the school library, or house your books in a separate storage area.

If you rely on the school library, your students will follow the library's procedures for obtaining books. However, if you keep books for your students, you will need a simple and efficient system for students to check them out. It is worthwhile to invest in the time it takes to keep a stock of your own books; what can be easier than a student getting a book from a shelf in your room?

If you build a class library, however, management will be a major concern. Most importantly, you'll need to maintain a record of your inventory. I use a Book Inventory Sheet, which is a lined sheet of paper with the words *Author, Title, Number of Copies,* and the *Condition* of the books written across the top. Always tag your books by writing or rubber stamping your name and the book number in the inside cover. This helps you in recording and maintaining your inventory.

When I first began building my library, I simply made a running list of titles according to author. As my stock of books grew, and I began to acquire several books by the same authors, I began using a separate sheet for each author, and kept it in alphabetical order. That soon became tedious, however, and it wasn't long before I transferred my inventory to a computer disk. Now, as new books are acquired, they are simply added to the file which is periodically updated. Virtually any word processing program can be used to set up a file containing the information of the book inventory sheet.

If you keep your inventory on a computer disk, I suggest that you maintain backup copies of the disk, as well as printouts. Power outages, electrical surges, and spilled coffee can ruin a disk, destroying all records of your inventory. I'm in the habit of upgrading the backup every time I enter new books. I save the file on one disk, and then save it on the copy.

BOOK BUYING CHECKLIST

Before purchasing books for your classes, ask yourself the following questions:

1. Have I considered the abilities of my students?

2. Have I considered literature that is interesting, yet challenging?

3. Am I providing a variety of literature for my students?

4. Have I selected both fiction and nonfiction titles?

5. Have I selected literature that depicts males and females in various lifestyles and roles?

6. Have I selected books that avoid stereotyped characters?

7. Have I considered the sensitivities of my students, particularly those of different ethnic groups, and chosen books that relate to them?

8. Have I provided literature that offers a rich experience in reading?

9. Have I selected literature that contains strong themes?

10. Have I selected literature that includes some "classics"?

BOOK SIGN-OUT SHEET

Name	Title & Copy #	Signed Out	Returned

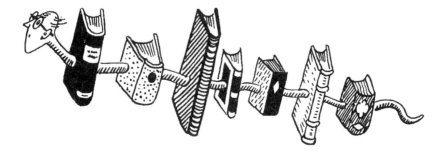

Although computers can be a great help in keeping lists of inventory, they are not practical for class sign-out records of books. In this case, it's easier to simply keep a "Book Sign-Out Sheet," which is included. Keeping a separate sheet for each class simplifies record-keeping. Students write their name, the title of the book, when they signed it out, and when they returned it on the sheet. You can keep the sheet on a clipboard on your desk and students can sign out the books themselves.

If you share books with other teachers, it's helpful to have teachers sign out books just like students. Maintaining a record of who has what eliminates the problem of not being able to find a book when you need it. A copy of a sign-out sheet for teachers should be kept in a safe but accessible place with the books. A desk drawer or file cabinet can serve this purpose.

Housing books on shelves should be kept simple. Storing books alphabetically by the author's last name makes it easy to find and replace titles.

Keeping Your Books in Good Repair

Along with maintaining an updated inventory, it's vital to keep your books in good repair. Paperbacks (or even hardcovers) will not last long if steps aren't taken to prevent and fix damage. Remind your students of some simple "don'ts" and one important "do" when using classroom or library books:

* Don't bend covers.
* Don't dogear pages.
* Don't spill food or drinks on books.
* Don't write on or in books.
* Do treat books like a treasure.

I always repeat this to my classes. It may sound a little corny, but it emphasizes the point and I'm convinced it reduces damage. Listing these points on a wall chart is also helpful.

Book repair should be an ongoing enterprise. Most book covers can be repaired and reinforced with transparent tape. A two-inch wide roll is good because it can be used to strengthen book spines as well as covers. Rolls of tape and applicators can be obtained at any office supply store. You might also be able to order them through general supplies. Your school librarian probably has some, too.

I find it's easier to repair books as needed rather than put them on the side and wait to repair a few dozen at once. I keep tape handy and fix books as necessary. I also encourage students to tape torn covers or weak spines. While book repair is ongoing in my classes, at the end of the year every book is checked and those needing repairs are fixed. During the last week of school, I'll have student volunteers help me in this.

Along with student volunteers, you should consider using adult volunteers. Many parents, grandparents, and senior citizens are willing to help in the schools. Adults can help record inventory, repair books, make sure books are returned to the shelves, and even help students select books. The presence of adult volunteers also helps to reduce discipline problems and time wasting. If you have a volunteer program in your school, utilize it; if you don't have one, try to set one up. A letter to parents will get you started.

When enlisting the aid of adults, take some time after school or during a free period to meet with your volunteers and explain what they are to do. Set up a schedule. If they are coming in just to update your inventory and repair books, perhaps an hour per week will be sufficient. If your volunteers will be helping students to select books, or checking to see if books are in the right place on the shelf, more time may be needed. Never have volunteers come in and not have anything for them to do.

Student volunteers can be quite helpful, too. Reliable students can help you keep track of your inventory and repair books during free periods or after school.

Occasionally, books will be lost or damaged beyond repair. When this happens, students should pay for the book. Books that are lost or irreparably damaged should be replaced as soon as possible. Make it a point to maintain your library. Even better, keep expanding it.

Managing Your Time

Since teachers never have enough time, effective time management is crucial. The more time you spend on non-teaching tasks, the less time you will have to spend with students.

To utilize time advantageously, organize routines and activities with efficiency in mind. Once routines are established, stick with them. Changing routines can be disruptive to students, and the time necessary to learn new routines is lost. When students understand the class's procedures, the day runs smoother. For example, when students know that they have writing workshop on Mondays, Tuesdays, and Thursdays, they will come to class on those days with their materials and prepared to write. Having reading when writing is scheduled will only cause confusion.

The handing in of assignments after due dates also disrupts efficiency. When you give assignments, be sure that students know when they are due. Suggest that they write assignments down in a notebook or assignment pad. For long-range assignments, remind students often of the due date. When students are late with the completion of assignments, there should be consequences. Some teachers simply count the assignment as a zero while others may schedule detention. Determine consequences based on how you wish to work with your class, but once set, you should discuss the importance of completing assignments and explain what happens when work is not done. Trying to track down students with late assignments can become a frustrating drain of your time.

Some teachers get bogged down with special projects and activities. The production of class magazines is a good example. The teacher announces the deadline for the magazine and begins collecting material. Unfortunately, some students who promise articles don't finish them, or the pieces are handed in but they need additional work. The deadline comes and goes and the magazine doesn't come out on time. The teacher is frustrated and the students are disappointed. Eventually the magazine gets produced, but instead of people being satisfied with it, they are simply relieved the job is done.

In planning any long-term project like a magazine, give yourself enough lead time. Set a deadline for students to hand in work, but leave enough time for the pieces to be revised.

Organize committees of students to help with the editing and proofreading. Remind students often of the deadline and work with those who might need extra help. As material is handed in, have it edited and revised. Don't wait for pieces to pile up and then a few nights before the deadline try to tackle them all at once. Break the work down into manageable parts. (For more information on producing a class magazine, see "Class Magazines" in the next section.)

Approach grading in the same way. Staggering the workload makes it easier. Rather than taking a hundred papers home over the weekend to read, take a few each night. Trying to read a tote-bag full in one sitting will only discourage you; further, you'll wind up rushing and lose objectivity.

The way you organize and manage group work can also result in time wasted, or time saved. If you intend to organize groups, it's usually better to set them up before class. Doing it with the students wastes class time. Prior to class list the names of group members on file cards, then during class simply call out the names. While it's beneficial to change groups periodically, avoid doing so too often. Established groups usually work more efficiently than new ones.

Collaboration can also aid efficiency in your class. In writing, encourage students to work with an editing partner. The editors read each other's work and offer suggestions for revision before the piece is submitted to you. Not only do students learn by sharing ideas about writing, but by middle and high school, students can often catch errors in mechanics on each other's papers. This frees you to concentrate more on the overall piece.

A well-run English class involves students in the class's routines and procedures. Design your classes so that class time is spent on learning.

The importance of sound management to your classes can't be overemphasized. Frequently, when people walk into a successful English class for the first time, they are impressed at how smoothly the class functions. Students are busy at various tasks, noise is purposeful, and the interest in language learning is evident. What's not usually seen is the strong management skills of the teacher. Yet it is those very skills that are responsible for the success of the class.

_3_

Reading, Writing, and Evaluation

There is a strong connection between reading and writing. Readers remain interested in what they are reading because of an author's ideas and skills. Since authors want their material to be read, they use their writing skills to express their ideas and keep their readers hooked. An English class built around these points permits students a wonderful opportunity to explore the bonds between good reading and writing.

Reading in Your English Class

No matter which reading model you use in your class—whole class guided reading, small group guided reading, paired reading, or individualized reading—your primary purpose is to develop competent, independent readers.

Because of the emphasis on reading in your class, you will find that many students read more than one book at the same time—the book that is assigned and a book of their own. To record their impressions of books they read individually, have your students answer some or all of the questions on the student "Book Completion Summary" sheet, which is provided. The questions may be answered on a separate sheet of paper or in literature response logs. Obviously, the sheet is meant to serve only as a guide, as not all of the questions are appropriate for every book. For example, question number 7, about characters, won't apply to nonfiction; I instruct my students to skip questions that aren't relevant. Since the questions are open-ended, you can easily determine whether a student read and understood a particular book, even if you are unfamiliar with that title.

Literature Discussion Groups

Literature discussion groups (also called response groups) provide students with the opportunity to share reactions about their reading. Ideally, the literature discussion group is heterogeneous and small, about 5 to 6 students. In the discussion group, students use their own experiences and knowledge to draw conclusions, analyze and synthesize ideas, and share opinions.

In the beginning of the year, it is likely that you will need to work closely with your groups. You will provide guidance and model appropriate behavior. You might wish to distribute copies of "Literature Discussion Group Guidelines," which is included. It highlights important characteristics of effective discussion groups.

BOOK COMPLETION SUMMARY

Answer the following questions.

1. Write the title of the book, the author's name, the publisher, place of publication, and copyright date.

2. Briefly describe what the book is about.

3. Describe the author's style. Give an example. Was it appropriate for the book? Why or why not?

4. Describe the setting.

5. What did you find most interesting about the book? Why?

6. What part of the book did you find the least interesting? Why?

7. Who was the most interesting character? Why?

8. What was the conflict in the story?

9. What did you learn from this book?

10. Did the book keep you interested? Why or why not?

11. Would you like to read another book by this author? Why or why not?

12. Would you recommend this book to others? Why or why not?

LITERATURE DISCUSSION GROUP GUIDELINES

You will be meeting in a literature discussion group this year where you will share your ideas and opinions about reading. The following suggestions will help your group work smoothly.

1. Remember that the purpose of the literature discussion group is to share reactions to and opinions about the reading.

2. Always be polite and considerate.

3. It's not necessary to raise your hand to be recognized, but don't call out and don't interrupt the speaker.

4. Speak clearly and back up your statements with facts. Cite pages and examples from the text to support your ideas.

5. Make your positions clear. Try starting your comments with phrases like—

   * I believe that . . .
   * I don't believe that . . .
   * I agree with that because . . .
   * I disagree with that because . . .
   * I don't see your point . . .
   * I'd like to add . . .
   * I'm not clear about what you're saying . . .

6. Be willing to give the floor to others.

7. Remember that everyone is entitled to his or her opinion. You may not agree, but you must be willing to let others offer their ideas.

8. Keep an open mind to new ideas. Don't dismiss the ideas of others without first reflecting on them.

9. Remember that everyone should get a chance to speak.

10. If you don't understand what someone said, ask for clarification. There are probably others who don't understand either.

As students become familiar with the discussion groups' routines, you should slip more to the background. You might appoint group leaders who take the responsibility for starting the discussion and making sure that everyone contributes. I like to appoint leaders for one-week intervals. This gives the group leaders time to gain some experience on the task, but also ensures that eventually everybody gets a chance. You'll find that students relish this opportunity of "taking your place." As students assume more responsibility for conducting the group discussions, you are freed to circulate and sit in on various groups. This is an excellent management strategy, for it allows you to monitor student behavior, evaluate individual efforts, and guide the discussions when necessary.

At the end of the discussion time, you might want to summarize the major points. This is particularly appropriate when the entire class is reading the same book and is on the same chapter. You can summarize for the whole class at once. If the groups are reading different books, you might designate the leader to summarize the points that were covered. In this case, designate a secretary, or recorder, to take notes during the discussion.

It takes time for students to become proficient at literature discussion groups, especially if they have never done them before. However, as they gain confidence, the discussions will go beyond the mere facts of the story to a thorough reflection and analysis of storylines, development, and themes.

Literature Response Logs

To ensure that students come to their discussion groups prepared, require them to keep literature response logs (also known as literature logs, reading logs, reading journals, literature journals, and probably a half-dozen other names I haven't heard of). Spiral notebooks, three-ring binders, or booklets can be used for students to record their thoughts and impressions of what they read, as well as answer questions you or others might pose. Require students to date their entries and number their notebooks, 1, 2, 3, etc. By the end of the year students may have several, which, together, will comprise an extensive collection of their reactions to literature.

The logs can be used in various ways. You might present students with a question to answer during their reading, ask them to respond to a particular scene in a story, examine a character's actions or motivations, or reflect upon the theme. You might simply assign an activity packet from Part II of this book, and instruct students to answer the questions as they read the book. I usually ask students to record at least one thing in the reading that impressed them, for example, the author's style, the action, setting, dialogue, imagery, or the emotional impact. What impressed them most might even be that the story bogged down and they began to lose interest. That's fine, as long as they support their opinions. I encourage students to note the page number and paragraphs of sections that support their views so that they can direct group members to specific examples.

Writing in Your English Class

While you can build your writing program around various models, you should teach the writing process, which focuses on the way real authors actually work. The writing process is composed of at least five stages: prewriting, drafting, revising, editing, and publishing.

Although each stage is characterized by different activities, the lines between them are fluid and authors easily move back and forth through the stages as necessary. If your students are unfamiliar with the writing process, you may wish to distribute copies of the "Stages of the Writing Process," which follows.

Writing for Authentic Purposes

Students, as well as professional authors, write best about subjects and topics that they find meaningful. Encourage your students to select topics of their own, as well as topics that naturally grow out of their reading experiences. Reading can be a powerful motivator for writing, as students react to the ideas they encounter in literature.

Your classroom should be a place where students can experiment with various kinds of writing. Some suggestions are provided in "Types of Writing," which I copy and distribute to my students. It emphasizes that they need not limit themselves to just essays and stories—which for some students are the only kinds of writing they've ever done in school.

Writing Journals

Writing journals are a fine way to promote writing in your class. Kept in a spiral notebook or booklet, journals become storage sites for an author's ideas, reflections, questions, and dreams. Entries may explore topics, or be simple musings. Not only do journals help build the habit of writing, but they provide the opportunity for students to experiment with written expression.

Before students start writing in journals, you should lay down the ground rules. Will journals be shared? If yes, with whom? Will you look at the journals? If you do, will they be used in evaluation? Once the rules are set, they should be maintained throughout the year.

While I encourage students to write about personal thoughts, I instruct them to turn down the pages of entries they don't want me to read. However, I also warn them that if I read something in a journal that indicates someone is in trouble, I am obligated to report it.

Writing journals frequently become a record of a student's writing experiences throughout the year. As such, they chronicle the growth of your students.

Writing Folders

I encourage students to keep their writing in folders. Only *writing* is to be kept in the writing folders, and I require students to bring them to class each day. This way works-in-progress are always handy.

Some teachers, particularly those who have their own rooms, prefer to keep writing folders in the classroom. This eliminates the problem of lost pieces and forgotten folders. If you have your own classroom, or can safely store folders in the room in which you meet, keep the folders of each class in a separate box or milk crate to prevent them from being spread around. (Permit students to keep their journals so that they may write in them at home.) Alphabetizing the folders makes retrieval easier, and storing them near the door enables students to pick up their folders on their way into class. This saves the time of passing them out. If you find it necessary to have the folders passed out, ask for two or three volunteers to do it. Assigning volunteers on a weekly basis eliminates the need of picking different people each day. Likewise, you can have students collect the folders at the end of class.

STAGES OF THE WRITING PROCESS

Writing is composed of at least five stages. Authors move back and forth through the stages as they develop their pieces.

* *Prewriting* is the stage in which an author decides on her topic, purpose, and audience. She generates ideas, gathers information, analyzes and organizes the information, and considers what form her writing should take.

* *Drafting* is the writing of a piece. During drafting the author often writes, then pauses to read what he has written. He may then rewrite some of the work, or find that he needs to go back to the prewriting stage to change some of the original ideas.

* *Revising* comes after drafting. The word "revising" means "re-seeing." Authors read through their work carefully, adding, deleting, and rewriting. If changes are major, they might return to drafting or even to prewriting.

* *Editing* is the stage in which the writing is prepared for publishing or sharing. Final corrections to mechanics are made and the piece is put in its finished form, either printed via computer or typewriter, or written neatly in longhand. If the author finds that more rewriting is needed, she can switch back to revising, drafting, or even prewriting.

* *Publishing* is the final stage of the writing process. It is the time the piece is shared. For students this includes simple sharing with teachers, peers, parents, or the public. It may also include publication in school newspapers or newsletters, as well as local, regional, or national magazines and newspapers.

© 1994 by The Center for Applied Research in Education

TYPES OF WRITING

There are many types of writing you can do in your class. Throughout the year, try as many of the following as you can.

advertisements

advice columns

allegories

anecdotes

anthologies

articles

autobiographies

awards

ballads

biographies

book reviews

books

brochures

comic strips

diaries

editorials

essays

fables

fiction (adventure, fantasy, historical, horror, mystery, romance, science fiction)

folk tales

greeting cards

how-to articles

informational articles

jokes

journals

letters (apology, thanks, business, complaint, congratulations, friendly, job application, to the editor)

movie reviews

myths

newspaper articles

plays

poetry—all kinds

posters

puzzles

quizzes

radio scripts

recipes

reports

research papers

résumés

song lyrics

speeches

sports articles

surveys

tall tales

TV scripts

yearbooks

Publishing the Work of Your Students

All authors need an audience. They need others to react to their writing. If your students know that their writing will be published, they will write better than if the writing is only something to be turned in for a grade.

Publishing refers to all the ways writing is shared—from reading a piece aloud to a partner, group, or class, to displays on bulletin boards and actual publication in magazines. Because it is so important, publishing should be an ongoing activity in your classes. See "Ways to Share Student Writing," which follows.

Class magazines are a high-profile way to share the writing of students. With access to computers and desktop publishing software, you can easily produce impressive magazines. The simplest class magazines, however, may be collections of works written neatly in longhand and produced on a photocopier. I usually produce both kinds of magazines. The important thing is that students see their work published. See "Guidelines for Producing Class Magazines," which follows.

Evaluating Reading and Writing

Several methods of evaluation are appropriate for English classes. Whichever methods you choose, evaluation should be based on authentic language experiences, should be consistent, and should be understood by both students and parents. Following are some of the more common evaluation strategies.

Logging

Keeping a daily record for each student in several classes each day, in which you enter letters, numbers, or checks and minuses in a grade book can become tedious at best and overwhelming at the worst. Instead, consider maintaining a log, or annotated list, of student accomplishments.

You might permit students to keep their own logs, and maintain a running account of what they do each day. You'll find that most students are quite honest. For those who "fudge," casually checking what they're doing each day can foster honesty. Allowing students to record their progress relieves you of the burden of daily record-keeping.

If you prefer, you can keep the log. Make the process a part of your class routines. As you circulate around the class, carry a clipboard or three-ring binder with individual student log sheets. (Each log sheet needs only the student's name and section. Remember to date each entry.) As you observe what students are doing, take notes, but avoid writing too much. Following is a sample log entry:

Date: 10/14
    Spent period reading independently. Worked well with discussion group.

Date: 10/15
    Worked on draft of essay, "Violence in Schools." Conferred with me about
    the lead.

WAYS TO SHARE STUDENT WRITING

Following are some ways students can share, or publish, their work:

- Reading a piece to a partner
- Reading a piece to a peer group
- Reading a piece to a class
- Displaying writing on class bulletin boards
- Displaying writing on hallway exhibits
- Reading a piece at special events or programs
- Publishing writing in class or school magazines or newspapers
- Publishing writing in district or PTA newsletters
- Reading a piece to students of other grades
- Producing anthologies of student writing
- Displaying student writing in the school library
- Photocopying pieces and distributing them to other students
- Submitting writing to local newspapers (See if a local paper is willing to run a "Students' Corner" and have your students write for it.)
- Submitting writing to magazines that publish student writing (A good list can be found in *Market Guide for Young Writers, 3rd Edition* by Kathy Henderson, Writer's Digest Books, 1507 Dana Ave., Cincinnati, OH 45207. You might also consult *Writer's Market,* Writer's Digest Books, at the same address. Both books can be found at many libraries.)

GUIDELINES FOR PRODUCING CLASS MAGAZINES

It's not that hard to produce class magazines of your students' writings. The following guide makes it even easier.

* Decide what type of magazine it will be. Will it contain only fiction? Only nonfiction? Only poetry? Or will it contain all three? If it is to be fiction, will it focus on one type of genre (for example, fantasy)?

* Decide on standards. How long will pieces be? Especially decide on what is unacceptable (for example, gory murders). Caution students that pieces must be original. Discuss plagiarism.

* Set your deadline for material well in advance of your publication date. As students hand in material, read it and have them revise ahead of time. Don't wait until the last week and hand back a dozen pieces for revision. You'll never get them all back in time.

* Store finished pieces in a separate folder. If students from more than one class are contributing to the magazine, store each class's work in a separate folder. This makes it easier to find particular pieces.

* Have students enter as much of the magazine as possible into computers. Working on computers makes revision easier. Good printers also produce sharp letters, which reproduce well on photocopiers. Desktop publishing software can produce high-quality magazines, and the software isn't that hard to use.

* Ask for parent volunteers to help in typing. Sending a letter home in advance helps to line up volunteers early. Whenever you send something home for typing by a parent, be sure that you provide adequate instructions of how you want the material set on the page. A copy of a page from a previous magazine is helpful.

* If you use artwork, stick with line drawings. Elaborate illustrations won't reproduce well on the typical photocopier. Have students do illustrations on separate sheets of paper, then cut them out and paste or use white tape to attach them to the page. Drawing directly on the printed page risks making a mistake and having to do the entire page over.

* For titles, subtitles, and page numbers, use transfer letters or stencils. (Of course, if you have access to desktop publishing, the software can do all this for you.) Use light, blue-lined graph paper to help position letters.

* Before printing have student proofreaders carefully check every page. Impress on students that the magazine should be error-free (at least as far as humanly possible). Working on a class magazine helps to teach students the importance of quality work.

* Print your magazine on a photocopier. If your school has a print shop, see if the printing classes can produce your magazine. You'll get a great-looking magazine, and the print shop students will have the chance to work on a meaningful project.

(Class magazines can also be produced on duplicators, but then all of the pieces will need to be put on ditto masters.)

* Print on both sides of each page. Not only does this save paper, but it improves the appearance of the magazine.

* To make the job of putting the magazine together, do it in parts. Do the first eight pages, then the next eight, and so on.

* Print enough copies of the magazine for students, as well as the principal, school library, and other interested parties.

To reduce the amount of writing, use phrases, abbreviations for procedures and activities (r. for reading, w. for writing, d. for draft, etc.), and be specific. If you find that it is too difficult to observe each student every day, focus on five or six in each class today and others tomorrow. The information contained in the logs can help you to follow student progress, zero in on weaknesses, and set objectives. You'll find that over time logging builds a fine profile of your students.

Portfolios

In recent years portfolios of student work have become popular tools of evaluation. A portfolio is a collection of a student's work, showing that skills have been mastered and class objectives have been met. Portfolios also enable students to see and reflect on their own growth, and can provide the basis of goal-setting.

The work is usually stored in a large folder or portfolio. You may select the work to be stored, based on specific criteria, or permit students to select work that they feel best demonstrates achievement. Over the length of the year, the portfolios become an excellent vehicle for showing student growth.

Students may also be enlisted in portfolio evaluation. Working in pairs or small groups, students may offer opinions on each other's portfolios, what they feel are strengths and weaknesses, and suggest what the portfolio owner could work on next.

Reviewing Logs and Journals

Periodically, I review literature response logs and writing journals. Monitoring the logs and journals enables me to follow the daily activities of students. While I may comment on their work, I don't red-pen or grade logs or journals. I'm concerned that if I did students would take fewer risks. They would pay more attention to mechanics, and write what they thought I wanted to see. They'd be writing for the grade instead of genuinely reflecting on their ideas.

Grading

No matter what type of program you have, it's likely you'll still have to grade your students. Many grading systems can be used.

To determine reading grades, you might test students on the various novels they read. Grades can be calculated on a percentage basis. You might also assign a specific percentage to the satisfactory completion of daily activities.

Writing can be graded according to various elements or pieces. Here's a breakdown I like to use:

Focus—20 percent
    The topic is clearly defined; all ideas and details relate to the topic.

Content—25 percent
    The piece contains fresh ideas. Main ideas are logically developed and supported with details.

Organization—25 percent
> The piece is developed logically from the opening to the conclusion. There is a clear progression of thought. The piece is unified.

Style—15 percent
> The author's tone and voice are appropriate for the topic.

Mechanics—15 percent
> The piece exhibits correct punctuation, grammar, and spelling.

Another system of grading that works well is the point system. You assign certain points for particular activities. Reading a novel and completing its accompanying activities might have a value of 10 points, completing a piece of writing satisfactorily might be worth 10 more, and completing a group project might be 15. During a marking period, the points are added up and at the end are converted into a grade.

Similar to the point system is the minimum plus. In this grading system, certain activities must be completed satisfactorily to achieve a specific grade. The base might be a "C", and additional work would raise that to a "B" and then an "A." This may or may not be used in conjunction with student contracts.

The success of your classes will depend in large part on your management skills. Classes in which students know the procedures, know what is expected of them, and are encouraged to do their best will be far more successful than those where students are unsure of the classroom routines and objectives.

PART II

READY-TO-USE ACTIVITIES

Ready-to-Use Activities

The following activities for novels are arranged in three sections—for grades *7-8, 9-10,* and *11-12.* Depending on the abilities of your students, however, you may find some of the books are useful in other grades.

The activities are reproducible and support whole-class, group, or individual reading. You may have your students record their answers in reading logs or notebooks, ask them to hand in answers daily, or turn in all the written work upon completion of the novel.

Each set of activities has three parts: (1) a "Writing Connection," which is a specific writing assignment that grows out of the reading, (2) a page of "Questions to Consider" that focuses on comprehension and interpretation, and (3) a page of "Projects and Activities to Consider" and "Curriculum Connections" that offers the students an assortment of challenging assignments for both individual and group work. (Activities under "Curriculum Connections" are coded for subject areas: SS for Social Studies, Sci for Science, M for Mathematics, and A for the Arts.)

Of course it is not necessary to assign all of the work contained on the reproducibles. You may, for example, instruct students to answer all of the items on the "Questions" page, but give them a choice of projects and activities and curriculum connections. You can eliminate some questions by simply having students cross the number of the question out on their sheet. The reproducibles make it easy for you to assign work to go along with the reading, and follow the progress of your students.

4

Novels for Grades 7-8

1. *Homecoming* - Voigt
2. *One Fat Summer* - Lipsyte
3. *Call It Courage* - Sperry
4. *The Outsiders* - Hinton
5. *A Wizard of Earthsea* - Le Guin
6. *Roll of Thunder, Hear My Cry* - Taylor
7. *The Chocolate War* - Cormier
8. *The Slave Dancer* - Fox
9. *The Princess Bride* - Goldman
10. *Julie of the Wolves* - George
11. *The Contender* - Lipsyte
12. *The Sword in the Stone* - White
13. *The Upstairs Room* - Reiss
14. *The Pigman* - Zindel
15. *Sing Down the Moon* - O'Dell
16. *I Will Call It Georgie's Blues* - Newton
17. *Durango Street* - Bonham
18. *House of Stairs* - Sleator
19. *Home Before Dark* - Bridges
20. *Farewell to Manzanar* - Wakatsuki Houston and Houston

1. *Homecoming* by Cynthia Voigt
(Ballantine Books, 1981)

Synopsis

Dicey Tillerman and her three younger siblings—James, Maybeth and Sammy—are abandoned in a Connecticut mall parking lot by their mother, who later is deemed mentally ill. They do not know their father or any other family; they have only the address of a great aunt. They set off on foot to cross Connecticut toward her house, and must survive with hardly any cash and no supplies. When they arrive they find that the aunt is dead, and they are taken in by her daughter, Eunice, a religious fanatic. It isn't long before they run away from her to find their grandmother, whom they have never met, in Southern Maryland. Along the way they meet many people. Dicey becomes more resourceful as their leader, and each of the children grows and emerges as a distinct personality. They find their grandmother, Abigail, a bitter recluse who refuses to accept them. By making themselves useful to Abigail, the children win her affection and she invites them to stay with her.

Ideas and Concepts to Highlight

1. Discuss the importance of parents to their children. Parents help their children to acquire the skills and understanding necessary to survive in the world.

2. Note how Dicey must assume the role of father and mother to her younger siblings.

3. Emphasize the many decisions that the children must make on their journey from Connecticut to Maryland. (This can be set up on a class or individual student chart with information filled in as students read the novel.)

4. Point out how the children grow and change because of their experiences.

Writing Connection: "How People Change Because of Their Experiences"

This topic lends itself well to the essay form. Explain the essay to your students. Note that most essays follow a structure of introduction, where the main point is offered; the body, which explains and supports the main idea with details; and the conclusion, which usually adds a final idea to support the argument. This activity can be done individually or as a small group exercise for part of the class period. If you wish to have students work independently, instruct them to complete Worksheet 1-1 to generate and organize ideas, and then write their essays. If you wish to use this assignment as a group activity, instruct students to finish the worksheet individually, and then meet in small groups to discuss and share their ideas before writing.

1-1. *HOW PEOPLE CHANGE BECAUSE OF THEIR EXPERIENCES*

Directions: Write an essay explaining how experiences can change people. Use examples from your own life or examples from others. Writing down ideas and notes under the appropriate sections will help you to organize your essay.

Opening: _____
_____
_____
_____
_____

Body: _____
_____
_____
_____
_____
_____
_____
_____
_____
_____
_____
_____
_____

Conclusion: _____
_____
_____
_____
_____

1-2. QUESTIONS TO CONSIDER FOR
HOMECOMING

1. Dicey confides to James that she was proud of Sammy for stealing food, yet she acted angry toward him. Why did she do this?

2. After the children were left on their own, Dicey assumed the role of parent over the other children, especially the two younger ones. For example, when necessary, she would console, discipline, and nurture them. Discuss Dicey's role as a mother and father figure for the two younger children. Use specific examples from the story.

3. List five values that Dicey holds, then list five that she tries to impart to the others. Is there much overlap? Discuss the saying "practice what you preach," and how parents do or do not follow their own advice.

4. Compare Stewart, Eunice, Father Joseph, Will and Abigail as moral influences and disciplinarians. How did each of them affect Dicey and the other children?

5. Dicey's "family" is quite different from many American families. In what ways does Dicey's "family" compare and contrast with the idea of the typical American family? Cite specific examples from the story in your answer.

6. Explain Dicey's reasoning at the New York bus station when she is buying tickets to Delaware and tells James, "Two and two is not the same as four."

7. Given the sharp characterizations the author draws for each of the children (and disregarding their uncertain futures), in what careers could each of them excel? What types of arts or sports? Keep in mind the kind of mind-set, mental preparation, discipline and self-control that each of these might require.

8. Suppose you were Dicey. How would you have managed to get the younger children to a new home? What would you have done differently? How would you have disciplined the children? What social services would you have sought out? How would you have traveled? Is there any way Dicey could have been more successful? Why or why not?

1-3. *PROJECTS AND ACTIVITIES TO CONSIDER FOR* <u>*HOMECOMING*</u>

1. During the story, Sammy grows from a "problem child" to a strong and cooperative boy. Describe some events that helped him to change. Use a chart like the one below to organize your ideas.

Events	**Changes**
1.	
2.	
3.	

2. Many novels are adapted into movies. Working in a small group, select a section of the book and write a screenplay for it. Produce and videotape your screenplay. (A good source for screenplay formats is *The Elements of Screenwriting: A Guide for Film and Television Writers* by Irwin R. Blacker, New York, MacMillan, 1986.)

3. In a small group, develop dialogue for a scene. Select various sections of the book. Then have them act out the scene.

4. Create an oral report, a panel, or small group discussion on catatonia, their mother's illness. Is it hereditary? Is there any treatment for it? Is there any chance for their mother's recovery? If their mother were to recover, what might then happen to Dicey and the children?

Curriculum Connections:

1. Why wouldn't Dicey hitchhike? Obtain a map of the Eastern United States and trace each trip, from Peewauket all the way to Crisfield. How many miles is it? How long would it take you to walk the distance at a steady pace? (SS)

2. Imagine you are planning the trip from Connecticut to Maryland. Consult the *New York Times* or your local newspaper, and follow the weather patterns for several days over the areas through which you will be traveling. Chart the patterns. Also consult an encyclopedia for geographical features, noting the important ones that you will need to take into account during your trip. How and when would you plan a trip from one destination to another? Prepare a short report about your trip. (SS or Sci)

2. One Fat Summer by Robert Lipsyte
(HarperCollins, 1977)

Synopsis

Bobby Marks is 14 and spending the summer at the family home on Rumson Lake, populated mostly by vacationing families, but with its share of generations-old local clans. At more than 200 pounds, Bobby is insecure and dreading the summer because more of his body will be exposed. His friend Joanie, also insecure because of her big nose, persuades Bobby to take a job keeping grounds for the stern Dr. Kahn. Bobby's parents are not very supportive, and, not wanting to be put down by his father, Bobby lies about the job. Bobby works hard, but is harassed by Willie Rumson, a local who worked for Dr. Kahn last summer and hates Bobby, who he feels stole his job. Bobby is eventually kidnapped by Rumson and his friends and left naked on an island. While there, he chides himself for always being put down and abused. One of the gang members retrieves Bobby, but his resolve is solidified. After a few weeks he loses considerable weight, and finally is cornered by Rumson toting a shotgun. They fight and Bobby topples him off a dock into the water and holds him under water until Rumson nearly drowns. Bobby learns much about manhood, self-confidence and getting along with others during his eventful summer.

Ideas and Concepts to Highlight

1. Discuss the insecurities and physical awkwardness that adolescents feel. Encourage dialogue about how children can keep from getting emotionally troubled by taunting.

2. Discuss the benefits of summer jobs in terms of physical and material gain and personal growth. Talk about interview techniques when someone is applying for a job.

3. Marital tension is present in the story, seen through Bobby's eyes. Talk about its effects on Bobby and adolescent behavior in general.

Writing Connection: "The Makeover"

Bobby feels badly about his weight. In the story, he becomes determined to lose weight, and he does. Most people would like to change themselves in some way, if they could.

For this writing assignment, ask your students to imagine that they, or a character they create, can change their personality or physical makeup. What would they change, and why would they change? Instruct them to complete Worksheet 2-1, and then write about "The Makeover" in an essay or story.

2-1. THE MAKEOVER

Directions: Few people feel that they are perfect. Most, if given the chance, would change themselves. Imagine that you, or a character you create, could change some thing(s) about your body or personality. Answer the questions below and then write an essay or story about these changes.

1. What would you change about your personality? _____

   _____

   _____

   _____

2. Why would you make these changes? _____

   _____

   _____

   _____

3. What would you change about your body? _____

   _____

   _____

   _____

4. Why would you make these changes? _____

   _____

   _____

   _____

5. Describe the type of person you would become because of these changes. _____

   _____

   _____

   _____

© 1994 by The Center for Applied Research in Education

2-2. QUESTIONS TO CONSIDER FOR
ONE FAT SUMMER

1. Bobby speculates that he and Joanie are best friends because of their physical detractions. Do you agree? What else draws them together? Compare their characters.

2. Define "defense mechanisms" and point out Bobby's and Joanie's. In the early chapters, when musing to himself, why does Bobby strike down people like Pete who are nice to him?

3. Explain the tension between Bobby and his father. Why is their relationship the way it is? In your opinion, how might they resolve it?

4. Define self-esteem. Compare Joanie's deliberate transformation with Bobby's naturally evolved emotional one. Which accomplishes more in terms of boosting self-esteem? What are their effects?

5. Discuss Bobby's relationship with Michelle. Trace its evolution, and write a few paragraphs about how you think their relationship will be in adulthood.

6. Bobby seems to lack positive role models in the story. Name some men whom you think Bobby would benefit from knowing. Consider both celebrities and people you know personally. Support your answer in the context of Bobby's story.

7. What is your opinion of Bobby at the beginning of the story? What is it at the end? How has it changed?

8. By the end of the story, Bobby has changed more than in just losing weight. Explain how else he has changed.

2-3. *PROJECTS AND ACTIVITIES TO CONSIDER FOR* *ONE FAT SUMMER*

1. In your group, discuss what types of summer jobs are available to students of your age. What are some jobs you'd like? What would you earn, and what kind of personal growth could you derive from it? Make a list of the jobs your group discusses, the qualifications (if any) that are required, and the type of pay you could expect to receive. Share your list with other groups.

2. Bobby's imagination is quite vivid, especially while he is working. Use your imagination to "see" a favorite place, activity, or item and write a physical description of it. Try to make your writing as detailed and vivid as you can by including your senses: sight, sound, touch, smell, and taste.

3. Imagine that you were a close friend of Bobby. What type of advice could you give him about his problems with Rumson? Write a conversation you would have with Bobby.

4. Research articles and books on divorce. Organize and conduct a panel discussion on the pros and cons of divorce, particularly the effects on the people involved.

Curriculum Connections:

1. Research weight-loss programs from books, magazine articles, and broadcast media. Prepare a short report on your findings. Pretend you are Bobby's dietitian, and include recommendations for him in your report. (Sci)

2. Weight-loss is often achieved better when the person also begins an exercise program. Imagine that you are a trainer and that Bobby has asked you to design an exercise program for him. Consult the necessary references and create an exercise plan for Bobby. (Sci)

3. Obtain copies of some of the recordings Bobby likes and listen to them. What do you think of them? What do they say about Bobby's personality? Expand your answer to include what you think your own choice of music says about you. (A)

4. Obtain a map of a popular recreational area similar to Bobby's summer home. Draw a map of Rumson Lake and the vicinity, using Bobby's description as a guide. Include landmarks, paths and roads like the map you read about. (SS)

3. *Call It Courage* by Armstrong Sperry
(Macmillan, 1940)

Synopsis

Mafatu, a Polynesian boy whose father calls him Stout Heart, fears the sea. When he is very young, he and his mother are caught on the sea during a great storm. Although she manages to save her son, Mafatu's mother dies. From then on Mafatu's haunting dreams make him avoid the sea until his people brand him as a coward: Mafatu, the Boy Who Was Afraid. No longer able to bear the scorn of his people, Mafatu leaves his home island in his canoe with only his small dog and pet albatross. A storm strands him alone on a volcanic island that he comes to find out is a sacred place to the eaters-of-men. While on the island Mafatu survives several tests of courage, including an escape from the savages who would kill him. When he finally returns home, he is truly Mafatu, the Stout Heart.

Ideas and Concepts to Highlight

1. Locate Polynesia on a map. Emphasize that it is made up of numerous islands scattered throughout the central and south Pacific.

2. Discuss that the story is based on a legend. Note the importance of legends to people.

3. Note that, being island dwellers, Polynesians find the sea vital to their survival.

4. Mention that throughout the story, Mafatu wants to make his father proud of him. Along with this, however, he also wants to be proud of himself.

Writing Connection: "Fear!"

Mafatu was known as the *Boy Who Was Afraid*. He not only struggled with the scorn of others, but he had to cope with his fearfulness as well. Discuss the issue of fear with your students, and note that everyone is afraid of something.

For this writing assignment, ask your students to consider their fears, and write about them. They may pick a fear from the past which they overcame, or one that still bothers them. Worksheet 3-1 can be used for a prewriting activity.

3-1. FEAR!

Directions: Everyone has fears. Mafatu, for example, was afraid of the sea. Explore your fears through writing. Answer the questions to help clarify and organize your ideas.

1. List some of your fears: _____

   _____

   _____

2. Which one bothers you the most? _____

   _____Why? _____

   _____

3. How have you tried to overcome it? _____

   _____

   _____

4. Have you been successful in overcoming your fear?_____

   If you haven't, what will you try to do next to overcome it? _____

   _____

   _____

5. Who can you go to for help in overcoming it?_____

   _____

   How might this person be able to help you?_____

   _____

   _____

   _____

3-2. QUESTIONS TO CONSIDER FOR
CALL IT COURAGE

1. Mafatu's father was Tavana Nui, Great Chief of the island Hikueru. Do you think that because his father was a chief, Mafatu was expected to be braver than other boys? Why or why not? Do parents usually have expectations for their children? Give some examples. Are parents' expectations good or bad for their children? Explain.

2. In what ways did the Polynesians rely on the sea? How did this reliance on the sea increase the scorn his people had for Mafatu?

3. Why did Mafatu leave Hikueru? What did he hope to do? Was he right in leaving? Why or why not?

4. When Mafatu dove into the water to fight the shark, he did so to save his dog. Do you think Mafatu thought about what he was doing? Or did he just react to save his dog? Do you think that heroes think about what they are doing, or do they just react to a situation? Explain.

5. How did Mafatu feel when he realized the eaters-of-men had come? Did he have any other choice except trying to get away from the island? Explain.

6. On his return home, in deep despair, Mafatu suddenly rages at Moana, the Sea God. He remembered always being afraid of Moana, but now he says, "I am not afraid of you! Destroy me—but I laugh at you. Do you hear? I laugh!" Why was this declaration important to Mafatu? What finally happened?

7. Do you think that Mafatu's triumph over his fear had a lasting effect on his character? Explain.

3-3. PROJECTS AND ACTIVITIES TO CONSIDER FOR CALL IT COURAGE

1. This story is based on a legend. What is a legend? Give some examples of other legends you know. Why are legends important and valued by people? Are legends as important to people today as they were in the past? Explain.

2. Mafatu wants to impress his father with his courage. Think of a time you wanted to impress someone. Who was it? When was it? How did you want to impress this person? What happened?

3. Write a poem celebrating Mafatu's victory over his fear.

4. Organize a debate over the statement: A person isn't born with courage; courage is an effort of will. Conduct the debate in front of the class and let the class decide who won.

Curriculum Connections:

1. Hikueru is a barrier reef. Describe what a barrier reef is. Consult references if necessary. (SS)

2. Mafatu becomes stranded on a volcanic island. What is a volcanic island? How is it different than a barrier island? Why is the soil of volcanic islands so rich? Consult references if necessary. (SS or Sci)

3. Based on a description of Mafatu's sailing canoe, draw or make a model. (A)

4. Research Polynesia. Give its location. Where did the people originally come from? Describe the traditions, customs, and livelihood of the islands. Based on your research, design a model that represents some aspect of Polynesian life, for example, a mask, hut, village, model of an island, a figurine, etc. (SS or A)

5. On his return home, Mafatu looked for constellations to guide him. Throughout history, sailors have relied on the stars to guide them. In the northern hemisphere the most familiar guiding star is Polaris, the North Star. Why? What makes the North Star unique among stars? Will Polaris always be the North Star? Consult references and write a brief report. (Sci)

4. The Outsiders by S.E. Hinton
(Viking, 1967)

Synopsis

Ponyboy Curtis lives in the urban Southwest with his older brothers Sodapop and Darry. They are the Greasers, members of a gang with four other teenagers, who are in constant conflict with the upper class, known as the Socs (Socials). Pony and another gang member, Johnny, are jumped by a group of Socs and Johnny kills one of them with a knife. Johnny and Pony hide in an abandoned church, which catches fire while kids wandering away from a field trip are trapped inside. Johnny and Pony save the youngsters, but Johnny is hurt and dies shortly after. Pony, only fourteen, grows up significantly during and after the killing.

Ideas and Concepts to Highlight

1. Note that this story is written in the first person. Explain that this point-of-view (POV) makes it seem as if Ponyboy is speaking directly to the reader. This POV is limited, however. The narrator can only relate those things Ponyboy has experienced or found out about in some way.

2. Discuss gangs and why people, especially teenagers, might belong to them. What does a gang provide its members? Expand the discussion to include peer pressure.

3. This book was written about the urban Southwest of the 1960s. That culture resulted in various pressures on teenagers. Discuss what some of these pressures were. Have students point out the similarities of today's pressures. What might be some solutions?

4. Discuss the differences between the Socs and Greasers, especially their values and actions. Also note their appearance versus the reality.

Writing Connection: "Why Gangs Are Bad (or Good)"

Explain that editorials, sometimes called persuasive writing, opinion pieces, or personal essays, express an author's opinion about a topic and usually try to convince readers to adopt the same position. Many newspapers contain editorials written by both staff and ordinary readers. Most editorials follow a simple structure of opening, which contains a strong statement about the problem, a body, which offers facts and examples to support the author's position, and a conclusion, in which the author suggests what should be done and often calls on the reader to take action. Distributing copies of Worksheet 4-1 will help students to formulate ideas for their editorials.

4-1. WHY GANGS ARE BAD (OR GOOD)

Directions: Teenage gangs are a problem in many American cities and suburbs. Consider your feelings about gangs. Are they good? Bad? What do they offer young people? Is there any other way of providing the same "opportunities" to young people? Write an editorial about teenage gangs. Use this worksheet to organize your thoughts and list some ideas for your editorial before starting to write.

Why Gangs Are Good	Why Gangs Are Bad

Alternatives to gangs: _____

_____

_____

_____

_____

_____

_____

_____

4-2. QUESTIONS TO CONSIDER FOR
THE OUTSIDERS

1. Why do the two groups, the Socs and Greasers, fight? What do they hope to accomplish?

2. Why did Darry pressure Ponyboy to get good grades? Do you think Darry was right to do this? Why or why not?

3. Describe the relationship between Johnny and Dallas. Why does Johnny look up to Dallas? Why does Dallas care so much for Johnny?

4. Why does Cherry Valance get along with Ponyboy?

5. What are some of the problems the Socs have? What are some of the problems the Greasers have? What do you think these problems arise from?

6. How is Ponyboy different at the end of the story than he was at the beginning?

7. Ponyboy describes other members of his gang as having "too much energy, too much feeling with no way to blow it off." What could the gang have done instead of fighting, drag racing, and shoplifting?

8. The story is written in the first person. It has a distinctive style and voice. Does it sound like it is written by a fourteen-year-old? Why or why not? Is the "voice" appropriate for this story? Why or why not? If the story was written in an adult's voice, how would the story be affected? Would it be as believable? Why or why not?

9. Does Johnny's act of heroism fit his character? Why or why not? What might he have done if Socs were trapped in a life-threatening situation?

10. What might have been S.E. Hinton's purpose in writing this story? Support your answer with examples from the story.

4-3. PROJECTS AND ACTIVITIES TO CONSIDER FOR
THE OUTSIDERS

1. Check a newspaper and find some articles about racial tensions. Compare the newspaper articles with the gang fights in the story. Prepare an oral presentation that describes some similarities and differences.

2. Imagine a court scene in which you are a lawyer defending a still-living Johnny Cade. What do you think the charge would be? How would you plan your defense? Working with your group, prepare a court scene. Determine roles for Johnny, witnesses, the prosecutor, defense attorney, judge, and jury. Write a script and act out the courtroom drama. Let the jury decide the case.

3. Write a poem, either rhyming or non-rhyming, from Pony's point of view about his feelings after Johnny's death.

4. Ponyboy says that "Nobody would write editorials praising Dally." Imagine that you are the exception. Write an editorial describing what you think were Dally's greatest qualities and achievements in the story.

Curriculum Connections:

1. This story was written about the urban Southwest in the 1960s. How does the culture of that time and place differ with yours today? How is it the same? Do teenagers still have the same kinds of problems? How do teenagers cope today? (SS)

2. Consult a reference and list the other major geographical areas that the United States can be divided into. Could this story have taken place in a city in one of those areas? Explain. (SS)

3. Consult references and list some "traditional" American values. Which, if any, of these values are held by the Greasers? Why might someone hold values that are different from the majority? (SS)

5. *A Wizard of Earthsea* by Ursula K. Le Guin
(Parnassus Press, 1962)

Synopsis

Earthsea is a group of island kingdoms at a time when wizards and magic were common in the world. As a young boy, Sparrowhawk learns simple magic from his witch-aunt. After defending his village against invaders, he becomes an apprentice to a master wizard. Impatient to learn more about the powers of magic, Sparrowhawk goes to a famous school for wizards. He learns quickly, but his pride makes him want even greater power. In attempting to summon the dead—a most dangerous spell—he unleashes a terrible evil. Regretful over what he has done, Sparrowhawk starts on a quest to hunt down the evil shadow in a journey that takes him across much of Earthsea. When Sparrowhawk at last finds the shadow, he finds himself as well.

Ideas and Concepts to Highlight

1. Point out that this story is a fantasy. While there are many types of fantasies, magic and the supernatural are essential to the plot. Most fantasy stories also have a quest of some sort.

2. Discuss magic. Primitive people often believed in magic as a way to gain control over their world, which was often unpredictable and frightening. Extend the discussion to magic today. Do people still believe in magic?

3. Talk about pride. Focus on how pride can be a positive thing and how it can be destructive.

4. Explain what an archipelago is. On a map, identify some archipelagos. (The islands in the Aegean Sea are a good example.)

5. Note that when Ogion advised Sparrowhawk to become the hunter it was just another way of saying face your problems.

Writing Connection: "A Fantastic Tale"

Fantasy is a genre in which stories contain magic. Fantasies can be set in any time or place. Many, like *A Wizard of Earthsea,* are set in mythical or magical kingdoms where societies are primitive. A good example of heroic fantasy are stories about Conan the Barbarian, while an example of a modern fantasy is *It's a Wonderful Life,* the movie starring Jimmy Stewart that airs during every Christmas season.

Instruct your students to write a fantasy. It can be either heroic or modern. Completing Worksheet 5-1 will help them organize their ideas.

5-1. A FANTASTIC TALE

Directions: *A Wizard of Earthsea* is an example of a fantasy. Fantasies are stories in which magic plays an important role. Write a fantasy of your own. It can be set in ancient or modern times, in a world of your design. Complete this worksheet to develop your ideas.

Setting

When my story takes place: _____

Where my story takes place: _____

Brief description of the setting: _____

_____

_____

Main Characters (Use the back if you need more space.)

1. Name: _____ Age: _____

Characteristics: _____

_____

2. Name: _____ Age: _____

Characteristics: _____

_____

Plot

1. What is the quest of the characters?_____

_____

_____

2. What is the major conflict in the story? _____

_____

_____

5-2. QUESTIONS TO CONSIDER FOR
<u>A WIZARD OF EARTHSEA</u>

1. After Sparrowhawk saves his village, Ogion offers to make him his apprentice. What is an apprentice? Why did he do this?

2. In Chapter 2 Ogion says, "Have you never thought how danger must surround power as shadow does light?" What does he mean? How might this be a warning to Sparrowhawk?

3. Why did Sparrowhawk become impatient with Ogion's teaching? Do you think Ogion was right in letting Sparrowhawk go to the school at Roke? Why or why not?

4. Why do you think Jasper makes Sparrowhawk feel foolish? How does Sparrowhawk feel about Jasper? Why does he feel this way?

5. Sparrowhawk had great pride in his magic-working. What is pride? How did his pride lead him to challenge Jasper to a sorcerer's duel? What happened? How did Sparrowhawk feel after the duel?

6. Why did the people of Earthsea hide their true names from all but their most trusted friends and relatives? Why did Vetch give Sparrowhawk his true name? What was so significant about this?

7. When Sparrowhawk returned to Ogion, his former master advised him to no longer run but to "hunt the hunter." What did he mean by this? Do you think his advice was sound? Why or why not? If you were giving a friend similar advice about a problem, how might you word it?

8. When Sparrowhawk finally confronts the shadow, he and it said the same word. What was it? Le Guin wrote: "Light and darkness met, and joined, and were one." What does this mean? What, or who, was the shadow?

5-3. PROJECTS AND ACTIVITIES TO CONSIDER FOR
A WIZARD OF EARTHSEA

1. Sparrowhawk was born with the ability to do magic. Give some examples of people you know who you believe were born with certain abilities. Do they have to practice their talents? Why?

2. Magic plays a prominent role in the story. Write a brief report about what magic is and why some people believe in it. Consult reference books.

3. What was sunreturn? What day of the year is it on our calendar? Why do you think sunreturn was so important to the people of Earthsea? Why do we mark such days as the beginning of spring, summer, autumn, and winter on our calendars today?

4. Either individually or with a partner or small group, write the lyrics of a song praising Sparrowhawk's ultimate victory. If you play an instrument, set the lyrics to music and perform the song for your class.

Curriculum Connections:

1. In Chapter 3 the Master Hand explains that the "world is in balance, in Equilibrium. A Wizard's power of Changing and Summoning can shake the balance of the world." What does he mean? Apply this to ecology and the concept of "balance of nature." Explain how nature is in balance. (Sci)

2. An archipelago is a large group of islands. How might living in such islands affect the way a people develop? (Hint: Think in terms of language, customs, traditions, trade, etc.) (SS)

3. Study a world map and list examples of archipelagos. (SS)

4. In the story, people sang songs of glory, great deeds, and celebrations. What do people sing of today? Give some examples. (A)

© 1994 by The Center for Applied Research in Education

6. Roll of Thunder, Hear My Cry by Mildred Taylor
(Bantam Books, 1976)

Synopsis

An African-American girl living in rural Mississippi during the 1930s, Cassie Logan and her family are owners of rich agricultural land coveted by their white neighbors. Strong and protected from most prejudice, Cassie becomes incensed when her school is given discarded books from the state and she is forced to kowtow to a white girl. Her parents, angry that a white grocery is extorting black families for their crops, decide to boycott and begin driving to a store in Vicksburg, taking orders for other black families. The well-connected grocery owners, upset by the boycott, attack Mr. Logan on the road and his wagon rolls over on him and breaks his leg. Cassie's brother Stacey's troublemaker friend T.J. gets mixed up with the lawless sons of the store owners; they break into a gun shop and assault its owner, who later dies. The white townspeople converge on T.J.'s home and mean to lynch him, but are stopped by a fire that breaks out and threatens a wealthy white man's land. The fire, supposedly caused by lightning, is actually set by Mr. Logan to stop the townspeople. T.J. is then arrested by the sheriff and taken away. As the story progresses, Cassie comes to understand the trials of African-Americans.

Ideas and Concepts to Highlight

1. Review the transitional period between the Emancipation Proclamation in 1865 and the Civil Rights Act of 1964, especially in terms of whites' treatment of blacks. Note the major milestones in that period, such as blacks' role in the World Wars, the Industrial Revolution, Reconstruction, and the 1963 march on Washington, D.C. A good source of information for this is *The African American Experience in U.S. History* (Globe Book Company, 1992), which is written at a middle school reading level.

2. Compare blacks' place in American culture during Cassie's day with modern times. Encourage the class to express their views about what has changed and what has not changed.

3. Discuss symbolism. Explain how people and events can function as metaphors for larger themes that occur frequently in other novels and everyday life.

4. Discuss self-respect and how most black people were forced to swallow their pride regularly. Elicit discussion on the importance of self-image and how its obstruction can affect people.

Writing Connection: "The Melting Pot—Is It What We Want?"

The United States is often referred to as a "melting pot" in which people of various cultures and races have come together to build America and share in the American dream. Whereas in the past most immigrant groups suffered discrimination but were assimilated in time, blacks have had difficulty achieving true equal rights and equal economic opportunities. Reasons given for this vary. Some people feel that because of their skin color blacks have not been able to "blend in" and join the mainstream. Others feel that their past slavery remains an obstacle, an invisible barrier. Also, many individuals today reject the value of the "melting pot," preferring a term like "mosaic" that recognizes the persistence of unique cultural identities.

Instruct your students to examine this issue through their writing. Encourage them to consult references and then write an essay examining the concept of the melting pot. After students complete Worksheet 6-1 you might suggest that they meet in groups and discuss their ideas before writing.

NAME _____ DATE _____ SECTION _____

6-1. THE MELTING POT—IS IT WHAT WE WANT?

Directions: The United States is often described as a "melting pot." While many people would agree with that statement, others would not. Consult the necessary references to answer the questions below, and then write an essay about the American melting pot.

1. What is the concept of the American Melting Pot?_____

_____

_____

_____

_____

2. Do you think all cultural groups would agree with the concept of the melting pot? _____
Why or why not? _____

_____

_____

_____

_____

3. Do you agree with the concept of the melting pot? _____
Why or why not? _____

_____

_____

_____

4. What might make the melting pot better? _____

_____

_____

_____

_____

6-2. QUESTIONS TO CONSIDER FOR ROLL OF THUNDER, HEAR MY CRY

1. Taylor uses strong and precise character descriptions throughout the story. Discuss how her characterization adds to the story's realism. Give some specific examples.

2. Describe the Mississippi of the 1930s where this story takes place. Compare it to your home. How is it alike? How is it different? Consider the physical area as well as the relationships between people.

3. Describe Cassie's reaction when she learns that the books her school received had been discarded by the state. How would you feel in that situation? What would you do about it? Explain.

4. Which character in the book is most like you? Why? Select a scene from the novel and write about what you would have done and said in that character's place.

5. When they learn that a white grocery is extorting blacks for their crops, Cassie's parents become angry and decide to boycott the grocery. Do you think they did the right thing? Why or why not? What else could they have done? Explain.

6. Describe your feelings about the Logans' continuous rejection of Jeremy Simms. Are they justified? How would you treat him if you were in their situation?

7. Discuss some of the symbolism in the book, such as T.J., the fire, Stacey's new coat and the thunder. What do they represent? What other symbols could you add to the story?

8. Cassie changes much throughout the story in her understanding of African-Americans' position in Mississippi in the 1930s. How did her opinions and feelings change from the beginning of the story? Give specific events that affected her the most.

© 1994 by The Center for Applied Research in Education

6-3. PROJECTS AND ACTIVITIES TO CONSIDER FOR ROLL OF THUNDER, HEAR MY CRY

1. Imagine that you are a modern-day Cassie. You go to a store or restaurant and are told that you will not be served and that you cannot buy anything. You are told to leave. How would you feel? Write an essay about your feelings over such an incident and share it with the members of your group.

2. Write a short poem similar to "Roll of Thunder" at the beginning of Chapter 11. Choose any character and write it in the spirit of that person's feelings.

3. Imagine that you are an attorney representing Cassie and her family. You intend to sue the local school system for not providing Cassie and the students at her school an education equal to that of surrounding white schools. What would your arguments be? Around what points would you build your case? Working with a group, write the court scene showing how this drama would be played out. Act the scene for the class.

Curriculum Connections:

1. Research the types of employment available to unskilled blacks in the 1930s. Compare the types of jobs open to them in the past to the types of jobs available now. Also compare incomes for blacks of the past with blacks today. Compare the income of blacks with the income of whites. Give your opinion on how much, or how little, economic conditions for blacks have changed. Include graphs with your report. (SS)

2. What was the period of Reconstruction? How did it affect race relations and the geography and government of the United States? Consult the necessary references and write a brief report. (SS)

3. Make a "family tree" for Cassie, including all the characters related to her who are mentioned in the story. Discuss the importance to Cassie of her family "roots." (SS or A)

4. Read newspapers and magazines that contain national news and cut out articles that involve the African-American experience. Write a few sentences about any trends or connections you discover. Make a collage of the articles and pictures, using your words as a caption. (A)

7. *The Chocolate War* by Robert Cormier
(Dell Publishing, 1974)

Synopsis

Jerry Renault, a freshman quarterback, attends the private Trinity School, which is engineering a large fund-raising chocolate sale. The school's assistant headmaster, Brother Leon, is desperate to raise cash and seeks the backing of The Vigils, a gang of upperclassmen who thrive on intimidation and serve at the pleasure of Archie Costello, an icy senior with little concern for anything except power. The Vigils assign Jerry to reject selling the chocolates for 10 days, but after that time he continues to defy both Brother Leon and The Vigils. He becomes a sort of folk hero, but his refusal is a threat to Archie, The Vigils (who decide to thwart him by selling all the chocolates except Jerry's 50), and the school. After threats and a beating, The Vigils force Jerry to box the school's most vicious street fighter, Emile Janza, in a match governed entirely by students who pay a dollar for the right to call a punch in the ring. The Vigils, on the verge of collapse, are rejuvenated through the fight and the support of Brother Leon.

Ideas and Concepts to Highlight

1. Discuss the power of fear, intimidation and blackmail.

2. Discuss the themes of victimization and "lost innocence."

3. Peer pressure, though the term is never used, plays a significant role in the story. Discuss some of its negative effects, as well as the concepts of individuality and self-respect.

4. Review the concepts of tone and rising tension, and their use in the story. Consider the book's theater-like format, including rising and falling action, climax and denouement.

5. Discuss shifting points of view, and how seeing through the eyes of each character makes the story more engrossing.

Writing Connection: "A Modern-Day Hero"

In *The Chocolate War*, after defying both Brother Leon and The Vigils, Jerry becomes a hero to many of the students. For this writing assignment instruct your students to write about someone they admire and look up to. Completing Worksheet 7-1 will help them to organize their thoughts.

7-1. A MODERN-DAY HERO

Directions: After he stood up to Brother Leon and The Vigils, Jerry became a hero to some of the students. Answer the questions below and write about someone you look up to and admire.

1. Who is the person you admire? _____
   _____

2. What qualities do you admire in this person?_____
   _____
   _____
   _____
   _____
   _____

3. Do others admire this person?_____ If yes, in your opinion, is it for the same reasons?
   _____ Explain. _____
   _____
   _____
   _____
   _____
   _____

4. What is this person's most important accomplishments?_____
   _____
   _____
   _____
   _____
   _____

7-2. QUESTIONS TO CONSIDER FOR
THE CHOCOLATE WAR

1. Who do you think is the most fascinating character in the book? Why? Which one is most like you? Elaborate on why you think so.

2. Many characters in the book are dishonest and deceitful. Do you think this is representative of the people you know? Could a "Chocolate War" happen in your school? Why or why not?

3. Where do you think Jerry gets his strength to resist? What events in his life contribute to his resolve? Create some of the missing background in Jerry's past to support your answer.

4. Why do you think the Brothers ignored The Vigils and their pranks?

5. If a gang like The Vigils was in your school, how might they affect it? Would they have much influence? Would school authorities be able to stop them? How would you feel about them?

6. Consider what effect these events will have on Jerry as an adult. What kind of man do you think he will become? Explain.

7. Define the term "fatal flaw." What is Archie's? How might Carter, Obie and the others topple him?

8. Were you satisfied with the ending? How else could you conclude the action?

9. The story's action is told from a third-person omniscient point of view. Why do you think the author shifts points of view? How would the novel be different if it were told only from Jerry's point of view?

10. How has the story affected your view of peer pressure? Explain The Goobers' feeling that something was "evil" at Trinity.

© 1994 by The Center for Applied Research in Education

7-3. PROJECTS AND ACTIVITIES TO CONSIDER FOR *THE CHOCOLATE WAR*

1. Obtain a book of poems. Select three that you think Jerry would like. Support your choices.

2. Write a prologue scene in the hospital between Jerry and his father, or between Jerry and Brother Leon.

3. Construct a character sketch of Archie Costello. Use examples from the book to support your ideas.

4. Picture Archie in a situation where he chooses the black ball; select any prank and write the scene as if Archie had to perform it. Try to imagine what techniques he would employ, whom he would ask for help and what would be going through his mind.

5. Select a worthy cause—money for a class trip?—and organize and carry out a fund-raiser. Your fund-raiser might be something as simple as a bake sale or a used book sale. If you are daring, you might conduct a candy sale or similar project.

6. List each act of intimidation inflicted on Jerry by the various characters. Taken together, how do they make you feel? Pretend you are Jerry reading this list, and you have been told you would experience them in the next few weeks. What would you do to prevent them, given your resources?

Curriculum Connections:

1. Imagine that the fund-raiser in the story was successful with big sales. Create a chart that records the sales. Include columns for total units, units sold, costs, summaries, etc. (SS and A)

2. Compare The Vigils, who thrive on mental intimidation, to a gang that asserts or defends itself through violence. Consider the tactics of each. Which is more convincing to you? More frightening? Which one would you rather belong to, if forced to choose? Consult references if necessary. (SS)

8. *The Slave Dancer* by Paula Fox
(Dell Publishing, 1973)

Synopsis

Jessie Bollier, a 13-year-old poor white boy living in 1840s New Orleans, is kidnapped by pirates and forced to sail on a slave ship to Africa. Talented at playing the fife, Jessie's main function as a crew hand is to "dance the slaves," so that they will move about on deck and prevent their muscles from atrophying. Although the crew is generally a cruel lot, a few befriend the boy and show him how to avoid trouble with Captain Cawthorne, first mate Nicholas Spark, and the treacherous Benjamin Stout. The ship sails to Africa and picks up a cargo of Africans. After three diseased and famine-riddled months at sea, the ship is overtaken by American law enforcers and flees into a storm, dumping slaves and other evidence in the ocean as it goes. Jessie and one young slave about his own age hide in the hold in the ship's belly, and when the ship is wrecked in the storm, only they survive. They swim to shore in Mississippi, and are taken in by Daniel, an aged black man hiding from captivity in the woods. The two boys, though they cannot communicate, become friends. The young African boy is smuggled to the north, while Jessie returns to his family. The experience has a lasting impression on Jessie, who never again can listen to music.

Ideas and Concepts to Highlight

1. *The Slave Dancer* was written by a woman, yet it is told from a boy's point of view. Discuss the concept of taking on such a challenge in writing, and how young writers might adopt a point of view so different from their own.

2. Slavery as an institution makes up a significant piece of American history, well-explored in literature and nonfiction and highly charged with emotion. Compare some of the history and lore with modern-day situations. Bring history to life by noting how some of today's news stories may be the stuff of future novels.

3. Jessie, as a 13-year-old, feels many emotions that are typical of children his age. Encourage students to imagine modern situations comparable to Jessie's plight, and predict how they would react.

4. Discuss slavery as an immoral act that benefited people like Cawthorne, who considered it his "God-given trade." Compare it to current world events, in which great evils may be committed by people who believe staunchly in their cause for political or religious reasons or personal gain.

Writing Connection: "Abduction"

Instruct your students to imagine that they, or someone they know, is abducted. They might review Jessie's feelings in the story when he was abducted and taken aboard the ship. Completing Worksheet 8-1 first will help students clarify their thoughts for writing. Upon the completion of the writing, consider having students share their stories in small groups.

8-1. ABDUCTION

Directions: Imagine that you are abducted. Write a story about this chilling event. Answer the questions below to help you generate ideas.

1. Who abducts you?_____

2. Where are you abducted? _____

3. How are you abducted?_____

_____

_____

_____

_____

4. Why are you abducted? _____

_____

_____

_____

_____

5. What happens while you are abducted? _____

_____

_____

_____

_____

6. How do you escape? _____

_____

_____

_____

_____

8-2. QUESTIONS TO CONSIDER FOR
THE SLAVE DANCER

1. Jessie, at the outset of the story, is disrespectful toward Aunt Agatha and feels scorn for her. How would you feel toward a woman like her? What do Jessie's thoughts and actions toward his aunt say about his character before his ordeal?

2. Trace the evolution of Jessie's feelings toward Benjamin Stout. Describe some of the foreshadowing in the story that warns Jessie of Stout's true character. Was Jessie justified in his initial assessment?

3. Compare the egg-stealing incident and the resulting punishment to a crime of theft today. Do you think modern punishments are more likely to stop people from committing crimes than old-time consequences? Why or why not?

4. Explore Stout's character. Is he the same as or different from the other men? Compare Stout to Purvis. How are they alike? How are they different?

5. Explain the crew's lack of remorse for the treatment of the slaves. Why do they feel they are superior? How might they feel threatened and defensive?

6. Jessie at one point says he hates the slaves. Explore this complicated emotion. Why does he feel this way? Where do you think his anger truly comes from?

7. Midway through the story, Ned emerges as one of the more moral characters. Why did he continue to work on a slave ship? Do you think he is any less to blame because he is not as harsh as the others and claims to dislike all men? Why or why not?

8-3. PROJECTS AND ACTIVITIES TO CONSIDER FOR THE SLAVE DANCER

1. Consider Daniel's complex emotions, as a black man, as he releases Ras. Compare it to what he feels toward Jessie, a white boy. Write the final scene of that chapter from Daniel's point of view.

2. Trace the development of Jessie's feelings toward blacks throughout the major events in the story. How is his attitude different in the end? Write an essay about how people's positive experiences with other races promote tolerance. Support your thoughts with concrete examples—from newspapers, television, magazines, movies or personal experience.

3. Ras and Jessie are unable to communicate verbally, yet play together in harmony. Imagine yourself on a vacation in an unfamiliar place and meeting someone who cannot speak your language. Create a short story about the experience.

4. Compare Jessie's distasteful "job" to an experience you have had, where you had to do something you didn't like or knew was wrong. If you cannot think of such an experience, create one. Pay particular attention to your feelings about it, and the pressures you experienced.

Curriculum Connections:

1. Research the Emancipation Proclamation of 1865, and the Civil Rights Act of 1964. What are the major achievements of each? Which was a greater step toward racial equality? Support your argument with factual examples of blacks' place in society at either time. (SS)

2. Research and report on diseases that plagued crew members and Africans on the slave ships. Detail the symptoms and suffering. What types of treatments and medicines are available today for these diseases? (Sci)

3. There are many situations in history that were accepted in their time but are considered wrong now. Indentured servants were common during colonial days. What was an indentured servant? (Consult references if necessary.) How was an indentured servant different than a slave? Why in your opinion are there no openly indentured servants today? (SS)

9. *The Princess Bride* by William Goldman
(Ballantine Books, 1974)

Synopsis

This story is a fast-moving spoof of the standard fairy tale. Buttercup, the most beautiful woman in the world, loves Westley, a farm boy, who is very handsome. When Westley sails to America to make his fortune so that he and Buttercup can have a fine future together, he is captured by the Dread Pirate Roberts. Fearing Westley dead, Buttercup vows never to love again. When Prince Humperdinck proposes marriage to Buttercup, she tells him that she can never love him. The Prince is unconcerned by that, however, for he plans to kill her anyway and blame her death on a rival kingdom. He arranges to have Buttercup kidnapped before the wedding, but Westley, who has survived and has assumed the identity of the Dread Pirate Roberts, saves her by defeating her kidnappers: Inigo, a master swordsman; Fezzik, a giant; and Vizzini, a Sicilian. Humperdinck captures Westley and Buttercup and decides to marry Buttercup after all, and then strangle her. He has Westley tortured and killed (so he thinks), but Inigo and Fezzik recover Westley's body and take him to a wizard who brings him back to life. Inigo needs Westley to help him find Count Rugen, who killed Inigo's father and who Inigo has vowed to kill in turn. In the end, Inigo kills the Count and Westley saves Buttercup.

Ideas and Concepts to Highlight

1. Discuss the elements of the classic fairy tale—the theme of good and evil, a beautiful princess and her handsome hero, the triumph of good over evil. Note how this story is a spoof.

2. Discuss Goldman's authorial intrusions. Why does he do this? Does it enhance the story?

3. Point out how Goldman describes the characters in physical detail, and keeps returning to the concept of beauty. Buttercup, for example, is the most beautiful woman in the world. Discuss the idea of beauty and handsomeness in American culture.

4. Note the writing style. It is light and fast. The dialogue is sharp, witty, and has a modern sound to it. How does this affect the story?

Writing Connection: "Beauty"

Throughout the story Goldman seems to be poking gentle fun at the idea of beauty. Discuss with your students the importance of beauty in contemporary American society. Consider the media, entertainment, and cosmetics industries. Is beauty really that important?

Instruct your students to complete Worksheet 9-1, and then write either an essay or story showing how beauty plays a major part in American culture today.

9-1. BEAUTY

Directions: Beauty (and handsomeness) seems to be very important in American culture. Just think about TV, the movies, and fashion models. But is it *really* that important? Answer the questions on the worksheet and then write an essay or a story about beauty.

1. Is beauty important?_____ If yes, why? If no, why not?_____
_____
_____
_____

2. What makes someone beautiful? _____
_____
_____
_____

3. Why might feeling beautiful, attractive, or "trendy" be important to people? _____
_____
_____
_____
_____

4. Which do you feel is more important in a person—appearance or personality? _____
Explain. _____
_____
_____
_____
_____

© 1994 by The Center for Applied Research in Education

9-2. QUESTIONS TO CONSIDER FOR
THE PRINCESS BRIDE

1. When did Buttercup decide she loved Westley? How did she come to realize this? What was Westley's reaction to her telling him that she loved him? Why do you think he reacted the way he did?

2. Why did Westley decide to go to America? What happened on his voyage? What was Buttercup's reaction when she heard?

3. Goldman uses an unusual format in which he interrupts the story at key points. Do his intrusions add to the story? Do they detract from it? Why? What might Goldman's reason for doing this be?

4. Buttercup tells Prince Humperdinck that she cannot love him. But then she agrees to marry him. Why?

5. Why did Inigo become a swordsman? What was his purpose in seeking the six-fingered man? How skilled a swordsman was he? Give some examples. What happened when Inigo couldn't find the six-fingered man? What does this say about his character?

6. What happened when Inigo dueled the man in black? How did Inigo handle his defeat?

7. Why did the Prince plan to kill Buttercup?

8. Describe Count Rugen's character. What did he like to do? Why?

9. Westley was able to withstand his torture by "taking his brain away." What does that mean? Is it possible for anyone to do that? Explain.

10. After he realized who the man in black was, Inigo decided it was necessary to save him. Why did he do this?

11. In the climax, Goldman keeps noting the time, in a type of countdown. Why do you think he did this? Explain.

9-3. PROJECTS AND ACTIVITIES TO CONSIDER FOR
THE PRINCESS BRIDE

1. Why do you think Goldman provided such detailed physical descriptions of the characters? Choose one of the main characters and write a paragraph describing him or her in detail.

2. The dialogue of the story is snappy and witty. How does it add to the story? Take a scene and rewrite it with a formal dialogue that fits in more with the setting of the story. How does a formal dialogue change the story?

3. Assume that Prince Humperdinck immediately begins hunting Westley, Buttercup, Inigo, and Fezzik. Write a new ending to the story.

4. Watch the movie, *The Princess Bride* (Twentieth Century Fox). How are the novel and movie version of the story alike? How are they different? Write a movie review of the film.

5. The Dread Pirate Roberts was unlike most pirates. Read *Captain Blood* by Rafael Sabatini (Grosset, 1922) and write a book review. Share the review with other members of your class.

Curriculum Connections.

1. Goldman gives little thought to real history. List several examples of how he bends history to fit the needs of his story. For example, he notes in one place that the story happens "before Europe," but then, when Westley announces that he is sailing to America, says, "This was just after America…" (SS)

2. Throughout history royal marriages were often arranged for political reasons. Consult references and find some examples where royalty married, not for love, but for politics. Compile your notes and present a brief oral report to your class or group. (SS)

3. Pick a favorite scene of the book and create a comic strip of it. Change the dialogue if necessary to fit your comic strip. (A)

10. <u>*Julie of the Wolves*</u> by Jean Craighead George
(Harper and Row, 1972)

Synopsis

When Miyax (Julie), a 13-year-old Eskimo girl, can no longer tolerate her life with her husband, Daniel, she feels that she has no choice but to leave. Leaving, though, means crossing the tundra. Taking only essentials that she needs to survive, she begins walking, her destination being her pen pal's home in San Francisco. Despite her knowledge of the Arctic (which she obtained from her father whom she believes is dead), Miyax soon learns that the tundra is more vast and dangerous than she had thought. She becomes lost and runs out of food. Her only hope of survival is to gain the acceptance of a nearby pack of wolves. Through great effort in learning their ways, she wins their confidence and they come to view her as one of their own. She develops a close kinship with the wolves, who share their food with her and help her to make her way across the tundra. As she does, she realizes much about civilization and the world of the far north. When she finally finds her father alive, he has changed much and Miyax understands that the old world of the Eskimo is gone.

Ideas and Concepts to Highlight

1. Discuss the world of the Eskimo and how it has changed in recent years. Note how Miyax tried to cling unsuccessfully to the old ways.

2. Locate the Arctic Circle on a map, and especially Barrow and the North Slope of Alaska. This area is a major oil-producing region; discuss how the coming of such technology would likely affect the lives of the Eskimo.

3. Note the climate and terrain of the tundra.

4. Emphasize the environmental overtones of the book, particularly how the animals and plants exist in a "balance of nature."

5. Point out the structure of the book, that it opens with Miyax lost on the tundra, then details her time up to leaving Daniel, and concludes with her finding her father whom she thought was dead.

Writing Connection: "Surviving in the Wilderness"

Miyax was alone on the tundra where she survived on her resourcefulness and the help of a wolf pack. For this writing assignment, ask your students to imagine that with a parent or an older sibling, they will be going on a two-week survival trek to a wilderness area of their choice. How would they plan for this journey? What would they take?

Instruct your students to complete Worksheet 10-1 and write a story of how they would survive in the wilderness.

10-1. SURVIVING IN THE WILDERNESS

Directions: Imagine that you and a parent or older brother or sister are going on a two-week survival trip. Could you do it? Answer the questions below and write a story about your imaginary experience.

1. Where would you go on your wilderness survival trip? _____
_____ Why? _____
_____

2. Who would go with you? _____
_____

3. Describe the area you are going to. _____
_____
_____

4. What items or materials will you need to survive? _____
_____
_____

5. How will you get to this place? _____
_____
_____

6. Where will you stay once you arrive? _____
_____

7. How will you spend your days? _____
_____
_____

10-2. *QUESTIONS TO CONSIDER FOR*
JULIE OF THE WOLVES

1. Why did Miyax believe that the wolves might help her get food? How did she hope to communicate with them? Think of some of the animals you know. Do they have certain actions that tell you how they are feeling? Give some examples in your explanation.

2. Why was Miyax alone on the tundra? How had she gotten lost? Do you think her attempt to cross the tundra alone was a wise one? Explain.

3. Throughout her ordeal on the tundra, Miyax recalls much of Kapugen's advice. At one point she recalls he said: "Change your ways when fear seizes, for it usually means you are doing something wrong." What did he mean? Explain how you could apply that advice to your own life.

4. What did Miyax learn from Amy? Why was having Amy as a pen pal important to her?

5. Why did Miyax agree to marry Daniel even though she was only 13 years old? Can you imagine being married at 13? Explain.

6. How did the hunters' killing of Amaroq change Miyax's thinking about civilization? How did this experience change Miyax?

7. What was Miyax's impression of Daniel? Was she right in leaving him and attempting to cross the tundra? What else could she have done?

8. When Miyax is reunited with Kapugen in Kangik, what does she find? How has Kapugen changed? How did Miyax feel about him?

9. At the conclusion of the story after Miyax buries Tornait in the snow, she said: "...the hour of the wolf and the Eskimo is over." What did she mean?

10-3. PROJECTS AND ACTIVITIES TO CONSIDER FOR
JULIE OF THE WOLVES

1. Miyax learned several ways that wolves communicate. For example, upon rising from sleep, they wagged their tails in greeting of each other. Observe a pet, or a bird, squirrel or other animal around your home, and record its actions and their possible meanings. Share your notes with the members of your group.

2. To pass the time and loneliness, Miyax invented rhymes about the tundra. Write your own rhyme about your own environment.

3. Describe the order of the wolf pack. Amaroq, for example, was the leader. Who was next? What position did Jello occupy? What position did the pups occupy? Which pup was the most important? Design a chart to display the order.

4. Miyax's knowledge of the tundra was impressive. Working with a group, compile a list of how she used her knowledge to survive. An example—she dug out a hole in the frozen ground and used it as a refrigerator. Share your list with other groups.

Curriculum Connections:

1. After Kapu brought Miyax a caribou leg, she cut it up and cooked it. As it cooked, she felt inspired to dance. Create your idea of Miyax's dance. (A)

2. Identify the areas wolves currently inhabit in North America. Once they were found on much of the continent. Why have their numbers declined? Consult references and write a brief report. (Sci)

3. When wolves hunt a herd of caribou, they single out the oldest, slowest, or weakest. How might this be good for the herd? Explain. (Sci)

4. Describe the climate and terrain of the tundra. What kinds of animals and what types of vegetation would you find there? Consult the necessary references. (Sci)

5. Life on the tundra is bound in cycles, particularly that of predator and prey. Give several examples of predator-prey relationships found on the tundra. Consult references if necessary. (Sci)

6. The Arctic is known as the "land of the midnight sun." What does this mean? When does night begin and how long does it last? Consult references if necessary. (Sci)

11. *The Contender* by Robert Lipsyte
(Harper Keypoint, 1987)

Synopsis

Albert Brooks seems to be going nowhere. A high-school dropout, he works at a dead-end job in a small grocery store. His friends don't have jobs and are slowly drifting into drug use and theft. They try to pull him in with them, but Albert resists. A vague something in Albert wants more. He begins going to Donatelli's gym where he starts training as a boxer. Mr. Donatelli, who has trained champions, tells him straight out "Nothing's promised to you," but Albert accepts the challenge. As he continues his training, he learns that it is not the win that is important, but that it is what's inside a person that really counts.

Ideas and Concepts to Highlight

1. Discuss the setting, which may be unfamiliar to students who don't live in a major city.

2. The book offers conflicting opinions of blacks toward whites. For example, Hollis blames whites for the condition of blacks, while Uncle Wilson and Jeff see the world changing into a place where there are many opportunities for blacks. Note the effects of these opinions on Albert and how he balances them with his own experiences.

3. Note that being a "Contender" represents more than just the boxing ring; it represents life as well.

4. Point out how Albert changes after he begins training. The training strengthens his self-esteem which in turn influences his outlook on life.

Writing Connection: "The Expert"

Through training, Albert becomes a good boxer. Ask your students about some of the things they do well. Some might take dance lessons, others might be good athletes, while still others may have artistic talent. Discuss what it takes to become really "good" at something.

For this writing assignment, instruct your students to think of something they do well. Either in the form of a personal narrative or a story, they are to write about being an expert. Completing Worksheet 11-1 will help them get started.

11-1. THE EXPERT

Directions: Think about something you do well. It might be a hobby, a sport, a craft, dancing, or other activity. Answer the questions below. Then write either a personal narrative or story about "The Expert."

1. What are you an expert in? _____

_____

_____

_____

2. How did you become an expert? _____

_____

_____

_____

3. Why do you like this activity? _____

_____

_____

_____

_____

4. Do you plan to pursue this activity as you get older? Why or why not? _____

_____

_____

_____

5. What advice could you give to others who are just starting this activity? _____

_____

_____

_____

© 1994 by The Center for Applied Research in Education

11-2. QUESTIONS TO CONSIDER FOR
THE CONTENDER

1. Why did Albert refuse to go with his friends to rob Epsteins' grocery store? How did he feel about not going? How did he feel after he found out that James had been caught by the police? Why did Albert care so much about James?

2. On the Monday after the attempted robbery, when Albert returned to work, the Epsteins no longer trusted him. Do you think they were being fair to him? Why or why not? How important is trust between people? Explain.

3. When Albert first met Donatelli, the trainer said to him: "Nothing's promised to you." What did he mean?

4. After he watched the fight at the Garden, Albert was confronted by Major and Hollis, who wanted him to disconnect the burglar alarm at Epsteins' grocery. When Albert refused, Major threatened him with a knife. What happened? Why is Albert's action significant? What does this tell you about his character? Explain.

5. Why did Albert accept Major's invitation to go to the clubhouse again? What happened when Albert met James? Why do you think Albert stayed when he knew he shouldn't because he was in training?

6. After the incident with Major and the stolen car, Albert tells himself that he "ain't gonna be a boxer anyway." Why does he say this? Do you think he really means it? Why or why not?

7. The title of the story, *The Contender*, has an obvious meaning of boxers "contending" in the ring. But it also can be applied to life. Explain. What does a person need to be a contender?

8. After his first fight, Aunt Pearl tells Albert how, when she was a young woman, she was offered a contract to sing in a stage show. Because she was only seventeen, her mother had to sign for her, but her mother refused. Why did Pearl tell Albert this? What was Albert's reaction?

9. Why did Albert fight once more? How did the fight with Hubbard turn out? Why did Albert stay in the ring so long, even when he was getting beaten?

1. Why do many of the blacks in the story distrust whites? Does this view mirror our society? What programs, actions, or laws might help to bring blacks and whites into greater understanding and harmony? Consult the necessary references and organize a panel to discuss this issue.

2. Imagine that you are a sports writer. Choose one of Albert's fights and write a sports article about it.

3. Create a scene in which Albert is able to steer James away from drugs before James becomes addicted. Write the dialogue and act it out with the help of your classmates.

4. What happened with Albert's fight with Barnes? Why did Donatelli want Albert to quit after the fight? Do you think Donatelli was right? Why or why not? Discuss this in your group. List reasons pro and con.

5. James turned to drugs. Why do you think he did this? Research how and where people who are addicted to drugs can get help. Create a poster or pamphlet with this information and share it with your class.

Curriculum Connections:

1. Study the Civil Rights Movement. Compare the general conditions for blacks in this country before the Civil Rights Act of 1964 with now. Have conditions improved since then? How? In what ways? Give some examples. (SS)

2. Many people tried to influence Albert in the story. Create a chart and record how people tried to influence Albert. Include Major, Hollis, James, Aunt Pearl, Henry, Uncle Wilson, and Mr. Donatelli. (Feel free to include some of the other characters as well.) Who do you think was the biggest influence on him? Explain. (SS or A)

12. *The Sword in the Stone* by T.H. White
(Putnam, 1939)

Synopsis

Wart is destined to be King Arthur, but before he can assume his role as England's king he must be educated. Although Sir Ector provides Wart and Kay, his own son, with the necessary learning of the day, he realizes it is not enough and he wishes to find a tutor. Not long after that, Merlyn, a magician, arrives. Merlyn's purpose (unknown to Wart, who is unaware of his destiny) is to educate Wart so that he will be an able ruler. To that end he provides an education built on magic and reality, in which he turns Wart into various animals, giving the boy the chance to gain valuable knowledge from different perspectives. When Kay is to become a knight, Wart is to be his squire. Although accepting his position, Wart nevertheless wishes that he could be a knight, too. He accompanies Kay and Sir Ector to London where Kay is to take part in a tournament. When Kay leaves his sword behind, Wart must find him another. The only one he can get is a sword stuck in an anvil at a church. It is the Sword in the Stone that only the new king of England can pull out. Not realizing the sword's significance, Wart pulls it from the anvil.

Ideas and Concepts to Highlight

1. Explain castle life of Medieval England. Emphasize how White uses vivid detail to paint a realistic setting.

2. Point out the blending of magic and reality in the story.

3. Explain personification and note some of the many examples of it.

4. Discuss the differences between Kay and Wart, and note how Wart grows in understanding and knowledge throughout the story.

Writing Connection: "A Humanlike Acquaintance"

Personification is a literary device by which the author gives human qualities to non-human things or ideas. Giving objects and animals human traits can add a rich element to fiction.

For this assignment, instruct your students to imagine that something in their house or yard suddenly assumes human qualities. Students are to write a short story about their suddenly humanlike acquaintance. Completing Worksheet 12-1 will help them to generate ideas.

12-1. A HUMANLIKE ACQUAINTANCE

Directions: Personification is a literary technique authors use to give human qualities to non-human things or ideas. Talking animals, an evil tree whose branches grab unsuspecting hikers, and a thinking, feeling river are all examples of personification.

Imagine that something in your home or yard suddenly takes on human qualities. Complete the worksheet and write a brief story about your new acquaintance.

1. What "thing" did you select to be personified? _____

_____

_____

2. How did it assume human qualities? _____

_____

_____

3. What does it do once it has human qualities? _____

_____

_____

_____

4. What would your parents or friends probably say about it? _____

_____

_____

_____

5. Does it return to normal? _____   If yes, how? _____

_____   _____   If no, what happens next?_____

_____

12-2. QUESTIONS TO CONSIDER FOR
THE SWORD IN THE STONE

1. What was Kay's reaction when he and Wart lost Cully? What was Wart's reaction? What do their reactions tell you about their characters?

2. Describe how Wart's education is different from yours. Give some examples. Merlyn says, "Education is experience." Explain what he meant.

3. Choose one of the animals that is personified in the story and describe his character. What did Wart learn from this character?

4. Kay became jealous of Merlyn's attention to Wart and said, "Merlyn does everything for you, but he never does anything for me." How did Wart feel about this? What did he do? Describe what happened when the boys went on their "adventure."

5. There is much humor in the story. What character did you find most amusing? Why? What scene did you find most amusing? Why? Would the story have been as interesting without the humor? Why or why not?

6. As Kay and Wart grew up, Kay no longer cared to associate with Wart. Why?

7. How did Wart feel about Kay becoming a knight? Why did Wart refer to himself as Cinderella?

8. The first time Wart tried to pull the sword from the stone, what happened? How did he gain the strength to pull it out?

9. Do you think that Wart's education will help him to be a good king? Why or why not?

12-3. PROJECTS AND ACTIVITIES TO CONSIDER FOR THE SWORD IN THE STONE

1. Imagine that you were a reporter at the time of the story. Write an article about the old king's death and the search for a new king who could pull the Sword from the Stone.

2. Based on the story, write a prediction of the type of king you would expect Arthur to be. Use examples from the story to back up your ideas.

3. The dialogue of the story is reminiscent of Medieval England. It also shows how language changes over the years. For example, many words that we use today were not known a few hundred years ago. Working with a group, generate a list of words that Wart would not be familiar with. Some examples—astronaut, computer, television. Share your list with other groups. Compile a class list and think of a title for it.

4. Read another book or account of King Arthur. A good suggestion: *A Connecticut Yankee in King Arthur's Court* by Mark Twain (Morrow, 1988). How does this book compare with *The Sword in the Stone?*

5. Working with a group of three or four students, create a storyboard showing Wart when he was changed into different animals. What did he learn from each? Share your findings with the class or your group.

Curriculum Connections:

1. Although much legend surrounds King Arthur, most historians agree that he was a real man. Consult reference books and present an oral report to the class on the real versus legendary King Arthur. (SS)

2. The time of knights is often referred to as the Age of Chivalry. What does this mean? Working with a group, consult references to learn about the Age of Chivalry. With another group, debate the question, "Was There Really an Age of Chivalry?" (SS)

3. When Arthur was king, the castle dominated much of English life. Consult references and write a report describing life at the typical castle. Include facts both about noblemen and women and commoners. (SS)

4. Using clay, create a model of a medieval castle. (A)

© 1994 by The Center for Applied Research in Education

13. *The Upstairs Room* by Johanna Reiss
(Thomas Y. Crowell Company, 1972)

Synopsis

World War II begins and Jews all across Europe are in danger. When the Germans attack Holland and occupy Winterswijk, the town where the de Leeuw family lives, Annie and her family are forced to separate and go into hiding. Eight-year-old Annie and her older sister, Sini, eventually come to stay with the Oostervelds, a farm family who keep the girls safe from the Germans, at considerable risk to themselves. Told from Annie's point of view, the story recounts the initial innocence she at first had about the war and the terror, anger, and sadness she felt during the long years in hiding. Her story also shows the courage, resourcefulness, and unbreakable spirit people can call upon when living through horrifying, life-threatening events.

Ideas and Concepts to Highlight

1. Provide background information on World War II. Although the causes of the war had their roots in the conclusion of World War I, World War II officially began in 1939 when Germany attacked Poland. In response, Britain and France declared war on Germany and the war spread rapidly. By the summer of 1940, Nazi Germany had overrun most of Western Europe. In 1941 the Germans attacked Russia, opening a second front. After Pearl Harbor, Germany, an ally of Japan, declared war on the United States. Just a few hours later, the U.S. declared war on Japan, Germany, and Italy, which was allied with Germany and Japan, together called the Axis Powers. The countries allied with the U.S. were called the Allies. The war finally ended in 1945, but only after millions of people had died, including an estimated six million Jews who were systematically murdered by the Nazis in what is now known as the Holocaust.

2. Explain that the story is written from Annie's point of view, that of a young girl. Note that throughout the story, Annie interjects her thoughts and feelings.

3. Emphasize that along with the barbarity of war there was also courage and kindness. Many people risked their own lives to save others.

4. Discuss propaganda and how countries use it during wartime.

Writing Connection: "Hatred"

The German persecution of the Jews underscores hatred on a worldwide scale. However, hatred, bias, and intolerance are found, unfortunately, just about everywhere. Your students are undoubtedly aware of this, and may have experienced prejudice themselves. For this writing, ask your students to consider why some people hate others. Ask students to complete Worksheet 13-1 first, then meet in groups to discuss their feelings before writing.

13-1. HATRED

Directions: Consider the issue of hatred. At the least, it might result in a nasty or hurtful remark to another person. At the worst, it can lead to violence. Answer the questions below and then write an essay detailing your views on the topic.

1.   What can cause people to hate others? _____

_____

_____

_____

_____

2.   Give some examples of hateful acts. _____

_____

_____

_____

_____

3.   Have you or someone you know ever been a victim of a hateful act? _____If yes, how,

when, and why?_____

_____

_____

_____

_____

4.   What can be done to lessen hatred? _____

_____

_____

_____

_____

© 1994 by The Center for Applied Research in Education

13-2. QUESTIONS TO CONSIDER FOR
THE UPSTAIRS ROOM

1. Why didn't Annie's mother want to go to America? Do you think the reason she gave was the real reason? Explain.

2. Did the de Leeuw family believe they would be safe in their new home outside of Winterswijk? Did you think they would be safe? Explain.

3. Compare the attitudes of Annie's father and mother about the German occupation. Which one do you think had a better understanding of what was "really" happening? Explain.

4. Several people, at great personal risk, were willing to help Jews during the war—Reverend Zwaal, the Hanninks, the Oostervelds, for example. Explain why you think they would do this.

5. Johann Oosterveld listened to what he called "the real news" on the radio. What did he mean by that? When might the "news" not be the news?

6. Pick an adjective to describe each of the Oostervelds—Johann, Dientje, and Opoe. Why did Annie and Sini feel safe with them?

7. Johann often referred to himself as a "dumb farmer." Do you think he was being accurate in referring to himself like this? Why or why not?

8. When Johann went to hide out in Enschede, Dientje sent the girls back to the Hanninks. Why did she do this? How did Annie feel about this?

9. How do you think Annie felt about the Oostervelds? Explain.

10. How do you think Annie's experience might have affected her? What kinds of values might she hold as an adult because of her ordeal? Explain.

13-3. PROJECTS AND ACTIVITIES TO CONSIDER FOR
THE UPSTAIRS ROOM

1. Research the term "propaganda." What is it? When is it used? When might propaganda be justified? Select an article from the newspaper and rewrite it as propaganda. Hint: An article about international conflict would be best for this.

2. Working with a group, research the causes of World War II. Organize a panel discussion of how the war might have been prevented. What should have been done? Did other countries such as Britain, France, and the United States have a right or responsibility to stop Hitler before he was strong enough to wage war?

3. Imagine that you are Annie, with the Oostervelds during the war. Write a letter to her father. What would she say?

4. Annie and Sini made up rhymes during their stay with the Oostervelds. Work with a partner and assume that you are in their situation. What kinds of rhymes would you make up? Share them with other groups.

5. Imagine that you had to remain hidden in your house every day with only the other members of the household knowing you were there. You had no TV, a radio that only offered news once a day, no books to read, no stereo, no games. Write a short description of how you would spend your days.

6. Write a tribute to the Oostervelds.

Curriculum Connections:

1. Research Kristallnacht. What was it? When and why did it happen? Describe what happened. Write a brief report. (SS)

2. Working with a partner or small group, create a timeline showing the major events of World War II. (SS)

3. Draw or create a model of one of Annie's and Sini's hiding places. (A)

4. Draw a map of Europe. Label the countries and major geographical features. Supply the names and dates of major battles, the dates of German occupation and subsequent liberation. (SS or A)

© 1994 by The Center for Applied Research in Education

14. *The Pigman* by Paul Zindel
(Harper & Row, 1968)

Synopsis

John and Lorraine are two lonely high school students who entertain themselves and each other by making crank phone calls. One of Lorraine's calls, as she poses as a charity worker, is to Angelo Pignati, an old widower who invites them over. They meet him, to his delight, and he treats them with respect, interest and kindness—unlike anything they are used to in their unhappy homes. They go to the zoo with him and gradually spend much of their free afternoons at his home and let him buy them things. One evening, after a shopping spree, the three race around the house on new roller skates and the Pigman—so named as much for his collection of pig figurines as his name—suffers a heart attack. John and Lorraine look after the house during his hospital stay, and decide to throw a party. Dozens of young people show up, and they explore all corners of the Pigman's house. Fights break out, and during the melee the Pigman comes home in a taxi. John and Lorraine are arrested but the Pigman declines to press charges, feeling only disappointment and betrayal. In their remorse they ask him to meet them at the zoo. During the visit, the Pigman discovers that his favorite baboon, Bobo, died during his absence. The Pigman suffers another heart attack and dies at the zoo. The book's format alternates, and the story is recounted as a "memorial epic," one chapter written by John, the next by Lorraine, and so on.

Ideas and Concepts to Highlight

1. Review the unusual format of the book. Discuss its effectiveness in the first person, and note the differences in point of view between John and Lorraine.

2. Discuss growing up through experience, in the context of platonic boy-girl relationships.

3. Have students share some of their experiences with elderly people, specifically those who are not related to them.

4. Explore the idea of loneliness, and point out how John and Lorraine lessened the Pigman's loneliness.

Writing Connection: "When Boys and Girls Are Just Friends"

John and Lorraine had a platonic relationship, which is quite different from the typical teen boy-girl relationship that centers around dating. Instruct your students to explore the topic, "When Boys and Girls Are Just Friends" by completing Worksheet 14-1, and then write an essay on it. At the end of the writing, you might like to compile the class's essays in a book by the same title.

14-1. WHEN BOYS AND GIRLS ARE JUST FRIENDS

Directions: John and Lorraine were friends. They weren't dating and they weren't in love. How was their relationship different from the usual boy-girl relationship?

Think about the pressures on boy-girl relationships. Answer the questions on the worksheet, and then write an essay on the topic.

1. Can teenage boys and girls be close friends? _____

Why or why not? _____

_____

_____

_____

2. How do boys and girls act toward each other when they are close friends? _____

_____

_____

3. How do they act toward each other when they are interested in dating? _____

_____

_____

4. Is there pressure on good friends to date each other? _____

Why or why not? _____

_____

5. If you have a close friend of the opposite sex, do you treat him or her differently than your

same-sex friends? _____ If yes, how? If not, why not? _____

_____

_____

_____

_____

14-2. QUESTIONS TO CONSIDER FOR
THE PIGMAN

1. What do you think draws John and Lorraine together? What draws them to the Pigman? Do you think that they like him as a friend, or do they "use" him to buy them things? What draws the Pigman to John and Lorraine? Who do you think values the relationship more—John and Lorraine or the Pigman? Explain.

2. What is an "alter ego"? How does the term apply to the book? Describe what your alter ego would be like.

3. Both John and Lorraine have unhappy family relationships. Do you think their portrayal of their parents is accurate? What might they do to help improve their family relationships? Explain and offer some examples.

4. Describe your feelings, as an observer, as you read about the events at the party. Compare them to John's and Lorraine's, who are participants.

5. John is an attention seeker, as is Lorraine to a lesser extent. Why do they do the provoking things they do? Are their purposes achieved or do they misfire? Explain. Think of some of the things you do for "effect" and write about why and how they make you feel.

6. What would you do if you met someone like the Pigman? Would you be friends with him? Would you let him buy you things? How would you treat him? If you did become friends with him, how would you react at his funeral?

7. Why do you think Zindel chose to alternate the format of this story, having John write a chapter, then Lorraine, and so on? Do you think that this was a wise choice? Why or why not? Could he have chosen a better format? Explain.

8. What is your opinion of John and Lorraine? Do you like them? Would you like to have either of them as friends? Why or why not?

14-3. PROJECTS AND ACTIVITIES TO CONSIDER FOR
THE PIGMAN

1. Create a chart that lists at least three values held by John, Lorraine, and the Pigman. Which ones, if any, do they share? What do their values say about each of them?

2. Read some magazine and newspaper advertising. Cut out a picture that resembles your mental representation of the Pigman. Discuss the amount of physical description in the novel, and explain whether or not you believe it is adequate.

3. Write and deliver a eulogy for the Pigman.

4. Notice the unusual tactic of shifting points of view. Select a few paragraphs and write them from the opposite point of view, keeping in mind the alternate character's style and values. Does the change in point of view change the impression on the reader? How?

5. Many elderly people live alone and consequently are lonely and isolated. Research what social agencies are available in your community to help the elderly. Imagine that you are a social worker and wish to inform the elderly about these organizations. Write a brochure explaining what organizations they can turn to for help and how they can be contacted.

Curriculum Connections:

1. Research heart attacks and present an oral report to your group or class. What are the major contributing factors? What can be done to reduce the risk of a heart attack? Do you think John and Lorraine considered the Pigman's age in their activities with him? If they had known about the risks, what would they have done differently? (Sci)

2. Go to a shopping center with a list of all the items the Pigman bought for John and Lorraine. Estimate how much he would have spent on them at your location. (Hint: Round off the prices.) How would you feel about a non-relative spending that much money on you? (M)

3. Recall the Pigman's game about the boatman. Whom or what do you think is most to blame for the Pigman's death? Be imaginative, and support your reasoning. Draw a diagram similar to the one he used, but fill in different names and situations as needed. (A)

15. <u>Sing Down the Moon</u> by Scott O'Dell
(Houghton Mifflin, 1970)

Synopsis

Bright Morning is a young Navaho girl who lives with her family in a village in Canyon de Chelly. The peace and promise of that spring of 1864 is soon shattered for Bright Morning when she is captured by Spanish slavers and sold to a wealthy white woman. After she escapes and returns to her village, the village is destroyed by U.S. soldiers who force the Navahos to march to a reservation at Bosque Redondo. The conditions are terrible and many Navahos die. As she recounts her experiences, Bright Morning also tells the story of Tall Boy, the young warrior who is wounded as he helps her escape from slavery, and who eventually becomes her husband. Together, Bright Morning and Tall Boy escape from the reservation and start a new life for themselves. This story tells of the removal of an entire people from their land, breaking their hearts and spirits; but it also is a story of courage and hope.

Ideas and Concepts to Highlight

1. Note that Navaho country was centered in what is now northeastern Arizona.

2. Point out that the story is told in the first-person. O'Dell likely chose this point of view because of the immediacy it offers. It is as if Bright Morning is speaking directly to the reader.

3. Mention that this story is based on historical fact. In 1863 the U.S. army began destroying Navaho villages, crops, and livestock in an effort to remove the Indians from their lands. By early 1864 most Navahos began to surrender. This was followed by The Long Walk to a reservation near Fort Sumner. Many Navahos died because of the hard conditions.

4. Discuss how during a great tragedy as befell the Navahos, some people's spirits are broken and they give up, while others find inner strength which helps them to courageously face the hardest situations.

5. Explain that O'Dell uses much symbolism for dramatic impact. For example, the death of Meadow Flower comes during the spring. Spring is a time of rebirth, growth, and hope, yet the little girl died at that time.

Writing Connection: "A Report on the Navahos"

Sing Down the Moon is set in the American southwest in the 1860s. The story revolves around the Navaho Indians, whose culture and customs are likely to be unfamiliar to many students.

Instruct your students to research and write a report on some aspect of Navaho history, culture, or traditions. For example, some students may choose to write about the Long Walk, while others might concentrate on tribal customs or mythology. Remind students that their reports should have an introduction, body, and conclusion. Briefly discuss the 5 W's and How as a technique to ensure that they include pertinent information in their reports. Because a subject like the Navahos is so broad, Worksheet 15-1 is designed to help students choose and focus a topic before writing.

NAME _____ DATE _____ SECTION _____

15-1. A REPORT ON THE NAVAHOS

Directions: The Navaho Indians of the 1860s lived in close harmony with their land and had many interesting customs and traditions. Choose an aspect of Navaho life and write a report on it. Complete the worksheet to find and focus a topic.

1.   List some possible topics for your report: _____

_____

_____

_____

_____

_____

_____

2.   Which (if any) of the topics overlap each other? _____

_____

How? _____

_____

Which can be combined? _____

_____

_____

3.   Choose a topic and define it by answering the 5 W's and How. (Use another sheet if you need more room.)

What is your topic about?_____

When did it happen? _____

Where did it happen?_____

Who was involved? _____

Why did it happen? _____

How did it happen? _____

107

15-2. QUESTIONS TO CONSIDER FOR
SING DOWN THE MOON

1. The story is written in the first-person. Would the story be as powerful if O'Dell had used the third-person point of view? Why or why not?

2. How did Bright Morning feel about slavery? Compare her feelings about it with those of Rosita. Give some examples to support your views.

3. Describe the Womanhood Ceremony. What was its purpose? Describe a ceremony that we have today in modern American culture. What is its purpose?

4. When the Navahos deserted their village, they didn't think the soldiers would stay long. When did they realize that the soldiers weren't going to leave? What did the Navahos then decide to do? Why do you think the soldiers destroyed the village? Why didn't the Navahos of Bright Morning's village fight?

5. Tall Boy throws his lance at the soldiers but it falls short. This is symbolic of the weakness of the Navahos against the soldiers. Explain. Give another example of symbolism in the story and tell what it represents.

6. How did Tall Boy feel about his useless arm? Explain.

7. Throughout the story Bright Morning is shown to be intelligent, resourceful, and sensitive. Identify examples in the story that support each of these descriptive words.

8. Describe how Tall Boy's character changes after he lost the use of his arm. Give some examples.

9. Why does Bright Morning decide to leave the reservation at Bosque Redondo? Why do you think so few Navahos tried to leave?

10. At the end of the story, why did Bright Morning step on the toy willow spear that Tall Boy had made for their son? What does her action signify?

15-3. PROJECTS AND ACTIVITIES TO CONSIDER FOR
SING DOWN THE MOON

1. The novel ends on a note of hope. If you had been writing this story and continued it, what would happen next?

2. Many Americans in the 1860s saw nothing wrong with forcibly removing Indians from their lands as the nation expanded westward. Such people believed that Americans had a right to take what resources they could. Others felt that such actions were wrong. Organize a debate and examine the issue.

3. Imagine that you were a reporter riding with the soldiers who rounded up the Navahos and marched them to Bosque Redondo. Write a newspaper account of the event.

4. Imagine that you were an 1860s public advocate, and the Navahos came to you to argue their case for leaving the Bosque Redondo and being able to return to their lands. Prepare a list of reasons why the Navahos should be allowed to go back to their lands. Write a scene in which you present your reasons to the Superintendent of the Reservation. With the help of classmates, act the scene out.

Curriculum Connections:

1. "Manifest Destiny" was a term used to justify the expansion of the United States across the continent. What does Manifest Destiny mean? How might the term have been used to justify the forcing of the Navahos off their lands? Consult references if necessary, and write a brief report. (SS)

2. Draw a map of Navaho country. Consult references. (SS)

3. Create an art object that represents some facet of Navaho life. (A)

4. Although the Navahos did not have any "hard" sciences, they knew much about nature and their world. Research the Navahos' understanding of nature and compare it to our modern understanding of nature. Present your findings orally to your group. (Sci)

16. I Will Call It Georgie's Blues by Suzanne Newton (Viking, 1983)

Synopsis

Neal Sloan's father is a Baptist minister in a small southern town. His father tries to show his congregation that he and his family are stable, exemplary members of the community. This isn't so, however. Beneath the facade he shows his congregation, Neal's father is slowly losing control of himself, with terrible consequences for his family. Each of the family members tries coping with the father's excessive demands in his or her own way. Neal retreats from the family's conflict by secretly immersing himself in playing jazz. His sister, Aileen, rebels outright. She infuriates her father by failing her English class, which will prevent her from graduating, and by dating Pete Cauthin, a noted troublemaker. Neal's mother struggles with divided loyalties between her husband and her children. But it is Neal's younger brother, Georgie, who suffers the most. Quiet, unassuming, Georgie is often ignored by the others, except his father, who demands as much of Georgie as he does the others. Only when Georgie begins fantasizing that his parents are false (he believes his real parents were abducted) does Neal realize how serious the family's problems are. Even then, it takes Georgie losing his sanity and running away for the family to seek the help they need.

Ideas and Concepts to Highlight

1. Note that the story is told from Neal's point of view.

2. Discuss the idea of presenting a false facade to others, giving others the impression that you are something you are not. Neal's father, for example, presented himself to his congregation as a steady, compassionate man. Another example is Neal, who did not want others to know that he loved playing jazz on the piano.

3. Discuss the various ways the family members tried to cope with the father's excessive (or even abusive) demands. Neal retreated from confrontation, Aileen openly rebelled, Georgie imagined that his parents weren't real, and Neal's mother tried to remain loyal to her husband yet also protect her children.

Writing Connection: "The Real Me"

Much of the Sloan family's turmoil is rooted in people not being themselves.

Instruct your students to write an essay entitled "The Real Me." Ask them to describe in their writing the type of person they feel others see them as, and the type of person they really are. Suggest that students may keep their writings private if they wish and need not share them with other students. Completing Worksheet 16-1 can be helpful in organizing their thoughts.

NAME _____ **DATE** _____ **SECTION** _____

16-1. THE REAL ME

Directions: Neal Sloan did not want others to know about his jazz playing. By keeping that part of himself hidden, others were not able to know the "real" Neal. Think about how others view you. Do others see you as the person you really are? Complete the worksheet below and write about the real you.

1. Fill in the appropriate information in the boxes.

What People Think I Am	**What I Think I Really Am**

2. Are you, or aren't you, what you appear to be? Why or why not? _____

_____

_____

_____

_____

_____

_____

16-2. QUESTIONS TO CONSIDER FOR
I WILL CALL IT GEORGIE'S BLUES

1. When Neal tells Pete that "Preachers' kids aren't any different from anybody else," Pete answers, "Maybe not, but they're supposed to be." Do you agree with him? Explain. Think of some other jobs parents may have for which their kids might be expected to behave better than other kids. What are they? Why?

2. What is Neal's opinion of his father? How was his opinion different from the opinions of church members? Explain.

3. What is your impression of Neal? Describe him. Would you like to have him as a friend? Why or why not?

4. Why did Neal like and respect Mrs. Talbot?

5. Why didn't Neal want anyone to know about his jazz playing? Was he right in keeping it a secret? Explain. Why was his music so important to him?

6. When Neal refused to tell others about his jazz, Mrs. Talbot told him, "It takes so much less energy to live an honest life." What did she mean? Do you agree with her? Why or why not?

7. How did Neal's mother feel about being a preacher's wife? What was Neal's opinion of his mother at the beginning of the story? How did it change toward the end? Explain.

8. If you were Neal, how would you have reacted when Georgie told you that he didn't believe his mother and father were his real parents? What would you have done?

9. After Neal's fight with Pete, how did his father act in the principal's office? What does his behavior tell you about his deteriorating mental stability? Explain.

10. In talking with Mrs. Talbot, Neal says, "Everything is connected...Changing one piece means changing all the pieces." What does he mean? Give an example of how things are connected in your own life.

© 1994 by The Center for Applied Research in Education

16-3. PROJECTS AND ACTIVITIES TO CONSIDER FOR *I WILL CALL IT GEORGIE'S BLUES*

1. At what point in the story did you realize that Georgie was very troubled? Discuss your opinion and reasons with the members of your group. List the different places. Did any of you agree? Discuss why not all of you chose the same place.

2. Write a scene in which Neal explains to his father and mother why he goes to Mrs. Talbot's. Think about how they would react before writing.

3. Listen to some jazz and compare it to one of your favorite kinds of music. How is it similar? How is it different?

4. Listen to the jazz of various musicians. Choose some songs that you feel Neal would have liked. Play the recordings for your group or class and explain why you feel that Neal would have liked the ones you chose.

5. Assume that the Sloans have entered counseling. Write a new ending to the story.

6. Imagine that you are Georgie. Write a letter to Neal telling him that you are planning to run away. Be sure to give your reasons.

7. Research and list the places family members might turn to for help if they are in trouble. In your opinion, what might be the best place to seek help? Why?

Curriculum Connections:

1. Research jazz in the United States. Describe jazz. How did jazz originate? Who are some of its greatest names? Write a brief report. (SS or A)

2. Research one of the great jazz musicians—Erroll Garner, Theo Monk, Charlie Parker, and Dizzy Gillespie are some possibilities. Present an oral presentation to the class and play some of his music. (SS or A)

3. If you play a musical instrument, compose a short piece that you feel Neal would write and title it "Georgie's Blues." If you're feeling brave, play it for the class or record it and play the recording. (A)

17. Durango Street by Frank Bonham
(Dell, 1965)

Synopsis

When Rufus Henry is released from the forestry camp detention home, he hopes to straighten out his life. He considers going back to school so that he can get a good job someday. Although he realizes that his future depends on not joining a gang, joining one is the only way to stay alive in the neighborhood of Durango Street. It doesn't take long for him to have an altercation with the Gassers, one of the local gangs. For protection, Rufus joins the Moors and soon fights his way to be headman. At the same time, he contends with Alex Robbins, a social worker who tries to guide the Moors and Gassers away from their destructive lifestyles and into positive activities. Only when the Moors, with Alex's help, sponsor a neighborhood graduation dance, does Rufus start to see how he can be a positive factor in life.

Ideas and Concepts to Highlight

1. Discuss life in the inner cities where poverty, lack of educational and economic opportunities, and violence are ever-present. Try to avoid stereotypes as you do so. It is likely that many students living in suburban or rural areas will have trouble identifying with the setting, and base their knowledge of it on television and other media.

2. Discuss the protection a gang can provide its members.

3. Explain how poverty and lack of opportunities provide a setting for gangs like the Gassers and Moors.

Writing Connection: "Ten Years from Now"

Rufus Henry has potential. He is intelligent, possesses leadership qualities, and is a good athlete. If he returns to school and begins playing football again, in 10 years he might be a star. An individual's future is tied to his or her expectations. For example, the student who expects and desires to go to college usually does. The student who expects to one day work in his or her parent's business often takes it over when the parent retires.

Ask your students to imagine that it is 10 years from now. What will they be doing? What kind of person will they be? Completing Worksheet 17-1 will help them generate ideas for writing about their futures.

17-1. TEN YEARS FROM NOW

Directions: Think about Rufus Henry. Based on his experiences and potential, what might he be doing 10 years after the last scene of *Durango Street?* Would he be successful in his life?

    Now think about you. Imagine it is 10 years from today. What will you be doing? What kind of person will you be? Answer the questions below and then write about your future.

1. What will you be doing 10 years from today? _____

_____

_____

_____

2. Why will you be doing this? _____

_____

_____

_____

3. Will you need any special skills, training, or education? _____ How will you obtain these?

_____

_____

_____

4. Describe yourself 10 years from now. _____

_____

_____

_____

5. Will you be married? Will you have children? Describe your family. _____

_____

_____

_____

17-2. QUESTIONS TO CONSIDER FOR
DURANGO STREET

1. Why did Rufus feel that he had to join a gang? How did Mr. Travers feel about gangs? What was his warning to Rufus?

2. What was Rufus's mother's opinion of him? Did she give him much support? Support your answer with examples from the story. How did he feel about her?

3. Describe the setting around Durango Street. Would you like to live there? Why or why not?

4. Why was Rufus so desperate for Ernie Brown to be his father? Do you think Ernie was his father? Explain. Why was the scrapbook Rufus kept so important to him?

5. After Rufus's altercation with Simon Jones and the Gassers, why did he need to join the Moors? Why couldn't he simply have called the police? Explain.

6. How did a person get into and out of the Moors? Why didn't Rufus run when he was attacked?

7. When Alex Robbins studied the files on the Moors, what did he find out about them? What did Rufus think of Alex when he first met him? Do you think Rufus's assessment of Alex was an accurate one? Explain.

8. When Rufus first agreed to have the Moors sponsor the graduation dance, what was his reason? How did his feelings about the dance change? What might Rufus have learned about himself because of the dance?

9. What do you think Rufus will be doing ten years after the story ended? Write a brief scene showing him at that time.

© 1994 by The Center for Applied Research in Education

17-3. PROJECTS AND ACTIVITIES TO CONSIDER FOR DURANGO STREET

1. Ernie Brown was Rufus's hero. Discuss with your group what makes a hero. Create a list of heroes, and include a reason why each person on the list qualifies as a hero. Discuss how a hero can influence your life. Share your list with other groups.

2. Imagine that Rufus returns to school, becomes a football star and makes it to the NFL. Interview him about his past and what advice he can offer to young people. Write an imaginary interview. What would he say? With a partner playing the part of Rufus, act out the interview for the class.

3. Imagine that you are a news reporter covering the Durango Street area. Select an incident in the story (perhaps a fight between the Gassers and Moors) and write a news article about it.

4. Working with your group, brainstorm ways that trouble between the Gassers and Moors could be minimized. Make a list of possible activities the two gangs could participate in that would improve their relations. Organize a panel discussion consisting of the members of various groups and discuss the various suggestions. Which ones are the most realistic? Why?

5. Imagine a conversation between Alex and Rufus about Rufus's future. What advice would Alex likely have given him. Write a dialogue between the two.

6. Compare the gangs in *Durango Street* to the gangs in *The Outsiders* by S.E. Hinton. How are they alike? How are they different? How are they alike and different from gangs today that you have heard or read about? Consult other sources if necessary.

Curriculum Connections:

1. Create a scrapbook of a famous sports star, celebrity, or other newsworthy individual. Include articles, photos, etc. (A)

2. Based on the information in the book, draw a map of the area around Durango Street. (SS)

3. Design a poster advertising the graduation dance. Provide an illustration and include all pertinent information such as cost, dress, entertainment, and refreshments. (A)

18. *House of Stairs* by William Sleator
(Dutton, 1974)

Synopsis

In this science fiction story, five 16-year-old orphans—Peter, Lola, Blossom, Abigail, and Oliver—are brought to a place that has nothing but stairs, a mysterious food machine, and a toilet. The teens have very different personalities, and none has any idea why he or she was brought to the house of stairs. There is no way out. At first they try to get along and work together, especially in attempting to make the food machine work. They are unaware that the machine is used by researchers to condition them. Eventually, Lola figures out that the machine works best when they hurt each other in some way—verbally or physically. Refusing to allow themselves to be manipulated, Lola and Peter decide not to eat. They vow to starve instead. Blossom, Abigail, and Oliver, however, lack the will to do this and they continue to cause each other pain for their reward of food. Only when Lola and Peter are near death do the researchers stop the experiment. Afterward, Blossom, Abigail, and Oliver continue to show the effects of their conditioning. Lola and Peter are labeled' misfits and are to be sent away to an island for misfits. That doesn't matter to them, though, because they know that they won.

Ideas and Concepts to Highlight

1. Note the mystery to the novel. The reader knows only as much about the house of stairs and why the teens are there as the teens do. This is a powerful technique for generating and sustaining suspense.

2. Note the point-of-view shifts. This allows the reader to experience the story from each character's perspective.

3. Discuss that food is a necessity for life. It is an excellent conditioning agent.

4. Explain behavioral conditioning and how the behavior of an organism, through the use of the appropriate stimuli, can be manipulated and shaped. You might want to talk about Ivan Pavlov and B.F. Skinner, both of whom did much work in behavioral psychology.

Writing Connection: "The Misfits"

At the end of the story Lola and Peter were to be sent to an island for misfits. Ask your students to imagine what will happen to Lola and Peter there and write a story about their experiences. Completing Worksheet 18-1 will help students to generate ideas. You might wish to let students discuss their ideas with a partner before writing to help them focus their ideas even more.

18-1. THE MISFITS

Directions: Imagine that Lola and Peter are sent to the island for misfits. Write a story about what happens to them there. Answer the questions below to generate ideas for your story.

1. Describe the island._____

_____

_____

_____

_____

2. Who do they find there?_____

3. What happens?_____

_____

_____

_____

_____

4. Do their experiences on the island change Lola or Peter? _____

If yes, how?_____

_____

_____

_____

5. Do they ever leave the island? _____ If yes, how? _____

_____

Then what happens to them?_____

_____

_____

_____

18-2. QUESTIONS TO CONSIDER FOR
HOUSE OF STAIRS

1. Describe the house of stairs. What was so unusual and frightening about it?

2. In what ways were the characters alike? How were they different?

3. In Chapter 9, when the teens heard the voice, each heard a different message. Speculate how that could be. Analyze each message and explain the meaning it had for the character who heard it.

4. Describe how the characters reacted to one another the longer they were trapped on the stairs. Why do you think they weren't able to get along better?

5. How did the machine shape the movements of the dance the characters did?

6. When did the characters realize what the machine really wanted them to do? How did each of them react to this understanding?

7. Why was Lola surprised when Peter came to her and told her that he didn't want to go along with what the machine wanted? Do you think each could have refused the machine alone? Or did they need each other? Explain.

8. How did Blossom, Abigail, and Oliver get food after Peter and Lola left? Why do you think they continued to act this way?

9. Do you feel that the machine could have made Blossom, Abigail, and Oliver act hatefully to each other if they were not inherently evil? Explain. Can anyone or anything make a "good" person act "bad"?

10. What was the purpose of the house of stairs? Did his five subjects give Dr. Lawrence the results he had expected? What was the purpose of Dr. Lawrence's research? Do you think he was justified in using the teens as "guinea pigs" without their consent? Explain.

18-3. PROJECTS AND ACTIVITIES TO CONSIDER FOR HOUSE OF STAIRS

1. If you had been included with the group in the house of stairs, how would you have acted? Would you have stayed with Blossom, Abigail, and Oliver, or would you have gone with Lola and Peter? Explain.

2. Research behavioral conditioning and discuss this question with your group: Can people be conditioned to do evil? Organize a debate with a group that feels differently than you do. Stage the debate for the class and let them vote on the winner.

3. Work with a partner and list at least three traits of each character. Which character do you like the most? Which one do you like the least? Why? Which one has the strongest personality? Which one has the weakest? Why? Which one grew the most because of the ordeal? Who deteriorated the most? Explain. Compare your conclusions with the conclusions of other groups.

4. Throughout the story, the characters reveal what society is like on the outside. For example, few diets contain meat, and there is mention of a past war. Review the book and, based upon such details, write a description of what you think the United States is like at this time. Would you like to live there? Why or why not?

5. With your group, discuss what the likely lasting effects of their experience in the house of stairs would be on each character. Use specific examples from the story to support your ideas.

Curriculum Connections:

1. Research behavioral conditioning. Write a short report on it. (Sci)

2. Select a major researcher of conditioning, such as B.F. Skinner or Ivan Pavlov. Research his contributions to the understanding of conditioning and present your findings orally to your group or the class. (Sci)

3. With four other students, create the dance that the characters did for the machine. (A)

4. Review some of M.C. Escher's drawings. Draw your own idea of what the house of stairs looked like. (A)

19. <u>Home Before Dark</u> by Sue Ellen Bridges
(Knopf, 1976)

Synopsis

For much of the first 14 years of her life Stella Willis lived out of her father's car as her family moved from one picking station to another. When her father finally takes his family to his boyhood home and they move into a small tenant house on her Uncle Newton's farm, Stella is thrilled. It is the first time she has ever had a real home and she views this as the start of a new life. She meets Toby, a boy her age whose friendship turns into love, and Rodney, an older boy who wants all her attention. Stella quickly learns that life, even when she lives in her own home, can be hard. Not only must she cope with the attentions of Toby and Rodney, but she struggles with her feelings over her mother's tragic death and her father's sudden remarriage. Unwilling to leave her "home" and move into her stepmother's house with her father and younger siblings, Stella stays in the tenant house alone. Only when she realizes that loving people is more important than loving things can she rejoin her family.

Ideas and Concepts to Highlight

1. Note that the story is told through multiple points of view. This enables the reader to experience the story through the eyes of the various characters.

2. Discuss how her early poverty helped to shape Stella's personality. Because of her past, her small house meant very much to her.

3. Explain what the lives of migrant workers are like, and how they move from place to place following the sowing and harvesting of crops. Discuss how difficult this type of life is on children, who are constantly uprooted as their family moves.

4. Discuss the value of relationships versus the possession of material things.

Writing Connection: "The Most Important Thing in My Life"

When Stella moved into the small tenant house, her "home" became one of the most valuable things in her life. After her mother died and her father began courting Maggie, Stella clung to her home because it offered her something tangible and steady, and for a while it was more important to her than her family.

Instruct your students to think about the thing (or person) that is most important to them. Ask them to complete Worksheet 19-1 and then write about this topic.

19-1. THE MOST IMPORTANT THING IN MY LIFE

Directions: Think about your life, and the things that mean the most to you. Answer the questions below and then write an essay on this topic.

1. What is most important in your life? _____

_____ Why? _____

_____

_____

_____

_____

_____

2. How would your life be different without this thing? _____

_____

_____

_____

_____

_____

_____

_____

3. Could something else take the place of this thing? _____

Explain. _____

_____

_____

_____

_____

_____

_____

19-2. QUESTIONS TO CONSIDER FOR
<u>HOME BEFORE DARK</u>

1. What was Stella's first impression of the tenant house her family was going to live in on Uncle Newton's farm? How did she feel about living in a real house? How did her mother feel about the house?

2. Why did Stella's mother want to leave the farm?

3. Compare Anne and Stella's mother, Mae. How were they alike? How were they different? Support your ideas with examples from the story.

4. In Chapter 7, Silas tells Toby that, "...what's fitting is for people like the Willises and the Biggers to be under the same bit of moonlight." What does he mean? Do you agree with him? Why or why not?

5. How did Mae's death affect Stella? How did it affect her father?

6. Why didn't Toby tell the police or his parents who gave him the beating? If you were Toby, would you have told? Why or why not?

7. How did Stella react to Toby's beating? How did her feelings about Rodney change? What does this tell you about Stella's character? Explain.

8. Why do you think Stella's father began courting Maggie so soon after his wife's death? Do you think he was in mourning long enough? Explain.

9. How did Stella react when her father told her that he was courting Maggie?

10. Why did Stella refuse to leave the tenant house after her father married Maggie and he and the other children moved in with her? Do you think Stella was being reasonable? Explain.

11. What did Stella finally learn from Maggie?

19-3. PROJECTS AND ACTIVITIES TO CONSIDER FOR HOME BEFORE DARK

1. Assume that Stella did not leave the tenant house. Write a new ending for the story.

2. List at least five adjectives that describe Rodney Biggers. What is your opinion of him? Based on his character revealed in the story, what type of man do you think he will grow up to be?

3. Suppose that Mae didn't die. How would that have changed the story? Discuss this question with your group, then create a list of possible changes in the story. Share and discuss your list with other groups. As a group select one of the changes and create a new scene for the story.

4. Imagine that you are Stella. Write about your feelings for the tenant house.

5. Imagine that Stella and Toby have graduated from high school. Do you think they would still be close at this time? Or would they have drifted apart? Consider their backgrounds and aspirations. Write a scene in which Toby says goodbye to Stella as he prepares to leave for college.

6. Consider the lives of migrant workers. If necessary, conduct research, then brainstorm with your group ways that the plight of migrant workers and their families might be improved. Organize a panel discussion of the topic.

7. Write a wedding announcement about James Earl and Maggie for the local paper in Montreet County.

Curriculum Connections:

1. Using maps, try to determine the state that Montreet County might be found in. Hint: Use clues from the story to help you. For example, tobacco grew in the area; there were hot summers, and cold winters. (SS)

2. Write a report about migrant workers. In what states are they found? What are the predominate ethnic groups that make up migrants? What are their wages? What laws have been written to protect them from being exploited? (SS)

20. *Farewell to Manzanar*
by Jeanne Wakatsuki Houston and James Houston
(San Francisco Book Co./Houghton Mifflin Co., 1973)

Synopsis

Jeanne Wakatsuki was seven years old when her family was forced out of their home in southern California and detained in the Manzanar internment camp. Manzanar was part of the U.S. government's attempt to maintain national security by imprisoning Japanese-Americans during World War II. Jeannie's large family endures many indignities, living in cramped quarters without privacy, and her father, Ko, is exiled to North Dakota for months while he is interrogated for disloyalty. Jeannie spends her formative years behind Manzanar's barbed wire. The camp evolves into a small city with stores, entertainment, services and schools. When the war ends, Jeannie and her family must return to a society from which they had grown apart, and the family itself breaks down from the extreme living conditions and community unrest. Jeannie, who grows up with low self-esteem and confused feelings that she somehow deserved to be detained in the camp, finally returns to the ruins of Manzanar 27 years later. She makes peace with her fears of rejection and racism, her buried anger at a government that imprisoned her, and her disappointment in her prideful, arrogant father. The book is a series of vignettes, some out of chronological order, combining her recollections of actual events with her adult feelings.

Ideas and Concepts to Highlight

1   Discuss the importance of family in Japanese culture, and the strain that living in an internment camp placed on the Wakatsukis.

2.   Compare, in relative terms, the detention of Japanese-Americans with the Nazi death camps in Europe. Encourage discussions about patriotism and morality, and government's role in preserving security during wartime.

3.   Discuss irony and its many manifestations in the book—that the children were actually afraid to leave the compound, that the Japanese-Americans interned were not even permitted to contribute to outside society, and so on. Encourage students to relate ironic situations from their own experiences to illustrate the meaning of the term.

4.   Discuss the long-term psychological effects that a childhood experience can trigger, especially in terms of racism and rejection.

Writing Connection: "Manzanar—A Question of Rights"

Although at the time during war hysteria, the internment of Japanese Americans was supported by most of the country, the episode has since been questioned by many people on moral and judicial grounds. Essentially, the question comes to this: Is it acceptable for a free country to imprison a segment of its population (or an individual) that is deemed a threat, even though those individuals have done nothing wrong?

Pose that question to your students for this writing assignment. Instruct them to complete Worksheet 20-1 and then write an essay about their views.

20-1. MANZANAR—A QUESTION OF RIGHTS

Directions: Manzanar symbolizes a time in American history when the rights of Japanese-Americans were suspended. Even though they had done nothing wrong, they were considered to be threats to security and were deprived of their basic rights as Americans. Supporters of internment camps justified the camps because of the war. If you were living during World War II, would you have been a supporter? Answer the following questions and then write an essay explaining your views.

1. Fill in the boxes with the appropriate information.

Basic freedoms Americans enjoy	Which should be suspended during war? Why?	What might happen as a result?

2. Would you "understand" having your freedoms denied for any reason?_____

Explain. _____

_____

_____

_____

3. What alternatives did the U.S. government have to internment camps like Manzanar?

_____

_____

_____

20-2. QUESTIONS TO CONSIDER FOR
FAREWELL TO MANZANAR

1. Jeannie maintains that the style of living in Manzanar caused her family structure to collapse. Give some examples of the major events that strained the family. What are some comparable situations today that can break down an existing family?

2. Describe Jeannie's feelings when she first arrived at Manzanar. How would you feel if you were suddenly forced into an internment camp as she was? Explain.

3. Describe Manzanar. In what ways is it like your community? How was it different?

4. Was Kiyo justified in punching his father to protect his mother? Compare the situation in the context of American versus Japanese culture. Does the event have differing significance from culture to culture? How?

5. Make a list of five values important to Japanese culture. How did the internment affect these values? Did the values change? If yes, how? If not, explain why.

6. What is irony? Discuss how it relates to Manzanar and the families' attempts to create normalcy in a virtual prison. Also, expound on the irony of the loyal Japanese-Americans being detained. Cite examples of ironic situations from the story.

7. Ko's pride is often his downfall. Trace some of his major failures. What are the effects on the family? How much is he to blame for the breakdown of its structure?

8. "What if" plays a significant role in Jeannie's childhood. Write five "what if" questions that she might wonder about, and answer them in the context of her experiences.

9. Jeannie's pilgrimage back to Manzanar helped her come to terms with her childhood. What does the term "pilgrimage" mean to you? How did Jeannie feel after her return to Manzanar? Was that trip important to her? Explain.

© 1994 by The Center for Applied Research in Education

20-3. PROJECTS AND ACTIVITIES TO CONSIDER FOR
FAREWELL TO MANZANAR

1. Manzanar functioned as a community on its own. Imagine that the inhabitants published a newspaper. Pretend you are a reporter, and interview classmates who pose as detainees. As a class, write news stories and create sections for the paper. Produce and distribute it, and discuss what effect a news organ might have had on the camp.

2. Write an essay about how _Farewell to Manzanar_ changed your feelings toward World War II, and your own nationalism.

3. Watch the film _Hiroshima_ or read the book (by John Hersey). Jeannie says that after the bombing, "internment camps were undeniably a thing of the past." Why? What did Hiroshima represent to Jeannie and to the Japanese culture?

4. Haiku is a poetic form of Japanese origin. Find out its format, then write two haikus from Jeannie's point of view regarding her experiences at Manzanar.

5. Imagine that the U.S. government did not detain Japanese-Americans in internment camps during the war. How would not having had experienced Manzanar changed Jeannie's life? Write a short biography of what this "different" life would have been like.

Curriculum Connections:

1. Research the current state of the laws applying to immigration into the U.S. from three countries of your choice. How are they different? Are they fair, in your opinion? Write a letter to a government official or to a newspaper expressing your views. (SS)

2. The author revisited Manzanar in 1972. Conduct some research to find out what currently stands on the spot where the camp was. Describe the climate, terrain, wildlife and any monuments or population. (SS)

3. During George Bush's presidency, Japanese-American survivors of the camps were compensated by the federal government. Obtain news, magazine, and/or broadcast reports or documentaries and research the feelings and opinions of the recipients of the compensation. Do you think they were adequately rewarded? Write an essay about the government response. Choose a specific angle and incorporate quotes from the survivors. (SS)

5

Novels for Grades 9-10

21. *A Separate Peace* - Knowles
22. *To Kill a Mockingbird* - Lee
23. *Animal Farm* - Orwell
24. *A Tale of Two Cities* - Dickens
25. *Of Mice and Men* - Steinbeck
26. *I Know Why the Caged Bird Sings* - Angelou
27. *After the First Death* - Cormier
28. *Dicey's Song* - Voigt
29. *I Never Promised You a Rose Garden* - Greenberg
30. *Flowers for Algernon* - Keyes
31. *Hiroshima* - Hersey
32. *The Miracle Worker* (play) - Gibson
33. *Dragonwings* - Yep
34. *Running Loose* - Crutcher
35. *Flowers in the Attic* - Andrews
36. *The Adventures of Huckleberry Finn* - Twain
37. *Something Wicked This Way Comes* - Bradbury
38. *The Pearl* - Steinbeck
39. *The Hitchhiker's Guide to the Galaxy* - Adams
40. *Night* - Wiesel

21. *A Separate Peace* by John Knowles
(Macmillan, 1960)

Synopsis

Gene Forrester returns to the Devon School 15 years after he graduated from it. He walks slowly through the campus, coming to a big tree by a river. At this point, Gene tells what happened when he attended the school during World War II. Although the Devon School tries to shield the boys from the war, the war is always lurking in the background. The boys realize that, at 16, they don't have much time before they will be fighting. Phineas, the best athlete in the school, is always devising games and challenges that symbolically represent the war. One of these is jumping from the big tree. Phineas considers Gene his best friend, and is always urging Gene to join him. However, Gene is not so sure of his feelings for Phineas, whom he both admires and envies. One night, as the boys are jumping off the tree, Phineas falls. Gene wonders if he jounced the branch to make Phineas lose his balance. Phineas breaks his leg and is crippled. Although Phineas does not blame Gene, Gene struggles with his uncertainty and guilt. The climax of the story occurs when other boys, led by Brinker Hadley, conduct a mock trial in which Gene is accused of causing Phineas's fall. Phineas ends the trial by erupting in anger. He rushes from the room and falls down the stairs. This fall leads to his death because some marrow from the broken bone escapes into his bloodstream and goes to his heart. After Phineas's death Gene is finally able to come to terms with the fear, jealousy, and guilt he feels.

Ideas and Concepts to Highlight

1. Note that the story is told in the first person. Gene returns to Devon School and tells the story of when he was a student there.

2. Discuss how this novel is a war story. Knowles makes continual reference to the war throughout the story.

3. Discuss the relationship between Phineas and Gene.

4. Point out that one of the major themes of the novel is how people must confront their own fears and hatreds and find their own separate peace.

5. Explain Knowles's view of the essential cause of wars—that wars are made "by something ignorant in the human heart."

Writing Connection: "My Own Separate Peace"

One of the major themes of this novel is an individual's search for personal peace, his or her attempts to reconcile internal conflicts. While not all conflicts are as dramatic as Gene's, everyone seeks his or her separate peace, often on a variety of issues.

Ask your students to think of a time they gained a separate peace and share the experience through their writing. (For students who may not have achieved a separate peace in some way, ask them to write about a separate peace they would like to achieve.) Instruct students to first complete Worksheet 21-1, which will help them to focus their ideas.

21-1. MY OWN SEPARATE PEACE

Directions: Everyone searches for his or her own separate peace. Answer the questions below and then write about a separate peace you've gained.

1. Describe the conflict that led to your separate peace. _____

_____

_____

_____

_____

2. How did you feel about the conflict?_____

_____

_____

_____

3. Why was it important to resolve the conflict?_____

_____

_____

_____

4. How did you resolve it?_____

_____

_____

_____

5. How did achieving your separate peace change you? _____

_____

_____

_____

_____

© 1994 by The Center for Applied Research in Education

21-2. QUESTIONS TO CONSIDER FOR
A SEPARATE PEACE

1. Why do you think Knowles opened the story with Gene returning to the Devon School 15 years after he graduated?

2. Compare and contrast Gene and Phineas. What are the strongest traits of each? How does Phineas feel about Gene? How does Gene feel about Phineas? Of the two, which one do you like better? Why?

3. How does his fall from the tree affect Phineas? How does it affect Gene? Do you think Gene was responsible for Phineas's fall? Explain, citing examples from the story.

4. What did the fall from the tree symbolize for Phineas?

5. How does Gene react to Leper's enlisting in the ski troops? Later, what effect did Leper's telegram have on Gene? Why, in your opinion, couldn't Leper adjust to life in the army?

6. Why does Phineas claim that the war isn't real?

7. Describe the war trial that Brinker Hadley organizes. Why did Brinker do this? How did Gene feel about the trial? Why did Phineas react the way he did?

8. In your opinion, who was responsible for Phineas's second fall? Explain.

9. Do you think Phineas's death affected the type of man Gene became? Explain.

10. Why do you think Knowles titled this novel *A Separate Peace?*

11. *A Separate Peace* has been widely acclaimed as a great novel. Do you agree? Explain.

21-3. *PROJECTS AND ACTIVITIES TO CONSIDER FOR A SEPARATE PEACE*

1. Write an essay explaining what you feel are John Knowles's feelings about human nature and war. Use examples from the story to support your ideas.

2. Working with a group, dramatize a scene from the book. (The trial organized by Brinker would be a good choice.) Feel free to improvise and expand the dialogue. Create a different ending for your scene, keeping in mind the personalities of the characters.

3. Read the book *Phineas* by John Knowles (Random House, 1968) which is a collection of six stories, including the one that *A Separate Peace* is based on. Compare the stories and Knowles's style, and present an oral report of your opinions to your group or class.

4. Phineas invented games in the story. Work with a partner and invent a game of your own. Write down its object and rules.

5. Imagine that you were a recruiter for the Devon School, and it was your job to convince young men to select the Devon School over others. Write a brochure in which you describe the benefits that the Devon School offers its students.

Curriculum Connections:

1. Create a time line of the major events of World War II. Consult the necessary references. (SS or A)

2. Research the causes of World War II. How did the war begin? Which were the major countries at war? How did the United States become involved in the war? How many people were killed? What were the monetary estimates of the total destruction? How did the war finally end? What were the results of the war? Write a report of your findings. (SS)

3. The Devon School was located in New England. Research that part of our country. What states make up New England? Describe New England's climate, geography, and economy. What influence did the Puritan religion have on New England? Does any of that influence remain today? Finally, why do you think Knowles located his story in New England? Write a report. (SS)

4. The inscription over the main door of the Devon School's First Building, where Phineas and Gene were taken to trial by Brinker Hadley, is "Here Boys Come to Be Made Men." How did those words apply specifically to Gene? Design a logo that includes these words. (A)

22. To Kill a Mockingbird by Harper Lee
(J.B. Lippincott Company, 1960)

Synopsis

Scout Finch, a young girl, tells this story that reveals the prejudice in a small Alabama town during the Great Depression. In the summer, Scout, her brother, Jem, and their friend, Dill, play on the street around Scout's home. A few houses down is the Radley house, a place of much superstition because of Boo Radley, a mysterious recluse. When Miss Maudie's house catches fire one night and everyone has to go outside because all of the nearby houses are made of wood, Boo slips a blanket around Scout's shoulders to protect her against the chill. Although Boo plays a major role later in the story, Scout's father, Atticus, is the central character. A lawyer, Atticus defends Tom Robinson, a black man accused of raping a white woman. Despite proving Tom innocent by showing that Bob Ewell, the girl's father, was responsible for her beating, Tom is still found guilty by the prejudiced jury. Furious at Atticus for making him appear a fool in court, Bob Ewell threatens Atticus. Later, Tom tries to escape from a prison farm and is killed; few people mourn him even though they know he was innocent. The story climaxes when Ewell tries to get back at Atticus by attacking Scout and Jem. He likely would have killed the children except that he is killed by Boo Radley. Scout and Jem grow up significantly throughout the story, learning to see prejudice for what it is, and judge people individually.

Ideas and Concepts to Highlight

1. Briefly explain the history of the South, and the changes brought by the Civil War.

2. Discuss prejudice and the place of African-Americans in the social order of the 1930s South, which is the setting of the story.

3. Note that Scout Finch narrates the story. She is a young girl and her point of view is limited by her age.

4. Point out how Lee, who comes from the South and is a relative of the Civil War general Robert E. Lee, captures the language and color of the setting.

Writing Connection: "Injustice"

A great injustice was done to Tom Robinson in *To Kill a Mockingbird*. Because he was a black man in the 1930s South, merely being accused of a crime by a white woman (despite its obvious falsehood in court) was enough for him to be convicted. Unfortunately, there are still many examples of injustice in our society.

For this assignment, ask your students to consider an injustice they perceive in society. (If you wish you can narrow the assignment to an injustice they perceive in their personal lives.) Instruct them to complete Worksheet 22-1, which will help them to generate ideas for their topic. Remind your students to include details to support their main ideas, and consult references if necessary.

22-1. INJUSTICE

Directions: Tom Robinson suffered a great injustice in *To Kill a Mockingbird*. Think about an injustice you see in the world. Answer the questions below and then write about your feelings.

1. Describe the injustice you will write about. _____

_____

_____

_____

2. Why do you feel this event or problem is an injustice? _____

_____

_____

_____

3. How can this injustice be corrected? _____

_____

_____

_____

4. Will some people be unwilling or reluctant to correct this injustice? _____
Why? _____

_____

_____

_____

5. How can such people be persuaded to change? _____

_____

_____

_____

137

22-2. QUESTIONS TO CONSIDER FOR
TO KILL A MOCKINGBIRD

1. Why do you think Scout opened the novel by mentioning her brother's broken arm? Why did she then tell about Simon Finch and provide so much information about Maycomb?

2. Compare Scout and Jem. As the novel progresses, which one of them seems to understand more of what is happening? Explain.

3. How do the white townspeople react to Atticus defending Tom Robinson? What does Atticus tell Scout and Jem to do about the "talk" they will hear? How do you think Scout felt about the remarks others made about her father? Explain, citing examples from the story.

4. Describe Atticus Finch. What kind of man is he? How does Scout feel about him in the beginning of the story? How does she come to feel about him at the end? Offer examples from the story to support your answers.

5. After Mrs. Dubose's death, why did Atticus tell Scout that Mrs. Dubose was the bravest person he ever knew?

6. How did Scout feel about Aunt Alexandra coming to spend the summer with them? How did Atticus feel about Alexandra's pride with the family background? What does this tell you about Atticus? Explain.

7. Describe how Atticus defended Tom Robinson. Was his defense a sound one? Explain. Why was Tom Robinson found guilty?

8. How do Scout and Jem react to the trial? What lasting impression do you think the result had on them? Explain.

9. Why do you think Boo Radley saved Scout and Jem?

10. At the end of the story, why does Heck Tate insist that Bob Ewell fell on his own knife? Why does Atticus finally agree? How does Scout show that she understands their decision?

11. What is a mockingbird? How does a mockingbird symbolize Tom Robinson?

22-3. PROJECTS AND ACTIVITIES TO CONSIDER FOR
TO KILL A MOCKINGBIRD

1. Write your own editorial about Tom Robinson's conviction and death.

2. This story is told from the point of view of a young girl. In that sense, it is limited by Scout's lack of experience. Working with a small group, discuss how using the POV of an older Scout, or a third person POV would have affected the story. Would the story have had as much impact? Why or why not? Appoint a recorder to write down your group's conclusions and then share them with other groups.

3. Form a panel and discuss this question: How is prejudice a major theme of the novel? Cite specific examples from the story in support of your ideas.

4. Work with a partner and try to determine who—Scout or Jem—changed more during the course of the novel. Write about your conclusion and share it with others.

5. Watch the movie *To Kill a Mockingbird*. How is the movie different from the novel? Which version of the story do you like better? Why? Write an essay comparing the two.

6. Imagine that you are Atticus Finch. Devise a different defense for Tom Robinson. Write the trial scenes over, using your new defense. Do you manage to convince the jury to find Tom not guilty? With the help of some classmates, dramatize your new trial.

Curriculum Connections:

1. Research the state of Alabama. What is its population? Describe its economy. What is its climate like? Compare the Alabama of today with the Alabama of the 1930s. Write a report of your findings. (SS)

2. Find out what a mockingbird is. Where is this bird found? Why is it called a mockingbird? Do you think *To Kill a Mockingbird* was a good title for this story? Explain. (Sci)

3. Consult newspaper and magazine articles written about the South. Based on your research, decide whether conditions for African-Americans have improved since the time of the novel. In your opinion, is there as much prejudice today as there was then? Present your conclusions to the class in an oral report. (SS)

139

23. *Animal Farm* by George Orwell
(Harcourt Brace Jovanovich, Inc., 1946)

Synopsis

Animal Farm is a political satire in which the characters and events mirror the rise of Communism in the Soviet Union. The story, set on a farm, begins with old Major, a prominent pig, sharing a dream with the other animals. He explains how humans oppress animals and urges the animals to revolution. Major dies three days later and the revolt comes shortly thereafter when Mr. Jones, the farmer, gets drunk and forgets to feed the animals and milk the cows. When the animals break into the feed bins, Jones tries to stop them, but they drive him, his wife, and the hired hands out. The animals, under the leadership of Napoleon and Snowball, two pigs, assume operation of the farm, now called Animal Farm. The pigs formulate *The Seven Commandments of Animalism,* which assert that "All animals are equal." In the weeks and months that follow, however, Napoleon and the rest of the pigs become pre-eminent. Napoleon forces Snowball off Animal Farm by claiming that Snowball is a traitor. Supported by the other pigs, and dogs he uses to ensure that his policies are carried out, Napoleon gradually becomes a totalitarian ruler, in effect, assuming Jones's old role. Most of the animals on Animal Farm work harder and have less to eat, but, because of skillful propaganda, believe they are better off than before.

Ideas and Concepts to Highlight

1. Explain that this story is often described as a fable. A fable is a story that uses animals to represent truths about human beings.

2. Point out that the story is one of literature's greatest political satires. Explain that a satire is a story that exposes human weakness or failings through irony or humor. Orwell satirizes Communism.

3. Note that this story is also quite ironic. Although the animals rebelled to gain freedom, they in fact only gained a new master.

4. Discuss the use of propaganda by leaders and governments.

5. Note Orwell's use of personification—the giving of human traits to nonhuman things (the animals).

Writing Connection: "Freedom"

The animals of Animal Farm were told that they had freedom. Of course, they had no freedom, but since they didn't remember what their condition was like under Farmer Jones they believed Squealer and the pigs. Instruct your students to consider the issue of freedom. What is it? Does it have any limitations? Do they feel that they enjoy freedom? After completing Worksheet 23-1 instruct them to write an essay about freedom.

23-1. FREEDOM

Directions: Think about freedom. Consider your own experiences as well as what you have read and heard about this important topic. Answer the questions below and then write an essay detailing your thoughts about freedom.

1. What does freedom mean to you? _____
    _____
    _____
    _____

2. Are there any limits to freedom? _____ If yes, what are they? If no, why aren't
    there any limits? _____
    _____
    _____

3. Does everybody enjoy the same amount of freedom? _____
    Explain and give examples. _____
    _____
    _____

4. What can be done to ensure that everyone enjoys the same amount of freedom? _____
    _____
    _____
    _____

5. What, if any, is the relationship between freedom and power? Explain. _____
    _____
    _____
    _____
    _____

23-2. QUESTIONS TO CONSIDER FOR
ANIMAL FARM

1. In Chapter 1, why does old Major tell the animals they should rebel against humans? Give some of his reasons. What final advice does he give the animals?

2. Soon after the revolution the animals worked together. When did this begin to change? Which animals assumed command? How were they able to do this?

3. How did Squealer explain to the other animals why the pigs got the milk and the apples? If you were one of the other animals, how would you feel about his explanation? Explain.

4. Napoleon eventually became the leader of the animals. In what ways was his behavior like that of Jones? Give some examples.

5. Do you think Snowball was responsible for the windmill being knocked down? Do you think he was responsible for the other acts of mischief? Why do you think Napoleon claimed that Snowball was responsible?

6. How were the original Seven Commandments changed as time passed? Why were the changes made?

7. How did Napoleon rewrite the history of Animal Farm? Why did he do this?

8. The pigs used propaganda, with Squealer as their "spokes-pig," to convince the other animals that things were better than they really were. Give some examples of Squealer's effective use of propaganda.

9. What is the significance of Animal Farm's name being changed back to the Manor Farm? Explain.

10. At the conclusion of the story, the animals could not tell the difference between the men and the pigs. What do you think was Orwell's message here?

23-3. PROJECTS AND ACTIVITIES TO CONSIDER FOR
ANIMAL FARM

1. Working with a partner or small group, consult newspapers, news magazines (such as *Time or U.S. News and World Report*), and TV newscasts, and list places around the world where political systems are being challenged. Find out the causes of the turmoil and the groups involved. After compiling your information present your information orally to the class.

2. Read some of Aesop's fables. Compare how Aesop used animals to convey morals and truths to the way Orwell did. Which in your opinion is more effective? Why? Share your opinion with your group.

3. The pigs use violence to bring about the new order of Animal Farm. They lead the fight against the humans and order the dogs to kill traitors. Organize a debate and examine this question: Is violence a necessary tool of leaders to establish and maintain order? Is such violence justified?

4. Working with your group, chart the pigs' rise to power. Identify the policies and decisions that ensured that the other animals would not challenge the pigs.

5. One of the major themes of *Animal Farm* is that power corrupts those who possess it. Explain how Orwell supports this idea throughout the story. (Hint: Think about Napoleon and the pigs.)

6. Irony is a situation in which someone expects one thing but gets the opposite. Working with a partner, list and describe as many examples of irony as you can. Share your list with others.

Curriculum Connections:

1. Napoleon, the Berkshire boar of the story, is often thought to be Napoleon Bonaparte, the French dictator. Research the historical Napoleon and compare him to Orwell's Napoleon. Write a brief report. (SS)

2. Research Communism and write a report. What type of political/economic system is it? Provide examples in your report. What countries currently adhere to a communist system? (SS)

3. Working with a partner, identify the major events in *Animal Farm* and find corresponding events of Communism in the Soviet Union. Create a flowchart showing how one event led to another. (SS or A)

4. Why did Communism in the Soviet Union collapse? Consult references and write a report. (SS)

5. Design a plaque that highlights the Seven Commandments of Animalism. (A)

24. *A Tale of Two Cities* by Charles Dickens
(Greenwich House, 1982)

Synopsis

Jarvis Lorry, accompanied by Lucie Manette, journeys from England to France in hopes of finding Lucie's father, Dr. Alexandre Manette, who has been jailed in the Bastille. They find the doctor in Paris. He has suffered greatly during his many years of imprisonment, and they return with him to London. Five years later, Lorry, Lucie, and Dr. Manette are called to testify at the trial of Charles Darnay, a Frenchman living in England who has been accused of treason. Although Lucie reluctantly provides evidence against him, he is acquitted because the evidence is circumstantial. Darnay and a lawyer at his trial, Sydney Carton, to whom Darnay bears a strong resemblance, both fall in love with Lucie. Because Carton is an alcoholic, Darnay wins Lucie's love and they are married. Carton, however, continues to love her and remains a friend. During this time, France is drifting toward revolution. The aristocracy oppresses the people who plan their vengeance. When Darnay's uncle, a cruel, heartless nobleman is assassinated, Darnay inherits his estate, but he renounces his claim, for he wants no part of the French nobility. The Revolution comes in 1789. In 1792, Darnay receives a plea for help from the family steward, who has been jailed. Darnay leaves for France, and is quickly jailed himself. Lucie, along with her daughter and Dr. Manette, go to France to help Darnay. Dr. Manette helps to get Darnay acquitted, but Darnay is arrested again. This time he is convicted and sentenced to death. Sydney Carton arrives in Paris and learns of Darnay's sentence. He works fast. Getting into the prison with the help of a spy he knows, Carton drugs Darnay and changes places with him. The resemblance between the two men ensures the success of his plan. Carton goes to the guillotine, and because of his sacrifice, Darnay, Lucie, their daughter, and Dr. Manette escape France and return safely to England.

Ideas and Concepts to Highlight

1. Note that the story is divided into three books, each dealing with a different period and focus, though all move forward to the climax.

2. Discuss the theme of resurrection that is woven throughout the novel. For example, when Carton sacrifices himself to save Darnay, Carton is symbolically reborn. Something good has come out of his wasteful life. Out of the destruction and death of the Revolution, a new society emerges.

3. Note Carton's pure love for Lucie, which enables him to make the greatest sacrifice to save her husband.

4. Provide background about the French Revolution. Begun in 1789, the country swiftly went over to mob rule. Unlike the American Revolution, which gave rise to a democratic republic, the French Revolution led to Napoleon.

Writing Connection: "A Great Sacrifice"

When Sydney Carton took Charles Darnay's place before the guillotine, Carton could offer no greater sacrifice. He gave his life because of his love for Lucie.

For this assignment, ask your students to write a story of their own in which a character sacrifices something. Have students complete Worksheet 24-1 to generate ideas.

24-1. A GREAT SACRIFICE

Directions: Sydney Carton sacrificed his life for his love of Lucie Darnay. Create a story in which your character(s) sacrifice something. While the sacrifice may not be as great as Carton's was, it should be significant enough to affect the story's climax. Answering the questions below will help you plot and organize your story.

1. What is the central conflict or problem of your story? _____

   _____

   _____

   _____

   _____

   _____

2. How do the characters solve (or fail to solve) the problem? _____

   _____

   _____

   _____

   _____

3. What sacrifice is made? _____

   _____

   _____

   _____

   _____

   _____

4. On a separate sheet of paper, list your main characters. Provide brief descriptions of their physical and personality traits.

© 1994 by The Center for Applied Research in Education

24-2. *QUESTIONS TO CONSIDER FOR*
A TALE OF TWO CITIES

1. Why does Dickens open the novel with a description of the period?

2. What is the significance of the title of each book?

3. Describe Dr. Manette when Lucie and Mr. Lorry first see him. Why is he in this condition? What does this tell you about prison conditions of this time?

4. Compare Charles Darnay and Sydney Carton. How are they alike? How are they different? Which, in your opinion, is the stronger personality of the two? Why?

5. Why did Dr. Manette, when distressed, take up his cobbling?

6. Why did Charles Darnay return to France in 1792? Do you think his decision to go back was a wise one? Explain. What happened to him soon after he arrived?

7. How did Dr. Manette save Darnay at his first trial in France? Why was he able to influence the jury?

8. Why was Darnay arrested again? Why wasn't Dr. Manette able to save him this time?

9. As Carton contemplates how he can help Darnay, he walks through the streets with the biblical passage, "I am the resurrection and the life," repeating in his mind. What significance does this have in his decision to save Darnay?

10. "Liberty, Equality, Fraternity" was the motto of the French Revolution. What does it mean? In your opinion, did the Revolution live up to its motto? Explain.

24-3. PROJECTS AND ACTIVITIES TO CONSIDER FOR
A TALE OF TWO CITIES

1. Assume that Carton didn't change places with Darnay. Write a new ending for the story.

2. Throughout the story Dickens gives several characterizations of nobility. Write an essay explaining what you think were Dickens's opinions of the French and English aristocracy. Use examples from the story to support your ideas.

3. A motif is a recurring idea in a story. One of the most important motifs in *A Tale of Two Cities* is the idea of resurrection. Working with a partner, find several examples of resurrection, then list and share them with your classmates.

4. Research the causes of the French Revolution and the eventual course the Revolution took. Organize a panel and discuss this question: Could the great violence have been averted, or at least minimized?

5. View the movie version of *A Tale of Two Cities* and compare it to the book. Which one did you find more interesting? Why?

Curriculum Connections:

1. This novel was written during England's Victorian Age. What was the Victorian Age? How might have the beliefs, attitudes, and customs of that time influenced Dickens's writing? Consult the necessary references and write a brief report. (SS)

2. Locate London and France on a map. How far apart are they? During the time of the novel, how did people travel between the two cities? How do people travel between them today? (SS)

3. Research the Bastille. What was it? Why did French men and women hate it so? What did its storming signify? (SS)

4. Research the French monarchy at the time just prior to the Revolution. Louis XVI and his wife, Marie Antoinette, ruled. Write an essay on how their attitudes and actions helped bring about the Revolution. (SS)

5. Consulting the necessary references, create a time line of the major events of the French Revolution. (SS or A)

6. Consult references and find out what happened to France after the Revolution. Present an oral report to the class about your findings. (SS)

© 1994 by The Center for Applied Research in Education

25. <u>*Of Mice and Men*</u> *by John Steinbeck* *(Viking, 1937)*

Synopsis

George Milton and Lennie Small are walking to a farm where they hope to find work. They stop by a stream for the night. George takes away a dead mouse Lennie has accidentally killed. (Lennie, who is mentally handicapped, likes to pet soft things.) George then repeats their dream for the future in which they will one day work their own place. George also tells Lennie that he should return to this spot if he (Lennie) gets in trouble. The next day they obtain work. Curley, the boss's son, picks on Lennie, but George comes to Lennie's defense. George's concern for Lennie's welfare grows when Curley's wife comes to the bunkhouse. George immediately sees her as a "tramp." Later, angry about his wife, Curley takes his rage out on Lennie, punching him in the face. Lennie doesn't fight back until George tells him to, and then he crushes Curley's hand. A few days later, Lennie is in the barn playing with a puppy Slim gave to him. Lennie plays too roughly with it and kills it. When Curley's wife comes into the barn, she gets Lennie to tell her that he likes soft things. She lets him touch her hair. He strokes it, she becomes frightened, and he accidentally kills her. Afraid, Lennie runs to the stream. When the men find Curley's wife, they want revenge. Curley leads them, but George finds Lennie first. He shoots and kills Lennie to prevent the others from hurting him.

Ideas and Concepts to Highlight

1. Discuss the relationship between George and Lennie. You might also wish to discuss mental disabilities.

2. Note the many examples of foreshadowing. For example, Lennie's accidental killing of the mouse and the puppy foreshadow his killing of Curley's wife.

3. Note the poverty of migrant workers like George and Lennie of the <u>1930s</u>. Compare their lives to the migrant workers of today.

Writing Connection: "A Mercy Killing"

George's killing of Lennie, from George's perspective, is an act of mercy. He believes that what would happen to Lennie if he were apprehended would be far worse than the merciful death George gave him. Lennie's last thought was of his and George's dream.

Ask your students to consider George's action in killing Lennie. Was he justified? After completing Worksheet 25-1 instruct your students to write an essay or story that examines this topic.

25-1. A MERCY KILLING

Directions: Think about George's killing of Lennie in *Of Mice and Men*. Was he right? Answer the questions below, then write an essay or story that explains your views.

1. Describe the relationship between George and Lennie. _____

_____

_____

_____

2. What crime did Lennie commit?_____ Why did he do it? _____

_____

_____

_____

3. What do you think would have happened to Lennie if he was apprehended?_____

_____

_____

_____

4. Why did George kill Lennie?_____

_____

_____

_____

_____

5. Was George justified to kill Lennie? _____ Explain. _____

_____

_____

_____

_____

© 1994 by The Center for Applied Research in Education

25-2. *QUESTIONS TO CONSIDER FOR*
OF MICE AND MEN

1. Describe the relationship between George and Lennie. What did Lennie get from their friendship? What did George get? How did their friendship separate them from the other farm hands?

2. Describe George's dream of the future for Lennie and himself. Do you think it was a realistic dream? Explain. Why was the dream so important to them? Why did Candy and Crooks want to share in the dream?

3. Give at least three examples of foreshadowing. How does Steinbeck's use of foreshadowing build suspense in the story?

4. Why did Candy finally agree to let Carlson shoot Candy's old dog? Do you agree with Carlson's reasons? Explain.

5. When Lennie first comes to Crooks's quarters, Crooks tells him to get out. Why does he then allow Lennie to come in? How are Lennie and Crooks alike?

6. Curley is described as being a "mean little man" who picks on bigger men to prove his manhood. Do you agree with that description? Explain.

7. Curley's wife often flirts with the other men. Why does she do this? What reasons does she offer?

8. Why did George shoot Lennie? Do you agree with what he did? Explain.

9. At the end of the novel Slim says to George, "You hadda, George. I swear you hadda." What does he mean?

25-3. PROJECTS AND ACTIVITIES TO CONSIDER FOR
OF MICE AND MEN

1. Assume that Lennie was caught and brought to trial. Write a scene, in the format of a play, of his trial. Working with a group, assume the parts of prosecutor, defense lawyer, judge, and witnesses. Other class members can be the jury. What would the outcome of the trial be?

2. Write a new ending for the story. George does not kill Lennie. Neither does Curley. What happens then?

3. Discuss with your group whether Lennie was responsible for his actions in killing Curley's wife. Appoint a recorder to write down the conclusions of your group—and your reasons—and share your results with others.

4. Lennie, George, Curley's wife, Curley, and Crooks, in his or her own way, are tragic characters. For which one do you have the most sympathy? Why? Write about your feelings in a short essay.

5. Watch one of the movie versions *Of Mice and Men* and compare it to the novel. Which in your opinion has the greater impact? Did the movie follow the storyline of the novel? How was it changed? Write a review of the movie for your classmates.

6. Imagine that George is arrested and goes to trial for the murder of Lennie. You were a worker on the farm and are called as a witness for the defense. What could you say to help George to be found innocent? Write a dialogue between you and the defense attorney. (This can be reversed. You can be a witness called by the prosecution. You would then be expected to support the state's case and help prove that George is guilty.)

Curriculum Connections:

1. Locate the Salinas River and Soledad on a map of California. Using an atlas or other reference, describe the topography and climate of the area. What types of crops are grown there? (SS)

2. Research the area around the Salinas River and Soledad. Compare the area of the 1930s when the novel is set to the area today. Include such things as population, crops, economic activity, and lifestyle. (SS)

3. Draw or sketch one of your favorite characters of the story. (A)

4. Research the conditions of migrant workers during the 1930s. In what ways, if any, have those conditions changed today? Write a brief report of your findings. (SS)

26. <u>I Know Why the Caged Bird Sings</u> by Maya Angelou
(Random House, 1969)

Synopsis

Marguerite Johnson, nicknamed Maya, is a product of a broken home and as a child is sent to live with her grandmother in Depression-era Arkansas. Her grandmother owns a large grocery and it is a solace for Maya to be a part of it. When she is seven, Maya and Bailey, her brother, are sent to St. Louis to live with their mother. While there, she is raped by her mother's boyfriend, and after his trial he is lynched. Her brooding is too much for the family to bear, and the two children are sent back to the grandmother in Arkansas, where Maya begins to realize how inferior blacks are considered to be. After Bailey witnesses the brutal treatment of a black corpse, their grandmother takes them to live in California. For a time Maya lives with her father in the south, then she joins her mother and Bailey in San Francisco. One summer during their teen years, she vacations with her father in the south, and has a fight with her father's girlfriend. She runs away and lives briefly in an abandoned junkyard with homeless children, then returns to San Francisco. She gets a job as the first black conductor on the city streetcars. During her first voluntary sexual experience she becomes pregnant, and gives birth to a son. Maya, always tall and feeling awkward, gains a sense of who she is and learns to make her way with the world instead of opposing it or shrinking from it.

Ideas and Concepts to Highlight

1. Discuss the importance of role models, and how they can affect a child's life and future.

2. Discuss the considerable interplay of poetry and prose in the book, recognizing Angelou's renowned poetic talent.

3. Recount the protagonist's ugly and beautiful growing-up experiences. Discuss how a person's adult character is formed by them.

4. Review autobiography as a narrative form, including such contexts as race relations, emotional development, and the difficulty of self-examination and exhuming painful memories.

Writing Connection: "Writing from the Heart"

Maya Angelou is an accomplished writer of poetry as well as prose. Her work examines many of the difficult issues of our time.

For this assignment, instruct your students to write a piece on a topic of their choice. Encourage them in the use of figurative language, such as similes and metaphors, and symbolism. Completing Worksheet 26-1 will help students with their ideas.

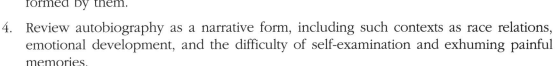

26-1. WRITING FROM THE HEART

Directions: Think of a topic that has great meaning to you. It might be a person, a place, an event, or an idea. Write about your feelings regarding this topic. Answer the questions below to organize your thoughts.

1. What is your topic? _____
    _____
    _____

2. Why is this topic meaningful to you? _____
    _____
    _____
    _____
    _____

3. Write two similes that might appear in your piece. _____
    _____
    _____
    _____

4. Write two metaphors about your topic that might appear in your piece. _____
    _____
    _____
    _____

5. How might you represent your topic symbolically? _____
    _____
    _____
    _____
    _____

© 1994 by The Center for Applied Research in Education

26-2. QUESTIONS TO CONSIDER FOR
I KNOW WHY THE CAGED BIRD SINGS

1. Compare the roles for black women in Maya's three societies: Stamps, St. Louis, and San Francisco. How was Maya affected by each?

2. What is a rite of passage? What are Maya's rites of passage, and how does each affect her?

3. At Maya's graduation, a white man "exposes" the black race, theorizing that black children's only role models were athletes. Was that true, or only Maya's interpretation? How are role models important for young people? Explain. Name at least one role model of yours. Why is this person a role model?

4. Choose three adults in Maya's life who you feel influenced her the most. Describe how each affected her.

5. Reread the anecdote at the end of Chapter 27. Write about another such anecdote if you have heard one. If not, create one. How do they make you feel?

6. In Chapter 28, Maya is delighted that Miss Kirwin treats teenagers with respect, stating parenthetically, "Adults usually believe that a show of honor diminishes their authority." Do you agree or disagree with this statement? Explain.

7. What do you think the book's title means? Why do you think Angelou chose it? Write three alternate titles.

8. Why do you think Angelou wrote this book? What was her purpose? Explain.

9. What, if any, effect did this book have on you? Explain.

26-3. PROJECTS AND ACTIVITIES TO CONSIDER FOR
I KNOW WHY THE CAGED BIRD SINGS

1. Maya Angelou, an accomplished poet, was featured during the inauguration festivities of President Bill Clinton. Find out what some of the President's favorite poems were. Why do you think he enjoyed them? How do you relate to them?

2. A "found poem" is a short, vividly described piece contained within prose that resembles a poem after only minor adjustments in punctuation and structure. "Find" a poem in the author's prose, and present it in verse form.

3. Read *Roll of Thunder, Hear My Cry* by Mildred Taylor and compare its protagonist, Cassie Logan, with Maya Johnson. Select a major conflict in each novel and reverse the two girls' places. How would each react in the other's situation? How are they alike and different? Who has the stronger voice, and why do you think so?

Curriculum Connections:

1. Using drafting tools and the author's descriptions, create an architect's design of the Store. (A)

2. Research the law in your state about rape. What is the punishment for a man raping a child like Mr. Freeman raped Maya? Why was his punishment so light? Would the sentence have been different if Maya were white? After compiling your research, debate this issue with the members of your group. (SS)

3. Research the emotional trauma victims usually suffer after rape. (Trauma can be especially serious in children.) Was Maya's withdrawal normal? Was her family justified in sending her back to Stamps? Do you think that situation turned out to be best? Support your answer from your research and the story itself. (SS)

4. Maya is struck by the racial diversity of San Francisco. Conduct some research to find out the city's racial and cultural makeup today. Then research the makeup of a large city near your home. How does your city compare with San Francisco? Include factors such as population, racial and ethnic diversity, and economies. Create a chart that compares the information. (SS or A)

27. *After the First Death* by Robert Cormier
(Dell Publishing, 1979)

Synopsis

Miro and Artkin are terrorists from an unnamed foreign country. They hijack a bus full of children and its woman driver, drug them and demand that their demands be met. They kill two of the children during the standoff. One of the demands is the dismantling of a secret government agency. The head of that agency, General Mark Marchand, is also required by the terrorists to send his only son, Ben, as a goodwill token to the bus. The son is tortured and shot but released in the ensuing firestorm. Miro, who is only a teenager, escapes with the woman and kills her. A year later, Marchand visits his son at school. They talk briefly, and the boy has never quite recovered from the shock and feelings of betrayal. While Marchand visits teachers, Ben kills himself. The book begins with the school visit and is recounted. Although much of the story is told from Miro's point of view, the point of view is shared by Ben, Marchand, and the bus driver in alternating chapters.

Ideas and Concepts to Highlight

1. The novel is told from varying points of view. Discuss point of view as a literary technique, and explain how a single story can change significantly when point of view is altered.

2. Discuss terrorism as a continuous threat. Encourage students to relate their feelings about it, and how they believe authorities should confront the problem of terrorist acts.

3. Discuss the father-son relationship, and how it can be affected by the father's career.

Writing Connection: "Terrorism"

No country is safe from terrorism. Because of the violence they are willing to do, terrorists are rewarded with prime coverage on the evening news. Even if their acts don't achieve their demands, the publicity they receive is often worth the risks they take.

Discuss terrorism with your students and talk about recent terrorist acts. Note that one of the most frightening aspects of terrorism is that perpetrators can strike anywhere and inflict great destruction. Seldom are they concerned with the lives of innocent people.

Instruct your students to reflect on their feelings about terrorism and write an essay that details their views. Completing Worksheet 27-1 will help them to organize their thoughts.

27-1. TERRORISM

Directions: Terrorism can strike anywhere in the world. But what can be done about it? Answer the questions below and write an essay expressing your opinions.

1. What is terrorism? _____

_____

_____

_____

2. Give some examples of terrorism. _____

_____

_____

_____

3. Why might an individual or group commit a terrorist act? _____

_____

_____

_____

_____

_____

4. Can terrorism ever be justified? _____ Explain. _____

_____

_____

_____

5. How can society stop terrorism? _____

_____

_____

_____

27-2. QUESTIONS TO CONSIDER FOR AFTER THE FIRST DEATH

1. What are your feelings toward Miro? The author alternately portrays him as a savage terrorist and a seeming tragic figure. Cite examples from the book where you feel anger for him as well as sympathy. Why do you think Cormier portrays Miro as he does?

2. Which, if any, of Miro's demands were realistic? In your opinion, could he have taken less violent action to achieve his goals? Explain.

3. Ben's father reads Ben's "diary." How would you feel if your parent read yours? Compare your feelings to how you think Ben would react.

4. Why do you think Marchand risked his son's safety for the sake of the children on the bus? Why did Ben agree to go? Do you consider him to have been brave or foolish? Why?

5. Interpret, in your words, the dialogue in Part 11. What is really being said?

6. There are numerous stories in *After the First Death* being told almost independently of one another. Do you think the unusual techniques served the book well? Which story touched you the most? Why?

7. In your opinion, was there anything Marchand could have done to resolve the situation with less violence? Explain.

8. How could Miro justify his actions, especially the killing of children? Imagine you are Miro, and try to explain why he did what he did.

9. Were there any "winners" in this story? Explain.

159

27-3. PROJECTS AND ACTIVITIES TO CONSIDER FOR AFTER THE FIRST DEATH

1. Cut out some newspaper articles about recent international terrorist acts. Find enough information to form a portrait of America's policy towards terrorists. Support your conclusions with specific case examples.

2. In the *New York Times Book Review,* a newspaper, or magazine, find a book review that you think is particularly well-written. Using its format as a guide, write a book review of *After the First Death.* Avoid simply retelling the story; critique the plot, point of view, and style.

3. What is an "ode"? Find some examples of this literary form, and write one for a character in the book.

4. Interview an adult and find out how that person would react in the general's situation. Be careful to spell out all the details, and do not reveal the outcome of the book to your subject. Deliver an oral report on your findings to the class, without identifying the adult.

5. Many parents today monitor their children's growth and learning closely, similar to Ben's father. Even if their intentions are good, do you think it is wise? Write an essay contrasting the encouraging of children and "pushing" them.

6. Imagine you were a TV journalist at the scene of the hijacking and following drama. Write a script in which you interview Marchand, Miro, or Ben. With a classmate assuming the other role, act out your script for the class. Consider videotaping the scene.

Curriculum Connections:

1. Write down all the instances Miro mentions his "homeland." Using an almanac, encyclopedia or similar source, find a country that could be his homeland. Write a short report on the state of that country's relationship with the United States. (SS)

2. Draw a picture of Miro in his mask, using the description provided in the story. (A)

3. Research newspaper or recent magazines and make a list of various countries that support terrorism. Try to find out why countries, or groups, resort to and support terrorism. Write a brief report and share it with your group. (SS)

28. <u>*Dicey's Song*</u> *by Cynthia Voigt*
(Ballantine Books, 1982)

Synopsis

In this sequel to Voigt's *Homecoming,* Dicey Tillerman and her three younger siblings, James, Maybeth and Sammy, are taken in by their estranged grandmother, Abigail, in Maryland. The children begin school and, since they are accustomed to total freedom, suffer some serious adjustment difficulties. Dicey, ferociously protective because she is the oldest, learns slowly how to make friends and adapt to a structured world. Their mother dies and Dicey and Abigail fly to Boston to have Liza cremated. They bring her back to Maryland, and the children are able to close the emptiness that they have felt since their mother abandoned them. Each child learns to carry on despite his or her impediments—James is arrogantly smart, Maybeth has a reading disability, and Sammy is a quick-tempered, unruly child—but as Abigail takes more interest in them the children flourish. At last Dicey is able to be a teenager instead of guarding her family like an adult.

Ideas and Concepts to Highlight

1. There is a strong theme of adolescent development in the story. Discuss the varying pace at which some young people grow up, especially runaways and abandoned children versus children in nurturing homes.

2. Discuss children taking on adult responsibilities and growing up too fast.

3. Point out how Dicey and Abigail both must let go of the past. Their strong pride alternately thwarts and supports them as they struggle to carry on and permit change.

4. Note that the novel's primary appeal is its strong characterization. Each person is drawn precisely and meticulously. Discuss the most distinguishing traits of each character.

5. Compare the story line with that of *Homecoming,* which contains more action as compared to this story's exploration of characters. Discuss the strengths and weaknesses of each.

Writing Connection: "A Major Responsibility"

Discuss with your students how Dicey assumed great responsibility in protecting the younger children. It is likely that your students, too, have responsibilities, although perhaps not as profound as Dicey's. Instruct your students to write about an important responsibility, task, or obligation they have. Completing Worksheet 28-1 is a helpful prewriting activity.

28-1. A MAJOR RESPONSIBILITY

Directions: Dicey assumed great responsibility in taking care of the younger children. Think of some responsibilities that you have. Answer the questions below and write about one of your responsibilities.

1. My responsibility is_____

_____

_____

2. To fulfill this responsibility, my duties, tasks, etc., include: _____

_____

_____

_____

_____

3. How I feel about this responsibility: _____

_____

_____

_____

_____

4. This responsibility is important because _____

_____

_____

_____

_____

28-2. QUESTIONS TO CONSIDER FOR
DICEY'S SONG

1. Gram's emotions varied widely, from cold-hearted to great worry to affection. What does such a wide display of emotions say about her? How does it affect the children?

2. Why do you think Gram is reluctant to take charity? What values does she hold that make her this way?

3. Dicey is very cautious in making new friends. Why is she like this? Could you be friends with Dicey, knowing her background? What do you like and dislike about her?

4. William Faulkner was noted for naming his characters according to some symbol attached to their personality or situations. Discuss Voigt's choice of the surname Tillerman. Why did she choose it? Relate it to and explain Dicey's attachment to boats and the sea. Create a surname for yourself that incorporates something about you.

5. Dicey did not like home economics. Why does she rebel against it so quickly? Explain your opinion in terms of her masculine and feminine traits.

6. Dicey attains a great deal of respect from others. Why is this so? Why do people respect her aloofness?

7. Discuss "reaching out," as Gram defined it. Relate how Dicey reaches out to make friends. How does it affect her? Why did Gram urge her to do it?

8. Explain Mina's attraction to Dicey. Why does she try so hard to befriend her, when Dicey constantly resists her? How would you feel about someone pursuing your friendship the way Mina does with Dicey?

9. Define feminism. Compare Dicey's brand of feminism with Mina's, and with Gram's. Contrast the gender roles that each female faces, or has faced.

28-3. PROJECTS AND ACTIVITIES TO CONSIDER FOR
DICEY'S SONG

1. Create a conversation between Gram and Dicey about her emerging sexuality, including what you believe to be Gram's moral beliefs about it. Why does Dicey resist these types of conversations? Why do you think most teenagers are uncomfortable discussing sexuality with adult relatives or authority figures?

2. Imagine you are Dicey's teacher. Construct a short conference about her attitude and study habits from the teacher's point of view. Have a classmate act as Dicey and act out the dialogue, incorporating what you and the classmate think their responses would be.

3. *Dicey's Song* won the Newbery Medal, given for excellence in juvenile novels. What do you think is the book's major strength? What criteria do you use to judge whether fiction is good or great? List them, and rank *Dicey's Song* in each category.

4. Write a short scene in which Dicey receives her first kiss, first from her point of view, then from Jeff's. Try to adopt Dicey's personality as you write, working through the moment as Cynthia Voigt would.

5. Write an obituary for Dicey's mother.

6. Write a scene in which any of the four children venture into the attic without permission. What would he or she find there? What would these items, which Gram has kept for so many years, say about Gram?

7. Imagine that Dicey is one of your classmates. What would she write in your yearbook?

Curriculum Connections:

1. Draw or sketch a boat that you think Dicey would like. (A)

2. Imagine that Dicey, who likes the sea, could take an all-expense-paid cruise around the world. As her travel agent, you are planning her trip. Where would you start from? Which countries and cities would you visit? When would you return? How many miles would you sail and how long, approximately, would the trip take? (SS and M)

29. *I Never Promised You a Rose Garden*
by Joanne Greenberg, as Hannah Green
(Holt, Rinehart, and Winston, 1964)

Synopsis

Sixteen-year-old Deborah Blau retreats from a reality she finds too hurtful into an imaginary world called Yr. It is in Yr that she hears voices that pull her farther into madness. Only after attempting suicide do her parents acknowledge Deborah's "problem" and seek help for her. When Deborah enters an institution for the mentally ill, she begins her journey back to reality. Under the compassionate and tireless counseling of Dr. Fried, an eminent psychiatrist, Deborah slowly starts to see that she created her imaginary world in response to the pressures of her real world. The book details the setbacks Deborah suffers, as well as her fragile victories. Along the way the reader shares vividly in Deborah's institutionalized life, coming to know many patients, whose only bond to each other is their insanity.

Ideas and Concepts to Highlight

1. Explain that schizophrenics have their own visions of reality. This is why it is so hard for them to cope in the real world.

2. Discuss schizophrenia, its potential causes and treatments. (Since this book was written, drug therapy has come to play an increasingly important role in treatment.)

3. Note the slow recovery and many setbacks many mentally ill patients suffer.

4. Point out the intrusions into Deborah's mind by the inhabitants of Yr. This author's technique underscores Deborah's fractured reality.

Writing Connection: "Walk in My Shoes"

Everyone has his or her own reality; no two people see the world in precisely the same way. This point is powerfully made by Deborah Blau. Even though the sane may not see things in the same way, they can at least agree on the general facts of the real world. Schizophrenics are deprived of this. How can anyone truly understand something he or she does not experience?

For this writing assignment, instruct your students to select someone they know well. They are to imagine being that person for a day and write a diary of their likely experiences, including their thoughts and feelings. To gain information about the individual's daily routine, it might be helpful for students to interview the person whose "shoes" they will assume. Completing Worksheet 29-1 will help students get started.

29-1. WALK IN MY SHOES

Directions: No two people can see or understand the world in the same way. Everyone has his or her own reality. But understanding others is necessary for people to get along.

Choose someone you know well and imagine what one of his or her days is like. Put yourself in this person's shoes. What does this person experience? How does he or she view life? Answer the questions below and then write a diary—a day in the life of your subject.

1. Whose "shoes" did you assume?_____

Why did you choose this person? _____

_____

_____

2. List the major events of his or her day. (You might wish to interview your subject for details.)

_____

_____

_____

_____

3. What part of the day does he or she like best? _____

Why? _____

_____

_____

_____

4. What part of the day does he or she like least?_____

Why? _____

_____

_____

_____

_____

© 1994 by The Center for Applied Research in Education

29-2. QUESTIONS TO CONSIDER FOR
I NEVER PROMISED YOU A ROSE GARDEN

1. Do you think that before she went to the hospital Deborah was aware that she was suffering from schizophrenia? Explain. If she was aware, why couldn't she help herself overcome her condition?

2. Describe Deborah's first meeting with Dr. Fried. What was her attitude at the beginning of the meeting? How had it changed by the end? Did the doctor give Deborah hope that she could get well? Explain.

3. How did Deborah's parents inform the rest of the family where Deborah was? Why were they so cautious in their telling? How did the members of the family react? Why do you think it was so difficult for the family members, especially her mother and father, to adjust to the fact that Deborah needed help? Explain.

4. Describe the Pit. How did Deborah behave in the real world after she had "fallen" into the Pit?

5. Why was Yr important to Deborah? Why did she have trouble letting it go?

6. Why did Deborah burn herself?

7. In Chapter 24, what is the significance of the dream?

8. When, in your opinion, did Deborah decide to keep living? Do you think it was her decision, or the voices of Yr? Explain.

9. Reflect on the title of the novel. Of what special significance do those words have for Deborah? Explain.

10. What did Deborah finally learn about herself through counseling?

29-3. PROJECTS AND ACTIVITIES TO CONSIDER FOR
I NEVER PROMISED YOU A ROSE GARDEN

1. Work with a partner and examine in what ways, if any, Deborah's parents may have contributed to her illness. Create a list and back up your ideas with examples from the story. Then share your list with others.

2. Assume that both Deborah and Carla were released from the hospital. Also assume that they remain in touch with each other, periodically informing each other of their progress. Pretend you are Deborah and write a letter to Carla, telling her how you are doing.

3. Write a final scene to the book, showing Deborah being released and going home. As you develop the scene, be sure to keep in mind the personalities of the different characters, particularly Deborah's parents and sister.

4. Write a dialogue in which Deborah breaks off with the inhabitants of Yr. With classmates assuming the voices of Yr, read the dialogue aloud to the class.

5. If Deborah was a classmate of yours before she entered the hospital, do you think you could be good friends with her? Explain.

6. Deborah's world of Yr was so real to her that she even invented a language for it. Working with a partner, invent your own language for Yr. Create an alphabet, words, and grammatical system. Write some sentences in your invented language.

Curriculum Connections:

1. Sketch or draw Lactamaeon, Anterrabae, or Idat. (A)

2. Sketch, draw, or using clay, create your impression of Yr. (A)

3. Research schizophrenia. Write a report including its causes, symptoms, and treatments. What advances in treatment have been made since this book was written? (Sci)

4. Research other types of mental illness, their causes and treatments and present an oral report to your group or class. (Sci)

30. *Flowers for Algernon* by Daniel Keyes
(Harcourt, 1966)

Synopsis

Charlie Gordon works at a bakery, has friends, seems happy, and is retarded. All this changes for him when he becomes the subject of an experiment that enhances intelligence. This novel is a series of progress reports, written by Charlie, that detail his experience. Before his operation, Charlie is capable of only cleaning toilets at the bakery. To determine if his intelligence is improving, his researchers test him against a mouse, named Algernon, whose intelligence has also been enhanced and who proves to be quite skilled at negotiating mazes. It is not long before Charlie's I.Q. begins to improve, and he is given a promotion at work. Soon his co-workers come to resent and fear him and his boss fires Charlie. As his intelligence increases more, Charlie realizes that he is becoming smarter than the researchers in charge of his experiment. Although he acquires the intellectual capacity of a genius, his emotions are much like those of an adolescent. He falls in love—or so he believes—with Alice, his teacher, but he is unable to achieve a satisfying relationship with her. Because no one is sure if the intelligence enhancement is permanent, Charlie begins working on the theory underlying his experiment. When Algernon starts showing signs of deterioration, Charlie becomes worried. Not long after that, he discovers that he, too, will deteriorate mentally. The final pages of the book show his deterioration, until he returns to his earlier level of retardation. He forgets all he had learned.

Ideas and Concepts to Highlight

1. Note that this book is written in the form of progress reports made by the main character, Charlie Gordon. Discuss how the reports reflect Charlie's intellectual capacity.

2. Discuss mental disabilities in general, and retardation specifically.

3. Note Charlie's relationships and his varying happiness.

4. Explain that this book is fiction. Researchers are, as yet, unable to conduct experiments that might enhance intelligence.

Writing Connection: "Improving Human Beings"

Charlie Gordon was the subject of an experiment to improve intelligence. At the time *Flowers for Algernon* was written, such experiments were impossible. However, with recent advances in understanding the human genetic code, the possibility of an "improved" human being might not be so far off. Already doctors are able to correct faulty genes in the treatment of some diseases. Some researchers predict that science will soon have the power to alter human genes before a baby is born. Parents will be able to pick the sex of their child, the color of its hair and eyes, its height, maybe even its I.Q. But should they? While few people would argue that using gene therapy to treat disease should be stopped, a controversy already exists over whether human traits should be manipulated.

Ask your students to reflect on this issue and write about their feelings in a story or essay. Encourage them to consult references if necessary to find out more about genes and gene therapy. Completing Worksheet 30-1 will help them to organize their thoughts.

NAME _____ **DATE** _____ **SECTION** _____

30-1. IMPROVING HUMAN BEINGS

Directions: Researchers tried to improve Charlie Gordon's intelligence. In the future, such experiments might be possible. But are they right? Should science tamper with improving human beings? Answer the questions below and write a story or essay on this topic.

1. In what ways might humans be improved?_____

_____

_____

_____

_____

_____

2. Who would decide which individuals should be improved? _____

_____

3. What would happen if an individual, marked for improvement, didn't want to be"improved"?

_____

_____

_____

_____

_____

_____

4. How would you feel if someone in authority decided you needed to be improved? _____

_____

What would you do? _____

_____

_____

_____

_____

171

30-2. QUESTIONS TO CONSIDER FOR
FLOWERS FOR ALGERNON

1. How do the progress reports Charlie writes tell you what kind of man he is? Give examples from the story to support your ideas.

2. Why is Charlie selected for this experiment?

3. Charlie views the other workers at the bakery as his friends. Do you think they were his friends? Explain.

4. Why do you think Charlie's co-workers become frightened of him and resent him as he becomes smarter?

5. Describe Charlie's feelings when he discovers that Gimpy deliberately undercharged a customer. Why did he feel this way? How would you feel about such a situation? Do you agree with the way Charlie confronted Gimpy? Explain.

6. Though flashbacks, Charlie recalls many events of his youth. Describe his relationships with his mother, father, and sister. Why does he feel he has to see them when he is smarter? How does his meeting with each of them turn out? Do you think he expected the meetings to turn out the way they did? Explain.

7. How does Charlie react to his realization that he has become smarter than Alice? Smarter than his doctors? He becomes critical of Nemur and Strauss. Do you think he was accurate in his assessment of these men? Explain.

8. When do you think Charlie was happier—when he was working at the bakery before the experiment, or when he was a genius? Cite examples from the story to support your ideas.

9. Would you describe Charlie Gordon as a tragic character? Why or why not?

© 1994 by The Center for Applied Research in Education

30-3. *PROJECTS AND ACTIVITIES TO CONSIDER FOR FLOWERS FOR ALGERNON*

1. Working with your group, discuss what society owes the mentally handicapped like Charlie Gordon. What should society provide for these individuals? Consider things such as education, training, jobs, and housing. Compile your ideas and present them to the class.

2. Imagine that you are Professor Nemur. After Charlie has reverted to his retarded state, write a letter to a colleague telling him about your experiment. Would you consider the experiment to have been a success? Think about Nemur's personality before writing.

3. Find out what facilities, programs, and institutions are available to the mentally handicapped in your area. Present your findings to the class in an oral report.

4. Work with a partner and speculate what might happen in the future if intelligence can be improved. Make a list of how society would be affected if such an opportunity became available to people. Share your list with others.

5. At the end of the story, Charlie was preparing to go to Warren. Imagine what his routine would be like. Write a scene describing it.

6. Although the researchers in Charlie's experiment took care of him, one must wonder if what they did was ethical. After all, they experimented with Charlie without really knowing what would happen to him. Work with a group and discuss the question of ethics in medical experiments—do doctors or researchers have the right to test experimental drugs or therapies on people if the test subjects might suffer adverse effects?

Curriculum Connections:

1. Charlie suffered from mental retardation. What does the term retardation mean? What are its causes? How can retarded persons be helped? Write about your findings in a report. (Sci)

2. What is a Rorschach test? How was it developed and what is its purpose? Consult the necessary references and share your findings with your group or class. If possible, provide some examples of Rorschach pictures. (Sci)

3. What does I.Q. mean? How is this measurement of intelligence arrived at? Do the experts on intelligence testing all agree on the validity of I.Q. tests? Write a short report on this topic. (Sci)

31. *Hiroshima* by John Hersey
(Alfred A. Knopf Inc., 1946, 1985)

Synopsis

Hiroshima follows the lives of six Japanese who survived the 1945 atomic bombing of the city that is the title of the book. The initial four chapters of the nonfiction book were written in 1946, and an additional chapter was added in 1985, briefly recounting each character's previous four decades. *Miss Toshiko Sasaki,* a clerk, had just sat down in her office when the bomb struck. For many hours she lay buried beneath a pile of books. Her leg was crushed. Finally, she was dragged out and left under a lean-to for days. When at last she was treated, her leg healed improperly and, despite several operations, she walked with a limp. Her fiancee abandoned her and she eventually became a nun, administering group homes. *Dr. Masakazu Fujii,* a wealthy physician, watched his house tumble into a river; he was trapped in tree branches while wearing only his underwear. After struggling free, he escaped to a friend's house in the north. Years later he drowned himself in alcohol and luxury, dying after spending nine years in a coma brought on by a suicide attempt. *Hatsuyo Nakamura,* a widowed seamstress, was caught in her home's rubble with her children, but managed to free them and escape to a relative's home. Impoverished, she suffered many years with radiation sickness, finally finding a job that accommodated her handicaps. She retired in 1966, moving into a pleasant old age. Jesuit *Father Wilhelm Kleinsorge,* later Father Takakura, was reading in his room. Upon impact he lost consciousness and later found himself wandering aimlessly through the home's gardens. Dedicated to service, Father Kleinsorge spent the next few weeks tirelessly ministering to the bomb victims. Despite his debilitating radiation illnesses, he continued similar ministry until his death in 1977. *Dr. Terufumi Sasaki* was in a hospital. He spent the next three days, as one of the only surviving medics in the area, treating thousands of patients with barely any supplies. He became a very wealthy physician in later years, only lightly affected by the bomb, but haunted by the mass cremations of unidentified bomb victims in the days following the blast. *Rev. Kiyoshi Tanimoto,* also barely affected physically, ministered to bomb victims immediately after the explosion, and spent the following decades lobbying for peace and the treatment of the disfigured. The responses of each *hibakusha*—bomb survivor—vary greatly and their lives curiously intertwine.

Ideas and Concepts to Highlight

1. Discuss the conflicting positions of civilians and military personnel, paying particular note to the fact that innocent civilians often "die for the cause" in war.

2. Discuss the author's style and how it evokes sympathy.

3. Discuss the ethics of the atomic bomb. Encourage students to express their views, and compare them to the characters in the book, who mostly avoided any moral discussion of it.

4. Compare the last chapter, which was added in 1985, to the first four. Discuss whether it adds to the book, by rounding out the lives of the characters, or detracts from it, by extending the drama to a 40-year versus a one-year reach.

Writing Connection: "The Controversy Over Nuclear Weapons"

Although at the time, during World War II, most Americans supported the dropping of the bomb, many people have since come to question the morality of using nuclear weapons. Such weapons, because of their great destructive power, can kill civilians on an unprecedented scale. Yet, the non-nuclear German bombing of Britain and the Allied bombing of many German cities also killed thousands of civilians.

For this assignment, instruct your students to reflect upon their thoughts about nuclear weapons. Are such weapons justifiable? Having students complete Worksheet 31-1 will help them to generate and organize their thoughts.

31-1. THE CONTROVERSY OVER NUCLEAR WEAPONS

Directions: The United States, along with several other countries, has a stockpile of nuclear weapons. While some people are convinced that nuclear weapons ensure the safety of the United States, others believe that all nuclear weapons—because of their great destructive force—should be dismantled. These people feel that nuclear weapons are immoral and their use can never be justified. Consider your thoughts about the controversy over nuclear weapons. Answer the questions below and write about your feelings in an essay.

1. Why were nuclear weapons designed? _____

_____

_____

2. What, if any, advantage(s) do nuclear weapons provide a country with? _____

_____

_____

3. What, if any, problem(s) do they give a country? _____

_____

_____

4. Should the United States, in its world leadership role, renounce and dismantle its nuclear

weapons?_____   Why or why not?_____

_____

_____

5. Was the United States right to drop an atom bomb on Hiroshima? _____   Why or why

not?_____

_____

_____

_____

_____

31-2. QUESTIONS TO CONSIDER FOR
HIROSHIMA

1. Create a list of the major characteristics of each hibakusha. Which individuals, in your opinion, were the strongest personalities? Which were the weakest? For which did you have the most sympathy? Why?

2. How does the destruction of the bomb and its after-effects make you feel about America? Have your sentiments about patriotism changed? Explain.

3. Describe what you think Mr. Fukai was feeling as he protested Father Kleinsorge's valiant attempts to save him. Is there a psychological basis for his reaction? Explain.

4. List five "miraculous" occurrences or bizarre coincidences that spared lives or had other freak effects during the bomb blast or soon thereafter. Describe how you would explain such incredible events, either from a religious or scientific viewpoint.

5. Select one of the six survivors and recount, briefly, that person's experience. Now substitute yourself for that person. How would you have reacted differently?

6. Hersey wrote that "A surprising number of the people of Hiroshima remained more or less indifferent about the ethics of the bomb." Why is this so? How do you feel about it as an ethical issue?

7. How does "The Aftermath," which was added to *Hiroshima* in 1985, change your perceptions of the incident itself and the story? Does it enhance or detract from its drama? Explain.

8. Describe the unusually close relationship between Father Takakura and Yoshiki-san. Why was their relationship such a close one? Explain.

9. What do you think Hersey's purpose was in writing *Hiroshima?*

31-3. PROJECTS AND ACTIVITIES TO CONSIDER FOR HIROSHIMA

1. Obtain publications about Japanese culture and customs. Explain (a) why the people felt "honored" by the emperor's public announcement that the war was over, and (b) why "disposal of the dead...is a greater moral responsibility to the Japanese than adequate care of the living."

2. The first four chapters of *Hiroshima* were written in 1946. Conduct research and review what scientists and the medical community have since learned about radiation sickness. Were the author's observations accurate? What sicknesses can today's nuclear weapons cause, short of death?

3. Research the explanations given as to why the bomb was dropped on Hiroshima. Organize a debate and discuss the question: Was it necessary to drop the atomic bomb? Be sure to consider such issues as the war being prolonged, with thousands more American lives likely being lost in an assault on Japan, as well as American anger over Japan's attack on Pearl Harbor.

4. Compose an interview for one of the characters. Create 10 questions you would like to ask, and share them with the class. Have classmates take on the role of the interviewee and answer your questions as they think the hibakusha would.

5. Imagine that you were a newspaper editor during World War II. Taking into consideration the emotions and feelings of the times, write an editorial either in support of or in opposition to the use of the atomic bomb.

Curriculum Connections:

1. Using the book and other sources, construct a geographical map of Hiroshima. Show the center of the bomb's explosions, and where each of the six featured characters was situated at that moment. (SS or A)

2. What other countries were allied with Japan in World War II? Why do you think the bomb was not used on those countries? Conduct the necessary research and present your findings to your group. (SS)

3. Conduct research and make a time line, tracing the development of nuclear weapons, beginning during World War II and continuing to the present. Write a short report to accompany your diagram. (SS or A)

32. *The Miracle Worker* by William Gibson
(Atheneum, 1960)

Synopsis

This play opens with a doctor assuring Captain Keller and his wife, Kate, that their infant daughter, Helen, will recover from a serious fever. Soon after the doctor leaves, however, Kate realizes that Helen is deaf and blind. The play then moves to when Helen is about six years old. She is a wild, undisciplined child. Though they try, her parents are unable to help or control her. In desperation they hire a young woman, Annie Sullivan. From the moment Annie arrives, it is clear that she and Helen will be gripped in a great struggle. But Helen is not the only problem for Annie. Annie must also convince the Kellers, especially the Captain, that she, Annie, needs complete control of Helen if she is to reach the child. Annie is certain that language is the key to gaining access to Helen's mind, and she constantly spells the names of things on Helen's palm. Although Helen can spell them back on Annie's palm, the understanding that the words represent things eludes her. After spending two weeks together in the garden house, Helen finally obeys Annie, but when the time is up and they return to the family, Helen quickly reverts to her former behavior. The Kellers are indulgent, ready to fall back in their old pattern of behavior, but Annie doesn't let them. When Helen spills a water pitcher on Annie, Annie takes her out to refill it. She spells "water" into Helen's hand, and suddenly the miracle happens. Helen understands.

Ideas and Concepts to Highlight

1. Explain the format of a play. Most plays are built around four important parts.

    a) *Opening*—reveals the problem.

    b) *Plan*—the characters try to solve the problem and reach a goal.

    c) *Obstacles and Complications*—events and situations that block the characters from solving the problem.

    d) *Climax*—the characters solve (or fail to solve) the problem and reach (or fail to reach) their goal.

2. Note Helen's behavior before Annie's arrival. Discuss why she was allowed to act in so undisciplined a manner.

3. Emphasize the clashing of personalities throughout the play—Helen and Annie, the Captain and Annie, James and the Captain.

4. Discuss the disabilities of blindness and deafness.

Writing Connection: "The Challenge"

Helen Keller was faced with a great challenge—the struggle to manage in life despite the enormous handicaps of being deaf and blind. Everyone, however, has challenges.

For this assignment, instruct your students to consider a challenge they face and write about it. The challenge they might face is how to obtain good enough grades so that they can go on to a good college, how to excel at a sport, dance or similar activity, how to get along with a brother, sister or other family member, or how to cope with a personal disability. Having students complete Worksheet 32-1 will help them get started.

NAME _____ DATE _____ SECTION _____

32-1. THE CHALLENGE

Directions: Helen Keller faced a great challenge in life. Think of a challenge you face. Answer the questions below and write about the challenge you must overcome.

1. What is your challenge? _____
_____
_____
_____

2. Why is overcoming this challenge important?_____
_____
_____
_____

3. How might you overcome it and be successful? _____
_____
_____
_____
_____

4. Who might help you? _____ How? _____
_____
_____
_____

5. What will you gain by overcoming your challenge? _____
_____
_____
_____

32-2. QUESTIONS TO CONSIDER FOR
THE MIRACLE WORKER

1. Before Annie's arrival, how did Helen's disabilities and behavior affect the Keller family? Be specific in discussing the Captain, Kate, and James.

2. Describe Annie Sullivan. What kind of young woman was she? Cite examples from the play to support your views.

3. Describe Captain Keller and Kate. Why do you think they had so much trouble in controlling Helen?

4. How do you think Annie's background, especially her memories of her younger brother Jimmie, influenced her behavior as an adult? Explain.

5. What are James's and Aunt Ev's roles in the story? Why do you think the author included them?

6. Why wouldn't Annie let Helen take food from her (Annie's) plate? Why was Annie's battle with Helen at the table so important?

7. Why was it necessary for Helen to be completely dependent on Annie during her learning? What was the Captain's reaction to Annie's demand of staying alone with Helen at the garden house? Why do you think he finally gave in?

8. When Helen and Annie returned from the garden house, why do you think Helen "tested" Annie and her parents at the table? What happened? In your opinion, was Annie right?

9. Why do you think "water," "wah, wah," was the first word Helen recognized?

10. The characters undergo profound changes by the end of the play. Explain how Helen, Annie, the Captain, and James changed.

32-3. PROJECTS AND ACTIVITIES TO CONSIDER FOR
THE MIRACLE WORKER

1. Research Helen Keller. Write a biographical sketch of this truly remarkable woman. Include her achievements and triumphs.

2. Write an additional scene to the play. What happens after Helen begins to understand words? Create a scene that shows how Annie continues to teach Helen. With the help of classmates, act out and dramatize your scene.

3. Toward the end of the play, Annie says to Kate, "We're born to use words..." With your group, discuss the importance of language. Brainstorm how different life would be without language. Appoint a recorder for your group to write down your ideas, and then discuss your ideas with the members of another group.

4. Research Annie Sullivan and present an oral report about her to your class. Include her background, education, and her accomplishments.

5. Before Annie came to the Keller house, Helen was wild and undisciplined. Her parents seemed unable to control her. Organize a panel to discuss this question: How important is parental discipline and guidance to children? Support your opinions with examples from the play as well as your own experiences.

6. Louis Braille created a method by which blind people can read. Research the Braille method. How does it work? Obtain a book or magazine written in Braille and see if you can read it through touch.

Curriculum Connections:

1. Research the cause of Helen Keller's blindness and deafness. Could her disabilities have been prevented using modern treatments and drugs? (Sci)

2. Annie suffered from trachoma. Research this affliction. What causes it? How can it be treated? (Sci)

3. Many researchers are concerned that listening to loud music too often might cause hearing loss or eventual deafness. Research this question and present your findings orally to your class or group. (Sci)

183

33. <u>Dragonwings</u> by Laurence Yep
(HarperTrophy, 1975)

Synopsis

When he is eight years old, Moon Shadow leaves China and his mother to sail for America to join his father, Windrider. Expecting to find mountains of gold, Moon Shadow is both surprised and awed by the real America. He is also fearful of the demons, the name given to Americans by the Tang, his people. Living with his father and other Tang in San Francisco's Chinatown, Moon Shadow settles into his new life. He works long hours helping his father, who he learns is a man of dreams and visions. Upon hearing that the Wright brothers built a flying machine, Windrider becomes determined to build one too. There is much work for the Tang men, however, and Windrider, even with Moon Shadow's help, can devote only his little spare time to his flying machine, which he calls Dragonwings. After fighting with Black Dog, who stole money from Moon Shadow to support his opium habit, Windrider takes Moon Shadow away from Chinatown. Moon Shadow now realizes that not all demons are evil. Their landlady, Miss Whitlaw and her niece, Robin, are kind, decent people who become friends with Windrider and Moon Shadow. Father and son continue to work on the flying machine, but their progress is interrupted by the great San Francisco earthquake. With Miss Whitlaw and Robin, Windrider and Moon Shadow help pull people from the destruction. As the city rebuilds, Windrider again begins work on Dragonwings. Finally, his flying machine is done and he flies; but the flight is short-lived and Windrider crashes, breaking his leg and some ribs. Knowing that he has flown is enough for him. Returning to Chinatown, Windrider makes plans to bring Moon Shadow's mother to America so that his family, at last, is together.

Ideas and Concepts to Highlight

MUSCH 45

1. Note that the story is written in the first person, with Moon Shadow as the narrator.

2. Discuss the Chinese customs and traditions that are shared with the reader.

3. Discuss the prejudice that the Chinese encountered.

4. Note that the late 19th and early 20th centuries were a time of great immigration. Discuss the reasons people from other countries come to America.

Writing Connection: "A New Land"

Moon Shadow's coming to the United States was an incredible journey filled with anticipation, excitement, and fear, for it meant going to live in a new land with different people and customs. Ask your students to think about what such experiences must have been like.

For this assignment, ask students to imagine that their family has decided to move to another country, where the language and customs are unfamiliar. How would your students manage in such a place? Instruct them to complete Worksheet 33-1 to organize their thoughts, and write a story about their move to a new land. Encourage them to consult reference books about their new country to find information about its customs and traditions.

33-1. A NEW LAND

Directions: Imagine that you, like Moon Shadow, are to move to a new country with your family where you can't speak the language and are unfamiliar with the customs and traditions. What would this experience be like? Answer the questions below and then write a story about your new land.

1. To which country will you move? _____

2. Why will you move there? _____

   _____

   _____

   _____

3. Where will you live? _____

4. Where will you go to school? _____

5. How will you learn the language? _____

   _____

   _____

6. What customs will you need to know about?_____

   _____

   _____

   _____

7. How will you make friends? _____

   _____

8. What will you do in your spare time? _____

   _____

   _____

33-2. *QUESTIONS TO CONSIDER FOR* <u>*DRAGONWINGS*</u>

1. Why did Moon Shadow's father go to America? Why didn't he take Moon Shadow and his mother?

2. Why did the Chinese refer to Americans as the "white demons"?

3. Describe Moon Shadow's vision of America. Compare the America he thought existed when he was in China with the America he found when he arrived here.

4. What is the significance of the story of the Dragon King that Windrider told Moon Shadow? Why did Moon Shadow feel as if he had found his true father?

5. Why did the Tang men wear a queue? What was the queue's original meaning? Why didn't many of the Tang men know what the queue really meant? If they did, do you think they would have continued to wear it? Explain.

6. How did Black Dog's opium addiction result in Windrider and Moon Shadow leaving the company?

7. What was Moon Shadow's impression of Miss Whitlaw? Why did he believe she had been a Tang woman in a former life?

8. Describe Moon Shadow's relationship with Miss Whitlaw and her niece Robin. What did he learn about "demons" from them?

9. Do you think that Windrider's decision to build a flying machine was a wise one? Explain.

10. Toward the end of the story, Moon Shadow says, "I had found my mountain of gold, and it had not been nuggets but people who made it up..." Explain what he means.

11. Describe Moonrider's flight with Dragonwings. What went wrong? Why didn't Windrider build another flying machine?

© 1994 by The Center for Applied Research in Education

33-3. *PROJECTS AND ACTIVITIES TO CONSIDER FOR DRAGONWINGS*

1. Every Tang can have several names—for example, a family and personal name, a name for when he comes of age, a nickname. Make a list of various names for yourself with reasons why you chose them.

2. Confucius was a Chinese philosopher who profoundly affected Chinese culture and tradition. Research his life and teachings, and write a report.

3. Black Dog was addicted to opium. Working with a partner, research the opium trade. What is opium? What effect does it have on the body? Why is it illegal today? Present your findings orally to your group.

4. Working with your group, review the story and list several examples of prejudice. Brainstorm and list reasons why Americans were biased against the Chinese immigrants. Then consider if Americans are less biased against immigrants today. Discuss your opinions and have your recorder present your conclusions to other groups.

5. What becomes of Moon Shadow after the story? Write a scene showing what happens to him in the future.

Curriculum Connections:

1. Consult references and research the great 1906 San Francisco Earthquake. Describe the destruction. Why is fire a danger in the aftermath of an earthquake? What causes earthquakes? Is science able to predict them? What are the chances of San Francisco experiencing a similar earthquake in the future? Write a report of your findings. (Sci)

2. Obtain some books on early aviation and study the diagrams and pictures. Draw or sketch what you believe Moonrider's Dragonwings looked like. (A)

3. The late 19th and early 20th centuries saw enormous immigration from Europe and China to the United States. Consult references and compare the immigration totals from 1890 to 1920 from the major European countries and China. Create a bar graph that represents your findings. Compare the immigration laws then to the laws now and write a brief report. (SS or A)

34. <u>*Running Loose*</u> *by Chris Crutcher*
(Dell, 1983)

Synopsis

Louie Banks is looking forward to playing football during his senior year in high school. He is a first-string receiver, and good friends with the team's star quarterback, Carter Sampson. When Louie begins dating Becky Sanders, one of the most popular girls in the school, he feels that life is great. And it is, until Coach Lednecky instructs the team to knock out an opposing player in an upcoming game. At first Louie doesn't believe it will happen, but when Boomer Cowens slams the player into the bench on the sidelines, Louie explodes. He demands of the referee to call a penalty against his own team, and confronts his coach. To Louie that kind of play isn't what football should be. For standing on his own principles, Louie is thrown off the team and ridiculed at school. Only his parents, Carter, and Becky support him. During this time, it is his growing feelings for Becky and hers for him that helps him to withstand the pressure. When Becky dies in a car accident, Louie's life is upended. Her death makes no sense to him and he questions God how such things can happen. When he comes to understand that life has its own set of random rules, Louie at last comes of age.

Ideas and Concepts to Highlight

1. Note that the story is written in the first person. Louie Banks is the narrator, and the story is written in a conversational tone as if Louie is speaking to the reader.

2. Discuss what it means to stand up for one's principles.

3. Point out Crutcher's excellent characterization and the sharp contrasts between many of the characters—for example, Carter and Boomer, Coach Lednecky and Coach Madison, Mr. Jasper and Norm.

Writing Connection: "Taking a Stand"

When Louie Banks confronted his coach about the cheap hit on Washington, he stood up for his principles even though it cost him his place on the football team and resulted in ridicule. It was a brave thing to do.

For this assignment, ask your students to think of a time they stood up for a principle. (If they didn't, ask them to think about a time that they wish they had or a situation in which they would like to.) Instruct them to complete Worksheet 34-1 and then write about taking a stand.

34-1. TAKING A STAND

Directions: Louie Banks took a stand on principle that cost him his place on the football team and led to his being ridiculed by many of his classmates. Think about a time you or someone you know took a stand on principle. Answer the questions below and write about this event.

1. When did you (or another person) take a stand on principle? _____

_____

_____

2. Describe the event and why the stand was taken._____

_____

_____

_____

_____

3. Who was involved in the event?_____

_____

_____

4. What happened when you (or someone else) took a stand?_____

_____

_____

_____

_____

5. Looking back, was taking the stand the right decision? _____

Why or why not? _____

_____

_____

_____

34-2. QUESTIONS TO CONSIDER FOR
RUNNING LOOSE

1. Compare Carter and Boomer. How does Louie feel about each? Do you agree with his opinions? Explain.

2. Describe Louie's relationship with his parents. Use specific examples from the story to support your ideas.

3. Louie asks Becky why she was willing to spend time with him when she could've dated any guy in school, and she answers, "Because if I was an animal in these woods and I saw you, I'd come up to you." What did she mean? What does that tell you about Louie?

4. How does Louie feel about Coach Lednecky's orders to deliberately knock Washington out of the game? What happened during the game? How did Louie react? Do you agree or disagree with his reaction? Explain.

5. What was Becky's advice to Louie after the Washington incident? Do you agree with that advice? Explain.

6. Compare Carter's and Louie's views about Lednecky and his orders to hurt Washington. Who do you think had the more practical opinion? Why? With which one do you agree? Explain.

7. How did Becky's death affect Louie?

8. After Becky's funeral Dakota tells Louie that "...knowin' the rules" is what separates a man from a boy. What did he mean? What did Louie learn about life from Dakota's "checker" game?

9. Coach Madison helped Louie get on the track team because he believed that Louie needed activity to get his mind off Becky's death. Do you think keeping active can help someone cope with a tragedy? Explain.

10. Why did Louie smash the plaque that was put up for Becky? Was he justified in this action? Explain.

11. What did Louie learn about life during his senior year in high school? Use examples from the story to support your answer.

34-3. PROJECTS AND ACTIVITIES TO CONSIDER FOR
RUNNING LOOSE

1. Imagine that Becky hadn't been killed. Write a scene to the story showing where Louie's and Becky's relationship would have gone.

2. What happens to Louie after high school? Write a scene showing what happens to him next.

3. Working with your group, brainstorm what Louie could have done to get back on the football team without compromising his principles. List possible solutions, discuss the merits of each, and share your list with the members of other groups. See if the class can come up with a solution.

4. Working with a partner, go through the book and identify the events that had a major impact on Louie. List the event and how it affected Louie. Share your list with others.

5. Imagine that you were a sports writer covering the game in which Boomer knocked Washington into the sidelines bench. Write an article about the game, especially noting Boomer's hit.

6. Write an obituary for Becky Sanders.

7. Work with a partner and identify the various conflicts in the story. Create a diagram that represents the conflicts. Share your diagram with others.

Curriculum Connections:

1. Design your own plaque for Becky Sanders. What would you write on it? (A)

2. Research the state of Idaho. Find out about its population, climate, and geography. Locate it on a map of the western United States. What states border it? Write a report and include a map. (SS)

3. Although baseball is often called America's favorite sport, football is king in the fall. Consult references and research the history of football. Trace its development and try to determine why so many boys and men play the game, and why so many fans enjoy watching it. Write a report of your findings. (SS)

35. _Flowers in the Attic_ by V.C. Andrews
(Pocket Books, 1979)

Synopsis

Christopher, Cathy, and twins Cory and Carrie have been shut in the attic of a mansion while their mother, Corrine, tries to win back her wealthy father's blessing. Corrine disgraced her family with her marriage, and when her husband dies, Corrine is destitute. Her father does not know of the children, but her mother does, and she assumes the responsibility for feeding and disciplining them, and monitoring their behavior as everyone waits for the grandfather to die. Because she considers them evil spawn, the religious-fanatic grand-mother punishes them through starvation, whippings and harassment. Corrine's visits to her children become less frequent as she re-enters genteel society, promising freedom but deliv-ering only gifts and promises, shaming them with guilt as she swears she will set them free when the grandfather writes Corrine into his will and dies. The children learn ways to steal out of the room and rob the house of small amounts of money and treasures, which they hope to use for escape. After two years, Chris, planning a large and final robbery, overhears from servants that the grandfather is long dead and Corrine has remarried and moved away, but not before Chris and Cathy's burgeoning sexuality leads to intercourse. They learn that Cory's death toward the end of their imprisonment is from arsenic poisoning, covertly sprin-kled on doughnuts delivered by their grandmother, and the three survivors flee bitterly from the house, Cathy plotting revenge.

Ideas and Concepts to Highlight

1. Melodrama plays a significant role in _Flowers in the Attic,_ both in plot and diction. Speculate on whether the author intends it or if it is her natural writing style. Discuss it as a literary technique and its successful use in the novel.

2. Cathy, the novel's narrator, is aged 12 to 14, and the story is told as a flashback through her eyes. Discuss the use of this young narrator and encour-age students to express opinions about it.

3. Discuss the need of children to grow up in envi-ronments where they interact with others and are free to go outdoors.

Writing Connection: "People's Needs"

In the story, the children were denied a normal life. Many of their needs were not met.

For this assignment, discuss with your students what the basic needs of human beings are. Obviously, things like food and water will be mentioned, but just as important are love, purpose, relationships, and the opportunity for personal growth. Ask your students to reflect on what they feel their needs are and then write an essay on the topic. Completing Worksheet 35-1 will help them to organize their thoughts.

35-1. PEOPLE'S NEEDS

Directions: All people have basic needs. Consider your needs, and then think about the needs of others. It is likely that many of them will be the same. Answer the questions below and then write an essay about the needs of people.

1.

List basic needs beyond food, water, oxygen.	What may result if needs are not met?

2.   Disregarding the needs for food, water, and oxygen, how would your life be affected if some of these other needs weren't met?_____

_____

_____

_____

_____

3.   What can you do to ensure that your needs are met?_____

_____

_____

_____

_____

35-2. QUESTIONS TO CONSIDER FOR
FLOWERS IN THE ATTIC

1. Compare Corrine Foxworth to characters you see in soap operas or similar television shows or movies. Is she more realistic? Is her character more like someone created by Hollywood or someone you know? Explain.

2. Describe the grandmother. What kind of person was she? What allowed her to try to kill her own grandchildren?

3. At what point do you think the children stopped believing their mother? At what point did you stop believing her? Support your answer with examples you find in the story.

4. After she views the Christmas party, Cathy says she has to "make herself over...better and become like Chris—eternally cheerful." How difficult is that for Cathy? How hard is that for a person in general?

5. Discuss the moral question surrounding Chris and Cathy's experience. Do you hold them accountable for their sexual incidents? Explain.

6. Trace the relevant events that lead to Chris's sexual assault on his sister. Which do you think was most significant? What might have prevented the attack?

7. In what ways do you think the grandmother was vulnerable? Was there any way the children might have won her over? Could they have stopped her? Support your answer with examples from the book.

8. Were you satisfied with the climax and ending of the story? If yes, why? If not, how would you have changed the plot to improve it?

9. Would you recommend this book to a friend? Why or why not? If you were a parent, would you recommend it to your own child? Why or why not?

35-3. PROJECTS AND ACTIVITIES TO CONSIDER FOR
FLOWERS IN THE ATTIC

1. In 1987, *Flowers in the Attic* was released as a movie. The movie was not well received by the public. Pretend that it is being remade this year, and you are the casting director. Which actors and actresses would you hire for the film? Justify your selections.

2. How do you think the rape will affect Cathy later in life? Find statistics and sources of information about the effects of incest on which to base your predictions.

3. Conduct research and write a report on the respective ailments that you think killed Malcolm and Cory.

4. Working with your group, assume you are the children. Brainstorm ways that you might be able to gain freedom. Appoint a recorder to write down your ideas and then examine them more closely, identifying both the strengths and weaknesses of the plans. Share your lists with other groups.

5. Imagine that you were one of the children and it was possible to smuggle a note for help out of the house. What would you write? And how could you manage to get the note to someone who could in fact help you?

6. Suppose that the children's grandfather doesn't die, and they escape from the house. Write a scene of their escape.

Curriculum Connections:

1. Using the author's description and your own imagination, draw one of the paintings mentioned in Chapter Three. (A)

2. Use your imagination to create a mental picture of the bedroom and attic. Draft a floor plan for both, creating measurements and dimensions. (A or M)

3. Make a Foxworth family tree from the "Momma's Story" chapter. Research the legality of the so-called "evil marriage" between Corrine and Chris. (A or SS)

4. In the story, Cory dies because of arsenic poisoning. Consult references and find out more about arsenic. Although the element is poisonous, it also has other uses. Write a brief report of your findings. (Sci)

36. The Adventures of Huckleberry Finn
by Mark Twain, pseudonym for Samuel L. Clemens
(Grosset and Dunlap, 1948)

Synopsis

Huckleberry Finn, son of the town's drunk, lives with the Widow Douglas and Miss Watson, the widow's sister. He likes the widow, but doesn't enjoy her attempts to "civilize" him. When pap, Huck's father, returns to town, he wants Huck to live with him, mostly because he wants to get his hands on money that Huck is entitled to. (Huck shares $12,000 with Tom Sawyer. In Twain's *The Adventures of Tom Sawyer,* which was written earlier, Huck and Tom found the money in a robber's cave. The money was then put in trust for them.) Since Huck doesn't want to go with pap, his father catches him and takes him to a cabin where nobody can find him. Huck escapes, though, and hides out at Jackson's Island. A few days later Huck finds Jim, Miss Watson's slave. Jim tells Huck that he ran away because he was afraid that Miss Watson was going to sell him to a slave trader in New Orleans. Huck promises not to turn Jim in. They begin traveling down the river on a raft, hoping to get Jim to the free states. Along the way they have several adventures. They take up with two con-men, one of whom betrays Jim by telling a man that Jim is a runaway slave. When Huck learns that Jim has been captured, he and Tom Sawyer, who has joined him, plan an elaborate scheme to save Jim, finally freeing him. The story is episodic with many adventures, rich in the dialects of the times, and provides vivid details of life along the Mississippi before the Civil War.

Ideas and Concepts to Highlight

1. Note that the story is told in the first person, with Huck as the narrator. Emphasize that Twain used the dialects of the times and that he wrote the story as if Huck were actually speaking. (Some students may have trouble with the dialects.)

2. Discuss the setting. The story takes place in the South prior to the Civil War. The country was divided into slave and free states.

3. Explain that the novel is episodic. The plot consists of numerous events, each of which is a very short story by itself. (Critics often complain that Twain wandered with the plot and occasionally needed to rely on coincidence to make things work out. Although this may be valid in some cases, it doesn't diminish the story's appeal and many strengths.)

4. Emphasize the powerful contrasts that are found throughout the book, the most striking being the differences between Huck and Tom, and slavery and freedom.

5. Note Huck's basic goodness. Although he has faults, he is willing to go against his society to help Jim.

6. Point out Twain's use of irony, which he frequently employs to give his opinions on the behavior of people. A good example is Huck's belief in the values of his society. He has been taught that slavery is right, and feels that it is wrong for him to help Jim. Yet, he helps Jim anyway and accepts Jim as an individual.

Writing Connection: "The Continuing Adventures of Huckleberry Finn"

Huck is truly an interesting character. Uneducated, he is intelligent; a product of his times, he nevertheless is willing to break social customs (and laws) that he feels are wrong. Although he has a keen understanding of people, he doesn't always make the right decisions. One of his most unwavering traits, however, is his desire to avoid being "civilized." That's why at the end of the novel he intends to go to "Injun" territory.

For this assignment, instruct your students to imagine that Huck did indeed go to Injun territory. Keeping in mind his personality, students are to write of his continuing adventures. Have students complete Worksheet 36-1 to generate ideas.

36-1. THE CONTINUING ADVENTURES OF HUCKLEBERRY FINN

Directions: Imagine what Huck Finn's next adventure will be. Answer the questions below and write a story about what happens to Huck next.

1. Where does Huck go after Jim is freed? _____

_____

2. Why does he go there? _____

_____

_____

_____

3. How does he get there? _____

_____

_____

_____

4. Who goes with him? _____

_____

_____

5. What happens when Huck arrives? _____

_____

_____

_____

6. How does this new adventure affect or change Huck? _____

_____

_____

_____

© 1994 by The Center for Applied Research in Education

36-2. *QUESTIONS TO CONSIDER FOR THE ADVENTURES OF HUCKLEBERRY FINN*

1. Describe Huck's feelings about living with the Widow Douglas and her sister, Miss Watson. Which one of the ladies does he like more? Why? What does he feel about their attempts to "civilize" him?

2. What kind of man was Huck's father? Use examples from the story to support your answer. How did Huck feel when his father returned to the village?

3. Why does pap forbid Huck to go to school? How would you react to pap's demand if you were Huck? Explain.

4. Why did Huck stage his own death?

5. When Huck finds Jim, he promises that he will not turn Jim in, even though Jim is a runaway slave. What does this tell you about Huck's character?

6. What did the river mean to Huck? Explain.

7. Huck quickly realizes that the Duke and Dauphin are con-men. What is a con-man? What does his ability to see these men for what they really are tell you about Huck? What does his decision not to confront them about their fraud tell you?

8. How was Jim betrayed? How did Huck react when he learned that Jim had been captured as a runaway slave? What did he decide to do?

9. The story contains several ironic episodes. Identify three and describe them. Explain why they are ironic.

10. Throughout the story, Huck rebels against civilization. At the end of the novel, has he become more "civilized"? Explain.

36-3. PROJECTS AND ACTIVITIES TO CONSIDER FOR
THE ADVENTURES OF HUCKLEBERRY FINN

1. In many ways, Jim assumes the role of a father to Huck. Working with a partner, find examples of this. Share your findings with the members of your group.

2. Select a favorite scene of the book and, with classmates assuming the necessary roles, act it out, reading the dialogue. This will give you a feel for the flow of the dialects that were common during the time of the novel.

3. Research Mark Twain (Samuel L. Clemens). Write a biographical sketch and share it with the members of your group.

4. Read Twain's *The Adventures of Tom Sawyer*. Write a book review of it, comparing it to *The Adventures of Huckleberry Finn*.

Curriculum Connections:

1. Research slavery and write a report about it. In your report answer the following questions: Which were the slave states? Which were the free states? How was it determined that a new state would be free or slave? What reasons did slave states give for justifying their need for slaves? How was slavery one of the issues that led to the Civil War? (SS)

2. Research the dialects of American English and write a short report. What are the major dialects? How do dialects arise? (SS)

3. Make a model of the raft Huck and Jim used to float down the Mississippi River. (A)

4. Using an atlas or other reference, locate the Mississippi River. How long is it? What states does it border? Research the Mississippi of the 1830s (about the time the novel takes place) and compare how the river was used then to the way it is used today. Make an oral presentation of your findings to your group or class. (SS)

37. <u>*Something Wicked This Way Comes*</u> *by Ray Bradbury*
(Simon and Schuster, 1962)

Synopsis

When Cooger and Dark's carnival comes to town, Will Halloway and Jim Nightshade, two thirteen-year-old friends, are fascinated by it and they stumble on to a fantastic sight: hidden, they watch as Mr. Cooger rides the carnival's merry-go-round backward and becomes younger. When they try to warn Miss Foley, their 7th grade teacher, that the young Cooger is posing as her nephew, Cooger becomes suspicious that they know the secret of the merry-go-round. Later, he makes it seem that the boys are stealing Miss Foley's jewelry. Will and Jim run after Cooger and chase him to the merry-go-round. While Cooger is on it, moving forward in years, Jim and Will scuffle at the control, breaking it and causing Cooger to go around so many times that he becomes an old man. Mr. Dark, the illustrated man, so called because his body is covered with tattoos, now tries to capture the boys to protect the secret. Will's father tries to help the boys. Although Dark tempts Will's father with renewed youth, Mr. Halloway recognizes Dark's evil and finds a way to stop him and his carnival.

Ideas and Concepts to Highlight

1. Note that the story is told from multiple points of view. This allows Bradbury to share the thoughts and feelings of various characters with the reader.

MUSCH 49

2. Point out that the story begins with a prologue. Mention that a prologue often serves to pique the reader's interest with a promise that something dramatic will happen in the book. Direct students to the last sentence of the prologue.

3. Discuss the theme of good versus evil.

4. Emphasize the fantastic allure of the merry-go-round—the possibility of eternal youth.

Writing Connection: "Riding Cooger and Dark's Merry-Go-Round"

Ask your students to imagine that Cooger and Dark's carnival came to their town or city, and that they could ride the merry-go-round. They could become any age they wished. Instruct them to complete Worksheet 37-1, and then write a story about their adventure.

37-1. *RIDING COOGER AND DARK'S MERRY-GO-ROUND*

Directions: Imagine that you could take a ride on Cooger and Dark's merry-go-round. Answer the questions below and write a story about your adventure.

1. Would you ride backward or forward? _____

How many years would you go? _____ Why? _____

_____

_____

_____

2. How would you be changed? _____

_____

_____

_____

3. How might your family, friends, and home have changed? _____

_____

_____

_____

_____

4. What happens to you in your new age? _____

_____

_____

_____

5. Would you ride the merry-go-round back to your current age? _____ Why or why not?

_____

_____

_____

© 1994 by The Center for Applied Research in Education

37-2. QUESTIONS TO CONSIDER FOR SOMETHING WICKED THIS WAY COMES

1. How does Bradbury use the lightning rod salesman to build early suspense in the story?

2. Describe Will's father. What type of man is he? Describe Will's relationship with his father. Use examples from the story to support your answer.

3. Compare and contrast Will and Jim. How are they alike? How are they different? Which one seems to be more adventurous? Which one is more cautious? Why do you think they are such good friends?

4. What special fascination did the merry-go-round hold for Jim? Did Will share this fascination? Explain.

5. Why do you think Bradbury chose a traveling carnival for the setting of evil?

6. What happened to Miss Foley?

7. What were the "autumn people"? Who did Mr. Halloway think Cooger and Dark were? Why did he consider them to be dangerous?

8. How did Dark tempt Mr. Halloway? Why was this the greatest temptation he could offer Mr. Halloway? Why did Mr. Halloway resist the temptation?

9. What did Mr. Halloway discover was the way to defeat the witch when she was trying to stop his heart? When he shot her with the wax bullet, what do you think really killed her? Explain.

10. How did Mr. Halloway finally defeat Dark? Why was evil, in the end, powerless against him?

11. What part of the book did you like the best? Why? What part did you like the least? Why?

37-3. PROJECTS AND ACTIVITIES TO CONSIDER FOR SOMETHING WICKED THIS WAY COMES

1. Think about a time you went to a carnival or circus. (One hopes it wasn't as frightful as the carnival of Cooger and Dark!) Write about your experience and share it with the members of your group.

2. Write a poem about the illustrated man.

3. Imagine that Mr. Halloway gave in to Dark's temptation of a ride on the merry-go-round. Write a story about how this would change Halloway's life.

4. Imagine that you were a reporter for the local newspaper in town. Write an article about the attractions one could see at Cooger and Dark's carnival.

5. Pretend that you are the barker at a side show at a carnival. Decide what type of show you'd be running. Write a sales pitch you would use to entice people to pay to see your show.

6. Watch the movie version of *Something Wicked This Way Comes* and compare it to the novel. How is the movie different? Which, in your opinion, has the greater impact? Write a movie review and share it with the members of your group.

7. Read *The Illustrated Man* by Ray Bradbury and write a review of the story.

Curriculum Connections:

1. Draw the illustrated man and some of the other characters of the carnival. (A)

2. Design an advertising poster for Cooger and Dark's Pandemonium Shadow Show. (A)

3. Science is rapidly unraveling the mystery of what makes people grow old. Working with a partner or small group, research aging. Find out the latest information on how scientists are trying to stop or turn back the biological clock. Present an oral report to the class. (Sci)

38. *The Pearl* by John Steinbeck
(Viking, 1947)

Synopsis

When Kino, a young Mexican fisherman, finds a pearl of great value—the "Pearl of the World"—his entire life is changed. He now has the means to pay the local doctor to treat his son for a scorpion bite (the doctor would not see the boy before this), Kino can afford the fee to marry his wife, Juana, in the church, and he will be able to provide his son with an education. All these dreams are quickly ruined, however. A man comes to steal the pearl in the night, and Kino fights him off. When Kino tries to sell his pearl to the pearl buyers, they offer him only a fraction of what the pearl is worth and he refuses to sell it. More men try to steal the pearl and Kino kills one of them. Knowing that he must leave the village, he and Juana take their son and set out, but they are followed by three men. Kino attacks them, but a stray bullet, fired by one of the men, kills his son. Kino and Juana return to the village, and Kino casts the pearl back into the sea.

Ideas and Concepts to Highlight

1. In the opening, Steinbeck describes the story as a parable. Explain that a parable is a simple story with a moral or lesson.

2. Discuss the symbolism in the story. The pearl, for example, represents material wealth and evil. Steinbeck seems to say that as one gains material riches he loses himself.

3. Discuss Mexico's rigid social structure that has come down from the Spanish colonization. The Spanish held positions of influence in government and business, while the mestizos and Indians occupied the lowest levels in the social order.

4. Note the theme of exploitation of the poor by the rich.

5. Locate La Paz, the setting of the story, on the Baja Peninsula.

Writing Connection: "Never Satisfied"

One of the themes of *The Pearl* is greed, that people are never satisfied with what they have. They always want more. In a prewriting activity, discuss this topic with your students. Then instruct them to complete Worksheet 38-1 and write about the subject. Encourage them to support their ideas with examples from the story as well as their own experiences.

38-1. NEVER SATISFIED

Directions: After Kino finds the "Pearl of the World," the greed of many people becomes clear. Even Kino refuses to get rid of the pearl when his wife begs him to. Do you feel that most people are never satisfied with what they have? Answer the questions below and write about your feelings.

1.   Give some examples (from the story or your own experiences) of people who *are* satisfied with what they have. _____

_____

_____

_____

_____

2.   Give some examples (from the story or your own experiences) of people who *are not* satisfied with what they have. _____

_____

_____

_____

_____

3.   In your opinion, are most people satisfied with what they have?_____
Explain. _____

_____

_____

_____

4.   What advice could you offer to those who are not satisfied? _____

_____

_____

_____

_____

© 1994 by The Center for Applied Research in Education

1. Describe Kino's life before he found the pearl. How did his life change after he found it? Give specific examples from the story.

2. Describe the townspeople's reaction to Kino finding the pearl. Why do you think the priest came? Why did the doctor come?

3. What were Kino's dreams? Given the reality of his position in the village, do you think his dreams were realistic? Explain.

4. Steinbeck writes: "From now on they (the neighbors) would watch Kino and Juana very closely to see whether riches turned their heads, as riches turn all people's heads." What does he mean by this? Do you agree or disagree? Why or why not?

5. What was Kino's opinion of the doctor? What was the doctor's opinion of villagers like Kino? How does Steinbeck use their opinions to show the rigid class structure of the village?

6. When Kino took his pearl to the pearl buyer, the man said, "This pearl is like fool's gold. . . . There is no market for such things." Was he being truthful? Why might he say this? How did Kino feel about his offer? What did he do? What would you have done if you were in Kino's place?

7. What did Steinbeck mean when he wrote that Kino "had lost one world and had not gained another"? Explain.

8. When he first found the pearl Juana was as happy as Kino was, but she soon began to view it differently than Kino. Describe their different opinions about the pearl. Who held the more accurate opinion of it? Why?

9. The pearl ends in tragedy. Given Kino's personality, is there anything he could have done to avert the sad ending? Explain.

10. What is the moral or lesson of the story? Explain, using examples from the story.

38-3. PROJECTS AND ACTIVITIES TO CONSIDER FOR
THE PEARL

1. Working with a partner, identify the major events of the story and show how they affected Kino's behavior. Create a chart and share your findings with your group.

2. *The Pearl* is often thought of as a parable. What is a parable? Relate it to another parable. How is it alike and different from the story of Kino and his pearl? Share your conclusions with your group.

3. Read *The Sea of Cortez* by Steinbeck and discuss with your group how his travels there helped him write *The Pearl*. Also discuss this question: Does an author need first-hand experience about a setting to write realistically about it?

4. What do you think happens to Kino and Juana after they return to the village? Write a final scene to the story. Especially consider how their experience with the pearl changed them.

5. Imagine you were a close friend of Kino. After learning that he had found the pearl, what advice would you have given him?

6. Working with a partner, identify several examples of symbolism in the story. List the symbol and what it represented. Compare your list with others.

Curriculum Connections:

1. Research the class structure in Mexico. Trace its development from the time of Spanish colonization. What efforts have been made to reduce the class structure? How successful have these efforts been? Write a brief report on your findings. (SS)

2. Write words to the "Song of the Family," or the "Song of Evil." (A)

3. Research how pearls are formed, and write a report. Illustrate your report. (Sci)

4. Consult an atlas or similar reference and study the climate of La Paz. What is its annual average rainfall? What is its annual average temperature? Create graphs that show its rainfall and temperature each month. Compare it to the climate of your own town or city. (Sci)

5. Based on the information of the story, create a map of Kino's village. (A)

39. *The Hitchhiker's Guide to the Galaxy* by Douglas Adams
(Harmony Books, 1979)

Synopsis

Arthur Dent is an unassuming Earthling buffoon whose house in England is about to be bulldozed for a freeway. Arthur does not know that Earth is about to be vaporized to make way for an intergalactic superhighway. His friend Ford Prefect, a hitchhiker from outer space who is researching Earth for his famous guide, rescues Arthur just before Earth is destroyed. They get away by grabbing a ride on the destroyers' spaceship. The marauding Vogons expel Arthur and Ford into space and they are picked up with a second to spare by Zaphod Beeblebrox, who is piloting the hijacked *Heart of Gold,* the premier method of space travel powered by the Infinite Improbability Drive. They arrive at Magrathea, a seemingly deserted planet that Beeblebrox is certain holds incredible wealth. The planet awakens after they arrive, and the galactic police that are pursuing Zaphod for stealing the *Heart of Gold* land on the planet. Arthur, Ford, Zaphod and his girlfriend Trillian, also an Earthling, escape and head for the Restaurant at the End of the Universe.

Ideas and Concepts to Highlight

1. Douglas Adams is a practitioner of a writing style that is kooky and playful, playing off the icons of contemporary culture. Discuss the relationship between technology and contemporary values and how technology can influence values.

2. Discuss comedic writing. Encourage students to explore humor in its many forms, and in their own writing.

3. Discuss science fiction as a genre, comparing it to other types of fiction. (Note that this book is a rare blend of comedy and science fiction.) Encourage students to share their favorite stories and authors.

4. Since many characters in the book are not Earthlings, they are described in great detail. Discuss the importance of character description, and encourage students to visualize such characters as Adams depicts them.

Writing Connection: "A Science Fiction Short Story"

Adams provides plenty of imaginative characters and situations in this book. For this writing assignment, ask your students to write their own science fiction story. Remind them that SF stories are technologically based and often have aliens. Good SF stories don't violate the physical laws of our universe, although futuristic devices allow characters far greater command over their realities than we currently have on Earth. Completing Worksheet 39-1 will help students to formulate their ideas for their stories.

39-1. A SCIENCE FICTION SHORT STORY

Directions: Science fiction is one of the most popular types of writing. Answer the questions below and write your own SF story.

1. Describe the world(s) on which your story will take place. _____

_____

_____

_____

_____

_____

2. List your main characters. (On a separate sheet, write a detailed description of each.) ____

_____

_____

_____

_____

3. List some of the technological advances your SF world will have. _____

_____

_____

_____

_____

4. Describe the central conflict of your story. _____

_____

_____

_____

_____

_____

© 1994 by The Center for Applied Research in Education

39-2. QUESTIONS TO CONSIDER FOR
THE HITCHHIKER'S GUIDE TO THE GALAXY

1. What is Arthur's reaction when he learns that the Earth is about to be vaporized? How would you react if you suddenly found out that the Earth was to be vaporized?

2. The typical science fiction story has advanced technology. Describe some examples of advanced technology in this story.

3. Name a celebrity or someone you know who attracts attention, like Zaphod Beeblebrox, whose very livelihood is dependent on doing so. Compare their styles. What is your opinion of their behaviors? Explain.

4. Explain why you think Marvin the robot was so depressed.

5. Do you think Arthur Dent was a suitable companion for Ford? Why do you suppose Ford brought him along? Explain Arthur's role.

6. Explain the author's fixations with alcohol and digital watches.

7. What did you find most plausible in the story? Why? What did you find the least plausible? Why?

8. Who is the "main" character in the story? The protagonist? The antagonist? Why do you think so? If you could adjust the personality of any character, whom would it be?

9. Would you describe this story as a comedy? As science fiction? Why or why not? Use examples from the story to support your views.

39-3. PROJECTS AND ACTIVITIES TO CONSIDER FOR
THE HITCHHIKER'S GUIDE TO THE GALAXY

1. Select another science fiction book, and compare the author's writing style with that of Douglas Adams in *The Hitchhiker's Guide to the Galaxy*.

2. Find 10 words that the author arbitrarily created for use in his book. Then invent five of your own, defining them. Write two paragraphs using all five, plus as many of the author's as you can.

3. Speculate for a few paragraphs how *you* think the Earth will end. Share your predictions with your group or class.

4. Write a stanza of Vogon poetry and illustrate it. (Work with your group to produce a volume of Vogon poems.)

5. Working with your group, create a new adventure for Arthur Dent. Appoint a recorder to write your story down and then share it with other groups.

6. Create a menu for The Restaurant at the End of the Universe.

7. Many people believe that the Earth is indeed doomed—not by invading Vogons, but by our own hand. What do you think is necessary to save the planet? Working with your group, discuss major pressing issues that you believe are necessary to preventing our self-destruction. As a group, write a letter to a newspaper or magazine editor expressing a collective viewpoint.

8. Obtain several editions of the comic strip "Calvin and Hobbes." Compare Bill Watterson's vivid imagination with the imagination of Douglas Adams. How are they similar? Where do you think such imaginations come from?

Curriculum Connections:

1. Design a new book jacket for *The Hitchhiker's Guide to the Galaxy*. (A)

2. Pretend you are a Magrathean designer of customized planets. Design a planet for Earthlings. Include all details, specifications, costs and time required. (A or Sci)

3. Magrathea was a legendary lost civilization. What are some similar legends on Earth? Research and report on one. (SS)

4. Research our Milky Way Galaxy. What does it consist of? How big is it? How did it form? What shape does it have? How many galaxies are there in space? Include the answers to these and similar questions in a report. (Sci)

40. *Night* by Elie Wiesel
(MacGibbon & Kee, 1960)

Synopsis

Eliezer Wiesel is a 12-year-old Hungarian Jew who yearns to become a mystic. He is learning from an older Jew until all foreign Jews are expelled from his town in 1941. When the old man returns months later, he tells stories of concentration camps and mass murders, but the townspeople remain complacent, expecting the Russian front to defeat the Nazis any day. The Germans, however, arrive in their town and within a few weeks they team with the Hungarian police and rob all the Jews of their possessions, cramming the people into ghettos. Soon they are deported, and after a horrific train ride, they arrive at Auschwitz, where Elie and his father are separated from his mother and sisters, and Elie sees the crematories for the first time. At that moment, he loses all faith in God. Elie and his father are sent to labor camps at Buna, where they survive for many months despite being surrounded by death. On numerous occasions they are nearly selected for death. As the Allied fronts advance, the German troops and their prisoners flee deeper into Germany, forcing a death march in the snow, first to Gleiwitz, then Buchenwald, where Elie's father finally dies after horrendous suffering. The prisoners at Buchenwald, aware that the American forces are near, revolt and scatter the German officers. That same day, the Americans arrive and liberate the camp. Elie survives, but sees himself in a mirror as a corpse.

Ideas and Concepts to Highlight

1. Discuss the death of Elie's religious faith, a focal point of many scholarly discussions of *Night,* and how religion is often the sole support of a person in great need.

2. Compare the Holocaust with other genocides, such as the "ethnic cleansing" in Bosnia, massacres of Native Americans, the slaughter of Kurds in Iraq or similar events in history. Discuss the long-term impact of such events.

3. Discuss the long-term effects of the Holocaust on individuals, and the varying ways in which survivors and their families deal with the experience in following years.

4. Mention the movement by Neo-Nazis in Europe and the United States, who promote the idea that the Holocaust never happened.

Writing Connection: "No More Holocausts"

Night is a chilling account of one of history's truly dark periods. Even while it was happening, many people refused to believe that it was. Afterward, people around the world vowed that it would never happen again. Unfortunately, one need only follow the news to see that hatred and brutality still exist in the world and the potential for new holocausts haunts us.

For this assignment, ask your students to reflect on the Holocaust and think how future holocausts can be prevented. Instruct students to complete Worksheet 40-1 and then write about this topic.

40-1. NO MORE HOLOCAUSTS

Directions: The Holocaust was a terrible episode in history. Answer the questions below and then write an essay explaining how new holocausts can be prevented.

1. What caused the Holocaust? _____

_____

_____

_____

_____

2. What might have ended the Holocaust before so many people were killed? _____

_____

_____

_____

_____

3. What can the United Nations, or other countries, do to prevent another holocaust? _____

_____

_____

_____

_____

4. What, if anything, can individuals do? _____

_____

_____

_____

_____

_____

40-2. QUESTIONS TO CONSIDER FOR
NIGHT

1. Why do you think the townspeople remained complacent, despite the advance of the German army?

2. Suppose you were Elie. What would you take with you when you were exiled? Why? What would your feelings be?

3. Justify Elie's reaction when his father was struck savagely by Idek. Why did he act that way? How did you feel after reading that paragraph?

4. Why did Elie lie to Stein, his relative, about Stein's family? Do you think he was morally right in doing so? Explain.

5. Define the following: Talmud, cabbala, Gestapo, Kaddish, Aryan, and Palestine.

6. Why do you think the Jews were made to strip, and constantly pass through showers?

7. Explain the author's meaning when he says after the hanging of the youth from Warsaw that "the soup tasted excellent that evening," yet after the *pipel* was hanged, "the soup tasted of corpses." Why did he utilize this juxtaposition?

8. Contrast the crucifixion of Christ with the many deaths in concentration camps. Why do you think the author continuously employs this specific image? Are they comparable? Support your answer.

9. What is the significance of "night" in the novel? Cite examples from the story to support your answer.

10. What effect do you think his experience had on the author in his later life?

11. What enables people to survive such horrible experiences as the Holocaust? Where, in your opinion, do they find the strength to live through such ordeals?

40-3. PROJECTS AND ACTIVITIES TO CONSIDER FOR
NIGHT

1. What is the purpose of a foreword? Write a new one for *Night*, based on the perspectives of the 1990s. Has understanding of the Holocaust changed since the book was written?

2. Obtain clippings, and if possible, a videotaped documentary about the Holocaust Museum, which opened April, 1993 in Washington, D.C. Discuss in your group your reaction to this monument. Is it sufficient remembrance or do you feel that it opens new emotional wounds? Arrive at a consensus, organize a debate with another group, and try to convince them of your position.

3. Recall the march in the snow, as the Russian front advanced through Germany. Consult references about other famous forced marches. (A good example is the Cherokee Nation's "Trail of Tears.") Choose one and compare and contrast it to the march in the snow. Write an essay.

4. Locate a person who survived or is the child of a survivor of the Nazi concentration camps. Have the person speak to the class about the Holocaust, and discuss your reactions.

5. With your group, discuss the historical significance of the Holocaust and how it is often cited when the world averts its eyes to tragedy. Why does the Holocaust still evoke such strong emotions? Share your conclusions with the members of other groups.

6. Imagine that you were Elie, and you were able to write a letter and have it smuggled out of Auschwitz. What would you write to tell the world what was happening?

Curriculum Connections:

1. Working with your group, print, in large block letters, the three paragraphs that begin with "Never shall I forget that night," the most well-known excerpt from the story. Make a poster, using illustrative or creative lettering to exhibit the drama of the words. Then have a group member read the words aloud, and discuss the impact and meaning of these words. (A)

2. Research the Holocaust and try to answer the following question: In a supposedly "civilized" world, how could it have happened? (SS)

© 1994 by The Center for Applied Research in Education

6

Novels for Grades 11-12

41. *Lord of the Flies* - Golding

42. *The Scarlet Letter* - Hawthorne

43. *All Quiet on the Western Front* - Remarque

44. *Wuthering Heights* - Brontë

45. *Brave New World* - Huxley

46. *Fahrenheit 451* - Bradbury

47. *A Raisin in the Sun* (play) - Hansberry

48. *Watership Down* - Adams

49. *A Little Love* - Hamilton

50. *Dune* - Herbert

51. *Gone with the Wind* - Mitchell

52. *Native Son* - Wright

53. *Jane Eyre* - Brontë

54. *Dinner at the Homesick Restaurant* - Tyler

55. *Slaughterhouse-Five* - Vonnegut

56. *One Flew Over the Cuckoo's Nest* - Kesey

57. *The House on Mango Street* - Cisneros

58. *Fallen Angels* - Myers

59. *Hamlet* (play) - Shakespeare

60. *Memory* - Mahy

41. *Lord of the Flies* by William Golding
(Coward-McCann, 1962)

Synopsis

During an atomic war, a group of boys are evacuated from England. When their plane is attacked, they are ejected in a passenger tube and land on a tropical island. Ralph and his companion Piggy soon find other boys, including a group led by Jack. Although Ralph is elected chief, he is unable to lead effectively, and soon he and Jack become rivals. The novel details a disintegration from order to chaos in which the boys return to a savage state. The darker side of human nature eventually dominates, resulting in two of the boys being killed by the others.

Ideas and Concepts to Highlight

1. Discuss the good and evil of human nature. Ask for students' opinions and feelings on what makes people "good." Do they believe that individuals can be both "good" and "evil"?

2. Discuss the question of innate good versus innate evil. Can anyone be truly either?

3. Emphasize the symbolism found in the novel. The conch represents authority; the fire represents hope, rescue and optimism; and the beastie represents the brutality in all human beings.

4. Note the significance of the title. The Lord of the Flies refers to Beelzebub, a prince of devils. In the novel, the Lord of the Flies is a fly-covered pig's head.

5. Discuss what happens when laws, regulations, and the conventions of society are removed.

Writing Connection: "Good Versus Evil"

A major theme of *Lord of the Flies* is good versus evil. Golding seems to be saying that without the constraints imposed on people by civilization, most people would do evil acts.

For this assignment, first lead a discussion about good and evil. Ask students to share their opinions, and then complete Worksheet 41-1, which will help them to clarify their thoughts further before writing an essay on the topic.

NAME _____ **DATE** _____ **SECTION** _____

41-1. GOOD VERSUS EVIL

Directions: One of the major themes of *Lord of the Flies* is good versus evil. Answer the questions below and then write an essay on this topic.

1. Can a person be born "good" or "evil," or does a person learn to be good or evil? _____
_____ Explain. _____

_____

_____

_____

2. Can a person be all good? Or all evil? _____

Explain. _____

_____

_____

3. Give an example of a good person you've read or heard about. _____

Why is this person good? _____

_____

_____

4. Give an example of an evil person you've read or heard about. _____

Why is this person evil? _____

_____

_____

5. Why might someone choose evil over good? _____

_____

_____

_____

_____

41-2. *QUESTIONS TO CONSIDER FOR*
LORD OF THE FLIES

1. Compare Ralph and Jack. Who is the better leader at the beginning of the story? Why? Who is the better leader at the end of the story? Is either one of them a good leader? Why or why not?

2. What is the conch? Why is it important? *symbolism*

3. How is the fire important to the boys being rescued? What might the fire, in the author's opinion, also represent?

4. In Chapter 5 during a meeting with the others, Ralph says, "Things are breaking up. I don't understand why. We began well; we were happy. And then—" What does he mean? What is happening? Why do you think this is happening?

5. The "beastie" throughout the story represents Golding's view that within all human beings is brutality. Do you agree with his assessment of people? Why or why not? *symbolism*

6. How does Jack change as the novel progresses? Give some examples. If the boys weren't rescued, what kind of person do you think Jack would have become in a few years?

7. The title of the story, *Lord of the Flies,* is a name for Beelzebub, a prince of devils. Why do you think Golding chose this for the title of his story?

8. At the end of Chapter 8, Simon has a conversation with the Lord of the Flies. What does the Lord of the Flies tell him? Does this foreshadow Simon's eventual death? How?

9. How did the British officer react when he first found Ralph? How did his attitude change when he began to realize what had happened on the island? Why did the boys begin to sob? Do you think he understood why the boys began to cry? Why or why not? *Response at end of novel*

10. After completing the novel, has your opinion about the basic goodness or evil of people changed? Why or why not? If yes, in what ways?

© 1994 by The Center for Applied Research in Education

41-3. *PROJECTS AND ACTIVITIES TO CONSIDER FOR LORD OF THE FLIES*

1. By the end of the novel, the boys have lost their civilization. Create a flow chart showing the events leading up to this. Why do you think this happened? Was it inevitable? What might they have done differently to stop their slide into savagery?

2. Authors often express their opinions or viewpoints about issues through their stories. Working with a group, research Golding's views in more depth. What do you think is Golding's likely opinion of the human race? Does he think that most people are inherently good? Bad? What do you think Golding would say is the reason most people act "good"? Organize a debate exploring Golding's views.

3. Imagine that you were marooned on a deserted island. What types of things would you need for survival? How would you manage to occupy your time? How would you overcome the loneliness? How would you feel if you were never rescued?

4. In the story, although Ralph was elected chief and assumed the role of "leader," he was unable to lead the boys effectively. Think of someone you feel is a good leader or role model. Write a biographical sketch of this person, focusing on the personal traits and accomplishments that make this individual a "real" leader. If necessary, consult reference books for background information.

Curriculum Connections:

1. Describe the island. Consult a resource on climates. What is the definition of a tropical island? Does the island the boys are on fit this definition? If yes, between what north and south latitude lines must it lie? Now study a world map. Which tropical islands are closest to England? Try to pinpoint the island the boys might have landed on. What island might it be? Why do you think this? (SS or Sci)

2. At the time this novel was written, nuclear war was a major worry for many people. The tensions between the United States and Soviet Union were often described as the Cold War. Research the Cold War. What was it? How did it begin? In your opinion, has it ended? Explain. Do many people worry about nuclear war today? What are some reasons for their attitudes? Present your findings in an oral report to your group. (SS)

3. When the boys hunted the pigs, they encircled the animals so that they would be easier to kill. Many animals—wolves are an example—hunt in groups or packs. Research the hunting strategies of wolves or other animals. Why do they hunt in packs? What advantage do they gain? How do they bring down their prey? How do these characteristics relate to human behavior? (Sci)

42. *The Scarlet Letter* by Nathaniel Hawthorne

Synopsis

Hester Prynne has committed adultery in Puritan Boston in the mid-seventeenth century. Brought out of prison with her infant daughter, and wearing an embroidered "A" which stands for adultery on her breast, she bears the ridicule of the townspeople. Although they demand to know the child's father, Hester refuses to tell them. Returned to prison, the baby becomes sick, and a doctor, who says his name is Roger Chillingworth, comes to treat her. Hester is frightened because Chillingworth is her husband, whom she hasn't seen in two years. He helps the baby, named Pearl, but demands to know the identity of the baby's father. When Hester refuses to tell him, he exacts a promise from her that she will not reveal his (Chillingworth's) true identity either. This is in exchange for his promise not to kill her lover if he is found out. Once Hester is released from prison, she moves to a small cottage where she raises Pearl. Meanwhile, Chillingworth comes to suspect Arthur Dimmesdale, a prominent young minister, as Pearl's father. Befriending Dimmesdale, Chillingworth begins a devious plan to psychologically "torture" the minister. Over time (the novel spans seven years) his plan works. Dimmesdale, who has never been able to admit his affair with Hester, becomes so distraught with guilt that his health begins to fail. Hester, on the other hand, has accepted her position and gains respect because of her willingness to help people. When she and Dimmesdale meet in the forest, she convinces him that their only hope is to leave Boston. He is afraid, but agrees when she promises to be his strength. Hester books passage on a ship which is to sail soon after Dimmesdale gives an important sermon. Although the sermon is one of his greatest, he is so weakened by his remorse and guilt that he struggles to the town's scaffold, where he confesses and dies.

Ideas and Concepts to Highlight

1. Note that "The Custom House. Introductory Sketch" is not essential to the novel. It has been suggested that Hawthorne added this extra material because he felt that the story was too short to be a novel. Still, the introduction provides valuable insight to Hawthorne's mind.

2. Point out the style, which is typical of writing at the time this story appeared in 1850.

3. Emphasize Hawthorne's use of symbolism—the "A," Pearl, the scaffold, and the forest are some of the more obvious.

4. Note Hawthorne's use of irony. For example, even as Dimmesdale struggles with his dark secret, his reputation as a minister grows.

5. Compare Puritan society with that of contemporary American society.

Writing Connection: "Breaking the Rules"

Hester Prynne broke an important rule of her society and paid a heavy price in ridicule and scorn. Although contemporary society is not Puritanical, there are laws and "unwritten" rules that, if broken, result in punishment.

Ask your students to create a character who breaks one of our society's laws or unwritten rules. What happens to this character? Is he or she, like Hester, eventually able to rise above the mistake? Instruct your students to complete Worksheet 42-1 and write a story about a character who b.eaks the rules. Note that answering the questions will provide a plot skeleton.

42-1. BREAKING THE RULES

Directions: Create a character who breaks one of society's laws or "unwritten" rules. Answer the questions below and then write a story of what happens to this character.

1. What is your character's name?_____

    _____

2. Describe your character. _____

    _____

    _____

    _____

    _____

3. What rule does your character break? _____

    _____

    _____

4. Why does he or she break it? _____

    _____

    _____

    _____

5. What consequences does your character experience?_____

    _____

    _____

6. How does your character cope with, or overcome, those consequences?_____

    _____

    _____

    _____

© 1994 by The Center for Applied Research in Education

42-2. QUESTIONS TO CONSIDER FOR
THE SCARLET LETTER

1. Describe the scene as Hester, with Pearl, emerges from the prison. What symbol is Hester wearing? What does it mean? How does the crowd treat her? What does the crowd's reaction to Hester's "sin" tell you about Puritan society?

2. Why do you think Hester named her baby Pearl?

3. Who did Chillingworth blame for Hester having "...fallen into the pit..."—her, himself, or her lover? Explain.

4. Why does Hester go to the Governor's mansion? Why do you think she dressed Pearl in the scarlet dress? Describe what happened at the mansion. Why do you think Dimmesdale argues in favor of Hester and Pearl?

5. Once Chillingworth comes to suspect Dimmesdale as Hester's lover, what does he do to "torture" Dimmesdale? Use specific examples from the story to support your answer.

6. Over the years the townspeople's view of Hester slowly changes. Describe the change and the reasons for it.

7. Describe several ways that Dimmesdale's inner turmoil is reflected in his behavior and appearance. Why do you think he couldn't admit his guilt to the town?

8. While with Dimmesdale in the forest, Hester convinces him that they should leave Boston and live with Pearl like a family. Given their personalities and their situation, do you think this was a practical decision? Explain.

9. Explain how Dimmesdale triumphed on the scaffold when he confessed that he shared Hester's sin.

10. In your opinion, which of the characters was the most tragic and suffered the most? Use examples from the story to support your answer.

11. The story actually ends with the final scaffold scene. Why do you think Hawthorne included the "conclusion"?

42-3. PROJECTS AND ACTIVITIES TO CONSIDER FOR *THE SCARLET LETTER*

1. Working with your group, discuss Hawthorne's likely opinion of Puritan society. Identify specific examples from the story that support your views. Appoint a recorder to take notes. When the group reaches a consensus, choose one of the members to report your conclusions to the rest of the class.

2. Working with a partner, go through the story and identify several instances of irony. Write down why each is ironic and share your findings with others.

3. The four main characters—Hester, Chillingworth, Dimmesdale, and Pearl—change significantly throughout the story. Work with a partner and create a chart that shows these changes.

4. Analyze Hawthorne's writing style and technique. Include his use of metaphors, similes, and symbols. What do you think his purpose was in writing *The Scarlet Letter?*

5. Select one of the scenes of the story. With the members of your group, act it out. Use Hawthorne's dialogue to achieve realism.

6. Imagine that Hester, Dimmesdale, and Pearl had managed to get on that ship and leave Boston. Write a scene that represents their new life together.

7. Think about Chillingworth. Why did he torment Dimmesdale? Was Chillingworth evil, or was he insane? Write an essay that attempts to explain his behavior.

Curriculum Connections:

1. Consult references and research Boston of the mid-1600s. Include the city's population, commerce, religious groups, and government. How is Boston's past reflected in the city today? Write a report that shares your findings. (SS)

2. Research Puritanism. Who was the movement's founder? What were the beliefs of Puritans? What was the Puritan Ethic? Present your information orally to your group. (SS)

3. Using clay or a similar material, design the letter "A" that Hester was forced to wear. (A)

43. <u>All Quiet on the Western Front</u> by Erich Maria Remarque (Little, Brown and Company, 1987)

Synopsis

In this novel, which has been called the greatest war story ever written, Paul Baumer is a young man in the German army during World War I. Soon after coming to the front, Paul realizes the terror of trench warfare. Through his eyes, the reader witnesses the destruction not only of men's bodies, but of their spirits and hopes as well. Unlike the people at home, the soldiers at the front quickly lose their passion for battle, their instinct for survival overriding all else. As he survives the attack-retreat-attack-retreat fighting in the trenches, the horror of gas attacks, the chilling and insensitive treatment in the war hospitals, the lack of proper food and enough munitions, and his stabbing and killing of a French soldier who falls into the same shell-hole, Paul comes to question the reason for war. As one by one his friends are killed or maimed, he understands that his generation is a lost one—young men who have experienced such unspeakable horrors that their lives will be forever altered. Despite all this, Paul's character is strong enough to continue with his duty until near the end of the war, when he, too, is killed on a day that was "all quiet on the western front."

Ideas and Concepts to Highlight

1. Note that Paul, who is the lead character, is also the narrator of the story. The reader experiences the story through Paul's eyes.

2. Note the use of present tense. Most novels are written in the past tense—it is assumed that since the story is being told the action has already happened. Discuss how Remarque's use of the present tense makes the action seem more real to the reader, almost as if the reader is there.

3. Mention that Remarque used a variety of techniques in the story such as irony, symbolism, and impressionism. Discuss examples of each. Perhaps the greatest irony of all in the book is Paul's death on a "quiet" day at the front. A good example of symbolism is the earth, which is like a protective mother to the soldiers. Finally, Remarque's focusing on details throughout the story created for the reader an overall impression of the grim reality of the trenches and horror of the war.

4. Discuss the background of World War I. Several reasons contributed to the war: British and German rivalry in trade, the French desire for revenge because of the defeat the Germans had given them in 1870, and the Austrian and Russian competition to dominate southeastern Europe. Prior to the war, the nations of Europe had aligned themselves into two great alliances—the Triple Entente of Britain, France, and Russia, and the Triple Alliance of Germany, Austria-Hungary, and Italy. Tensions were high throughout the continent. The flashpoint was the assassination of Archduke Francis Ferdinand, the heir to the Hapsburg throne, and his wife in Sarajevo by a Serbian student in June of 1914. World War I was the first modern war, and it resulted in unprecedented destruction and death.

Writing Connection: "A Great Novel"

Some critics have called *All Quiet on the Western Front* the greatest war novel ever written. That is powerful praise. For this assignment, ask your students to share their opinions and impressions of the novel by writing a book review. Ask students to refer to *The New York Times* "Book Review" section that appears each Sunday for examples of reviews. Completing Worksheet 43-1 will help them to clarify their ideas.

43-1. A GREAT NOVEL

Directions: *All Quiet on the Western Front* has been called the greatest war novel ever written. What are your opinions and impressions of the story? Answer the questions below and then write a book review sharing your thoughts.

1. On a separate sheet of paper, describe the characterization of the story. Include Paul, Kat, and at least two other characters. Were Remarque's characters believable?

2. How did Remarque use realism in the story? (Give examples.)_____
_____
_____
_____

3. How did Remarque use techniques such as irony, symbolism, and impressionism? (Choose one and give examples.)_____
_____
_____
_____

4. What was Remarque's likely purpose in writing this story? _____
_____
Did he stray from his purpose? Explain._____
_____
_____
_____

5. What is your opinion of the book?_____
_____
_____
_____
_____

43-2. QUESTIONS TO CONSIDER FOR
ALL QUIET ON THE WESTERN FRONT

1. What is Paul's opinion of Muller scheming to get Kemmerich's boots? What does this tell you about the conditions of the German soldiers during the war?

2. What was Paul's training like under Corporal Himmelstoss? How did Paul feel about the corporal? How did that training prepare him for war in the trenches? Later, when Himmelstoss joins Paul and his company at the front, how do they treat him?

3. How does Paul describe the "consciousness of the front..."? How does that consciousness help him to survive?

4. Compare Paul's life as a student to his life in the war. How does the war change him? Cite examples from the story to support your answer.

 5. Describe the horror of trench warfare that Paul experienced. According to Paul, how did a man survive that kind of fighting?

6. When Paul returns home on leave, he feels "a sense of strangeness." Why do you think he feels this way? Why does he find it difficult to talk about the war to his parents, especially his father? How are the opinions of the townspeople about the war different than Paul's?

7. Describe Paul's thoughts about the Russian prisoners he guards. He says, "A word of command has made these silent figures our enemies, a word of command might transform them into our friends." What does he mean?

8. How does his stabbing of Gerard Duval in the shell-hole affect Paul? When he gets back to his own lines, how do Kat and Albert help him overcome his feelings?

9. Toward the end of the war, did Paul feel there was any hope for himself? Did he feel there was any hope for the generation of young men who fought the war? Explain.

10. What do you think Remarque's purpose was in writing *All Quiet on the Western Front?*

43-3. PROJECTS AND ACTIVITIES TO CONSIDER FOR ALL QUIET ON THE WESTERN FRONT

1. Poison gas was used for the first time during World War I. It was considered to be so hideous that nations refrained from using it during World War II out of fear of retaliation. Still, some countries have reportedly used it against minority populations. Research the use of poison gas in recent years. When was it used? By whom? Why? What action was taken by the rest of the world? Write a report of your findings. (Hint: Magazine articles will be a good source of information. Consult the *Reader's Guide to Periodical Literature.)*

2. Remarque's writing has often been called impressionist. Impressionism is a literary style characterized by the use of powerful details and mental associations that evoke sensory impressions. Working with a partner, identify several examples of impressionism. Explain how the examples are indeed impressionistic and share your findings with others.

3. Remarque served in World War I, and was wounded five times. Discuss with your group how his experiences helped him write the story. Appoint a recorder to take notes, and then share your conclusions with the members of other groups.

4. Imagine that Paul wrote a letter to Gerard Duval's family. What would he say? Pretend you are Paul and write that letter.

5. Read Stephen Crane's *The Red Badge of Courage* (New York: Harcourt, Brace & World, 1962). Compare it to *All Quiet on the Western Front*. Write a report that analyzes the characterization, style, action, and realism of the two books.

Curriculum Connections:

1. Research World War I. What were the causes of the war? Which countries were involved? What were the major battles, and how did they affect the course of the war? What finally led to the ending of the war? Write a report. Include maps. (SS)

2. World War I has been called the first "modern" war. Why is it referred to in that way? Write a report on the new weapons introduced during the war. (SS)

3. Create an illustration or model of the trenches that Paul described. (SS or A)

4. Paul mentions various diseases the soldiers suffered, including dysentery, typhus, and influenza. Research each of these. What were the disease's symptoms? What treatments are now available for it? (SS)

44. Wuthering Heights by Emily Brontë

Synopsis

Mr. Lockwood, a new tenant at Thrushcross Grange, visits his landlord, Heathcliff, at Wuthering Heights. Lockwood finds Heathcliff to be a dark, brooding man. Becoming curious about the residents of Wuthering Heights—so named because of the weather to which the house is subjected during storms—Lockwood asks his housekeeper, Nelly, about Heathcliff. Nelly, who has been a servant at the Grange and the Heights for years, takes over the narration of the story and tells Lockwood how Mr. Earnshaw, the owner of the Heights, returned home from a trip one day with an abandoned boy he named Heathcliff. Mr. Earnshaw was more pleased with Heathcliff than he was with his own son, Hindley. Upon Earnshaw's death, Hindley inherited Wuthering Heights and he treated Heathcliff harshly. He tried to keep Heathcliff away from his (Hindley's) sister, Catherine, but in spite of his efforts Heathcliff and Catherine come to share a strong and hopeless love. In time Catherine becomes friends with the children who live in Thrushcross Grange, Edgar and Isabella Linton. When Hindley's wife dies while giving birth to his son, Hareton, Hindley rapidly declines into alcoholism. His torment of Heathcliff increases until Heathcliff leaves Wuthering Heights. Three years later, Catherine marries Edgar Linton. Soon afterward, Heathcliff returns, well-dressed and wealthy. He stays at Wuthering Heights as a paying guest and soon has Hindley indebted to him. Heathcliff visits Catherine often. When Edgar orders him to stay away, Heathcliff elopes with Edgar's sister, Isabella. Catherine becomes sick over the hate between the two men, and she dies giving birth to a daughter, also named Catherine. Heathcliff is never able to forget his love for her. Because of his brutal treatment of Isabella, she runs away from him, but not before she becomes pregnant. When Hindley dies, Wuthering Heights falls into Heathcliff's hands because of Hindley's debts to him. Heathcliff's ultimate plan for revenge now takes shape: he wishes to unite the Grange and Heights. Some years later, after Isabella's death, Heathcliff manages to bring his own son, Linton, to Wuthering Heights. As Edgar approaches death, Heathcliff kidnaps Cathy and forces her into marriage with Linton. Thus, when Edgar dies, soon followed by Linton, Heathcliff, through Cathy, gains control of both properties. Mr. Lockwood then leaves the Grange. When he returns some time later, he finds that Heathcliff is dead and Cathy and Hareton have fallen in love. Nelly tells him that once his revenge was achieved, Heathcliff yearned more and more for his dead Catherine. He stopped eating and one day was found dead.

Ideas and Concepts to Highlight

1. Explain that *Wuthering Heights* has a framed structure. The story begins with Lockwood as the narrator, but then the narration switches to Nelly. At the end of the story, Lockwood again becomes the narrator. His narration frames the narration of Nelly.

2. Emphasize and discuss the complex relationships in the book.

3. Discuss Heathcliff's unrelenting anger and desire for revenge and how it touches everyone in the story.

4. Discuss the story as being both a mystery and a romance.

5. Note the powerful use of symbolism in the story. The wind in Lockwood's dream, for example, represents the power of nature and the passion of human beings.

Writing Connection: "Where You Come From"

Everyone is influenced by the way he or she was raised in his or her home. Although it is not always true that coming from a good home ensures that a person will be upstanding and honest, environment does affect behavior. In *Wuthering Heights* Heathcliff's unrelenting quest for vengeance arises from his mistreatment by Hindley, and Hareton's oafishness is a direct result of Heathcliff's refusal to allow the boy an education.

For this assignment, ask your students to consider the effect environment plays on the behavior of people. They should use personal experience as well as information they have gained through reading or the media. Instruct them to complete Worksheet 44-1 and then write an essay or story about this topic.

NAME _____ DATE _____ SECTION _____

44-1. WHERE YOU COME FROM

Directions: The behavior of people is often influenced by their environment. Because of Hindley's mistreatment, Heathcliff set upon a course of revenge. Hareton turns out to be an oaf because Heathcliff denied the boy the opportunity of an education. Think about how the environment affects a person's behavior. Answer the questions below and then write an essay or story on this topic.

1.   How has your environment influenced you? _____

_____

_____

_____

_____

_____

2.   Give examples of how their environment has influenced other people you know. _____

_____

_____

_____

_____

3.   Is it possible for people to overcome the influence of their environment?_____   If yes,

how? If not, why not? _____

_____

_____

_____

_____

_____

44-2. *QUESTIONS TO CONSIDER FOR*
WUTHERING HEIGHTS

1. Why is Heathcliff's house named Wuthering Heights?

2. How does Heathcliff's past influence the man he has become? Cite examples from the story to support your answer.

3. What reason does Catherine give Nelly for marrying Edgar instead of Heathcliff? Do you agree with her? Explain.

4. After a three-year absence, Heathcliff returns to Wuthering Heights. Compare Heathcliff now to the person he was three years ago. How has he changed? How does Catherine react to his return? What is Edgar's reaction?

5. Why does Heathcliff marry Isabella? How does he justify his treatment of her to Nelly? How is Isabella's marriage much like Catherine's?

6. How does Heathcliff react to Catherine's death?

7. When he finds out that Isabella died and Edgar has brought Linton to Thrushcross Grange, Heathcliff sends Joseph to demand that Linton be brought to Wuthering Heights. Why does Heathcliff want the son he never saw?

8. Explain how Hareton's character was shaped by Heathcliff. Cite specific examples from the story to support your answer.

9. Upon Edgar's and Linton's deaths, how does Heathcliff manage to claim all of Thrushcross Grange?

10. As Lockwood returns to Wuthering Heights after having left, he notices the setting sun and rising moon. Explain what they symbolize.

11. In the story, Lockwood's narration frames the narration of Nelly. In your opinion, as each tells his or her part of the story, are they objective narrators? Explain.

12. Explain how revenge is one of the story's major themes.

44-3. PROJECTS AND ACTIVITIES TO CONSIDER FOR
WUTHERING HEIGHTS

1. Throughout the story Brontë relied on foreshadowing to prepare the reader for coming events. Working with your group, identify several examples of foreshadowing. Create a list of your examples and decide what event each example hints at. Share your list with the members of other groups.

2. Conflict is the fuel of any story. Conflict sets the stage for action, allowing character to be revealed. Work with a partner and identify the major conflicts in the story. Create a chart, showing how the conflict affected the characters.

3. Heathcliff is an example of a dark hero. An extremely complex character, at times he seems to be a devil, yet he also inspires a certain amount of sympathy. Analyze the character of Heathcliff and discuss his traits in an essay.

is Heathcliff good or evil?

4. The novel spans two generations. Working with your group, discuss how the first generation of characters influences the second. Cite specific examples from the story. Appoint a recorder to take notes and then share your conclusions with other groups.

5. Imagine that Lockwood and Cathy married. Keeping in mind their personalities, write a scene showing what their marriage would be like.

6. Watch the film version of *Wuthering Heights* (1939), and compare it to the novel. Did the movie follow the novel closely? Why do you think some parts of the novel were left out? Which version did you like better, the movie or the novel? Why?

7. Read *The Complete Poems of Emily Brontë* (New York: Columbia University Press, 1941, edited by C.W. Hatfield). Do any of the ideas in her poems appear in her novel? Explain.

Curriculum Connections:

1. Design a genealogical chart to delineate the various characters in the story. (A)

2. Locate northeastern England, which is the setting of the story. Describe its geography and climate. (SS)

© 1994 by The Center for Applied Research in Education

45. <u>Brave New World</u> by Aldous Huxley
(Harper and Row, 1946)

Synopsis

As the Director of Hatcheries and Conditioning takes a group of students on a tour of a hatching and conditioning center, the reader sees how people are "produced" and "conditioned" in the World State of the future (about the year 2532). The Director explains how conditioning ensures that people will be happy in the job selected for them so that they will contribute to society. However, once in a while, the process breaks down. Bernard Marx is unhappy and dissatisfied, although he is not sure why. His friend, Helmholtz Watson, is too perfect, and likewise suffers a vague feeling of not fitting in. When Bernard, accompanied by Lenina Crowne, visits the Savage Reservation, he finds people who have not been conditioned. Bernard and Lenina meet John, whose mother, Linda, was conditioned but had a baby (no woman in the World State has babies!) and was sent to the Reservation. John is unlike anyone Bernard has ever met. Like the other Savages, he is an individual, but he also reads Shakespeare. Bernard and Lenina bring John and his mother back to London where John becomes an oddity. Known as the Savage, people wish to meet him. In the meantime, John helps Bernard and Helmholtz become aware of new ideas. Lenina falls in love with John, but the differences in their value systems keeps them apart. After John's mother dies, he realizes that the people of the World State are being controlled and he tries to warn them. They won't listen. Brought before a World Controller, it is decided that Bernard and Helmholtz are to be sent to an island while John is forced to remain. Unable to accept the World State, John hangs himself.

Ideas and Concepts to Highlight

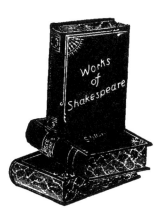

1. Emphasize the theme of the story—while the advancement of science brings great benefits, it also brings dangers.

2. Note that the story is an example of science fiction, which Huxley used as a vehicle to express his ideas about where he felt society was heading.

3. Explain that Huxley took the title, *Brave New World,* from Shakespeare's play, *The Tempest.* One of the characters, Miranda, says, "How beauteous mankind is! O brave new world that has such people in it." Unwittingly, she says this of people who had plotted against her and her father. Miranda does not see the evil of the people she praises. Huxley felt that way about people who support the rapid advancement of science—they see only the good and not the potential problems.

4. Discuss the value system of the World State and compare it to our contemporary system of values.

Writing Connection: "The Advancement of Science"

One of Huxley's themes in *Brave New World* is that the advancement of science offers great benefits as well as dangers. For this writing assignment, ask your students to select an issue in science that supports Huxley's contention. Some possible topics include genetic engineering, machines that can extend the survival of terminally ill patients, and powerful medicines that can treat disease but may also result in potent side effects. Encourage students to consult references if necessary, and instruct them to complete Worksheet 45-1 and then write an essay about their topics.

45-1. THE ADVANCEMENT OF SCIENCE

Directions: In Huxley's future World State, science has advanced to the point where people are controlled for the benefit of society. In Huxley's opinion, such advancement always has a price. Select a current issue or topic in science, answer the questions below, and then write about the benefits and dangers of your subject.

1. My topic is:_____

2. List the benefits and dangers of your topic.

Benefits	Dangers

3. How can the dangers be avoided or lessened? _____

_____

_____

_____

_____

45-2. *QUESTIONS TO CONSIDER FOR* <u>*BRAVE NEW WORLD*</u>

1. How does the World State make sure that its citizens conform to the ideas of the government? Give examples in your answer. Why is conformity so important to the World State?

2. Who is Ford? Why has he replaced God? What significance does this have for the people of the World State?

3. What is soma? Why do the people of the World State take it?

4. Why does Bernard Marx feel alone? What do he and Helmholtz Watson have in common?

5. Describe the Savage Reservation. How is it different from the rest of the World State? In your opinion, were the Savages really "uncivilized"? Explain.

6. Why is John different from the other Savages? How does he introduce Bernard and Helmholtz to new ideas?

7. Lenina and John fall in love. How does their relationship symbolize the differences between the values of the World State and the values of the Reservation?

8. It is the belief of Mustapha Mond, a World Controller, that people are unable or unwilling to act intelligently and reasonably, and that they prefer comfort and happiness to truth. Do you agree or disagree? Explain.

9. Which value system—that of the World State or the Savage Reservation—is most like yours? Why?

10. At the end of the story, John commits suicide. What do you think Huxley is saying by this act?

11. If you had a choice to live in the World State or the Reservation, which one would you choose? Why?

45-3. PROJECTS AND ACTIVITIES TO CONSIDER FOR
BRAVE NEW WORLD

1. Work with a partner and create a chart showing the main groups of the inhabitants of the World State. Provide a description of their intelligence and the types of jobs the members of each group are likely to have.

2. Work with your group and discuss the ways that the World State has replaced God and taught a new set of values. List the ways the State makes certain that people conform and work to contribute to the betterment of society.

3. Huxley chose the names of his characters with care, using the names to imply ideas. For example, Ford refers to Henry Ford, who developed the assembly line method of production. Bernard Marx represents Karl Marx, Lenina Crowne represents Nikolai Lenin, and Benito Hoover is a combination of Benito Mussolini and Herbert Hoover. Consult references to find out who these people are, and explain why you think Huxley chose them to appear symbolically in his book.

4. Write an editorial in favor of or opposition to the World State.

5. Read *1984* by George Orwell, which also offers a view of what the future might be like. Compare it to *Brave New World,* and write an essay about your impressions.

6. Imagine that you are a "civilized" Savage in the World State. Write a dialogue in which you discuss with a World Controller why he should allow individuality in the World State. Upon completion, have a classmate take the part of the World Controller and together read the dialogue aloud to the rest of your group or class.

Curriculum Connections:

1. Design a banner showing the World State's motto of "Community, Identity, Stability." (A)

2. Research conditioning. Is it possible to condition a person to the degree that is practiced in the World State? Based upon your research, do you think it will be possible in the future? Write a short report about your findings. (Sci)

3. Choose one of the following men and write a report: Henry Ford, Nikolai Lenin, Karl Marx, Benito Mussolini or Herbert Hoover. Include the subject's accomplishments. Why do you think Huxley used him symbolically in his book? (SS)

46. *Fahrenheit 451* by Ray Bradbury
(Del Rey, 1953)

Synopsis

Guy Montag is a fireman. Not the kind we would recognize, though. In the future world of the story, buildings are fireproof and firemen burn books and the places where they are found. Montag enjoys his work until he meets Clarisse, a teenage girl who admits that she is "peculiar." Clarisse is an outcast of society because she is interested in life and rejects the meaningless existence people have come to accept. After speaking with Clarisse a few times, Montag begins to wonder about his life and question what he is doing. He admits that his life is without happiness. His relationship with his wife is empty, he sees people everywhere committing suicide and murder, and the world is at the edge of war, although he is not sure why. After the burning of a house in which an old woman dies with her books, Montag gets in touch with Faber, a man he once met, who still remembers what the world was like before books were banned. At first Faber is afraid of Montag, because he is a fireman, but when he realizes Montag's dilemma he lets him in and they talk. Montag learns how books were banned and learning was lost. Faber also tells him about people who live in the country and who still cherish books. When Montag falls under suspicion by his captain, Montag's own house is burned. He learns that his wife called in the alarm. Uncertain of his feelings, but sure that he can no longer accept his reality, Montag, rather than being taken prisoner, kills his captain and flees. Briefly he stops at Faber's house, and then makes his way to the country where he finds other "fugitives," men who are waiting for the chance to bring their knowledge of books back to society. The war starts and the city is destroyed. Perhaps out of the ruin will come their chance.

Ideas and Concepts to Highlight

1. Explain that this story is science fiction. Note that SF stories are usually set in the future with some form of high technology being important to the plot.

2. Explain and discuss censorship and its effects on society.

3. Note how history has been rewritten in the story.

Writing Connection: "Censorship"

Fahrenheit 451 is about censorship in the future. Although the United States is a free country, with freedom of the press guaranteed by the Constitution, censorship is always a threat when someone or some group wishes to suppress information. Discuss censorship with your students. Is censorship ever justified? For example, during wartime, is the government right in suppressing information that might protect its troops? What about the efforts of special interest groups to censor or ban books? Does any minority have the right to prevent people from reading a book because the "minority" objects to something in the book? Is one group's morality better, or higher, than another's? Are the ideas of censorship and freedom in opposition? Undoubtedly, these are difficult questions and you should encourage students to consult additional sources if necessary.

For this assignment, instruct your students to complete Worksheet 46-1 and then write an essay explaining their views about censorship.

1984

NAME _____ **DATE** _____ **SECTION** _____

46-1. CENSORSHIP

Directions: Guy Montag in his role of fireman was really practicing censorship. Despite the United States being a free country, censorship is often an issue. What are your feelings about this important issue? Answer the questions below and then write an essay about your views.

1. What is censorship? _____

_____

_____

_____

2. Is censorship limited to just books?_____ If no, what else can be censored?

_____

_____

3. Give some examples of censorship._____

_____

_____

_____

4. What might be the reasons for censorship? _____

_____

_____

_____

5. Can censorship ever be justified? _____ If yes, when? _____

_____

_____

_____

_____

© 1994 by The Center for Applied Research in Education

46-2. QUESTIONS TO CONSIDER FOR
<u>FAHRENHEIT 451</u>

1. Clarisse described herself as being "peculiar." Do you think Montag would agree with her? Why or why not? Would you agree? Explain, citing examples from the story.

2. Describe the relationship between Montag and his wife, Mildred. Why do you think they had so much trouble communicating?

3. Why was Montag unhappy? What do you think was missing in his life? Describe what happiness, over the course of life, means to you. Do you think that most people would agree with you? Why or why not?

4. Why, according to Beatty, was it necessary to burn books? How did society come to that point?

5. Why do you think that Bradbury selected the Bible as the book Montag took to Faber?

6. Faber said, "Those who don't build must burn. It's as old as history and juvenile delinquents." What did he mean? Do you agree with him? Explain.

7. What was Montag's and Faber's plan? When you first read about it, did you think it had a chance of being successful? Explain.

8. Faber spoke of himself as being a coward. Do you agree with his assessment of himself? Explain.

9. Why do you think Mildred turned in the alarm on Montag?

10. Describe how Montag changed throughout the story. Use examples to support your answer.

11. At the end of the story, did you feel that there is hope for Montag's world? Or did you feel that his society will merely continue as it is? Explain.

12. What do you think Bradbury's purpose was in writing this story? Explain.

46-3. PROJECTS AND ACTIVITIES TO CONSIDER FOR
FAHRENHEIT 451

1. Imagine that you are a friend of Guy Montag and that you could share a book with him. What book would you give him? Why? If you could share a poem with him, which one would it be? Why? Write a scene in which you explain to Montag your reasons for giving him these. Share your writing with the members of your group.

2. Write a scene that shows what happens after the war has ended. Has Faber or Mildred survived? Does Montag find them? What does Montag do about the books?

3. In the story, history has been rewritten. For example, firemen don't put out fires; they burn books. Working with a partner, review the story and list instances where history was rewritten. Include how history was changed, and why you believe it was changed. Share your results with your group.

4. Imagine that you were Montag. What books would be most important to you? Why?

5. Organize a debate on the issue of censorship and try to answer this question: Is censorship ever justified?

6. Work with your group and select ten books that you feel are the most important to the world. Which ones would they be? Create a chart, listing the books, and provide a reason why you chose each one.

Curriculum Connections:

1. Granger referred to the current world as a Dark Age. Consult references to learn about the Dark Ages in Europe. What were they? Why were they called the Dark Ages? How did they start and how long did they last? How did they finally end? Were they *really* "dark"? Present your findings in an oral report to your group or class. (SS)

2. Research censorship in other countries. Who is responsible for the censorship? What is censored? Why? How does censorship affect the people's ability to understand the truth? Write a report of your findings. (SS)

3. Design an emblem for Montag's fire company. What would be written on it? (A)

© 1994 by The Center for Applied Research in Education

246

47. _A Raisin in the Sun_ by Lorraine Hansberry
(Random House, 1966)

Synopsis

The Youngers are an African-American family living in a small apartment on Chicago's Southside between World War II and the late 1950s. The family is headed by Lena, the mother. Her son Walter and his wife, Ruth, her daughter, Beneatha, and her grandson, Travis (the son of Walter and Ruth), make up the family. Walter is unhappy with his life because he can't get ahead, and his bitterness is straining his marriage. He tries talking his mother into giving him the insurance money ($10,000) she is to receive because of his father's death. He wants to invest it in a liquor store with two of his friends. He is convinced that this will be the opportunity he needs. His sister also wants the money to pursue her schooling; she hopes to become a doctor. When the check arrives, Lena refuses to give it to Walter, instead putting some of the money down on a house in a white section of town. Walter is furious. Seeing how much the money meant to him, Lena relents and tells him to put half of the remainder into an account for his sister's schooling and keep the rest for himself. Shortly thereafter, a Mr. Lindner, a man representing the white property owners, comes with an offer to buy the house from the Youngers. The whites don't want them moving into their neighborhood. Walter sends him away. After one of Walter's friends comes and tells him that the other friend stole the money they had invested for the liquor store—Walter admits that he used Beneatha's money as well as his own—he calls Lindner, hoping to make a deal. As upset as the rest of the family is over the money, they are more upset that Walter would sell out the family's pride. Realizing they are right, Walter sends Lindner away again and the family prepares to move to their new home.

Ideas and Concepts to Highlight

1. Note the setting of the play—somewhere between World War II and the present, which was 1959, the time when the play was first performed. Explain that the play is still relevant today.

2. Discuss employment opportunities for blacks as opposed to those for whites, and focus on good jobs as being a key to overcoming poverty.

3. Note the strong characterizations in the play.

4. Discuss the effects of prejudice in our society.

Writing Connection: "Prejudice"

The United States is composed of people of various races and ethnic origins. While much of our country's great strength grows out of the rich diversity of its people, that diversity is also a source of friction and hostility. Prejudice is a serious issue in America today.

For this writing assignment, ask your students to reflect on the differences of Americans—skin color, ethnicity, and religion, for example—and how these differences result in bias and hostility in some people. Conduct a class discussion on the topic to draw out students' feelings and opinions. Instruct students to complete Worksheet 47-1 and then write about this topic in the form of an essay or story.

Othello

NAME _____ **DATE** _____ **SECTION** _____

47-1. PREJUDICE

Directions: Consider the issue of prejudice, which is often a result of differences in skin color, ethnic origin, or religion. Answer the questions below and then write an essay or story that offers ideas of how we can overcome our differences.

1. List reasons why you feel differences in skin color, heritage, or religion make some people suspicious or hostile to others:

_____

_____

_____

_____

_____

2. Have you ever witnessed an act of bias?_____ If yes, describe it. If not, offer an example you have read or heard about or seen on TV.

_____

_____

_____

_____

3. What can government do to promote more understanding and mutual respect between people? _____

_____

_____

4. What can individuals do? _____

_____

_____

_____

47-2. QUESTIONS TO CONSIDER FOR
A RAISIN IN THE SUN

1. Walter blamed much of his problem for not being able to get ahead on Ruth, claiming that she wasn't behind him and wouldn't build him up to help him. Do you think he was being fair to her in that accusation? Why or why not?

2. What is the cause of Walter's unhappiness? How does Lena feel about it? How does Ruth feel?

3. Walter believes that "money is life." Do you agree with him? Explain.

4. Why do you think Ruth considers abortion when she finds out that she is pregnant? If you were a close friend of hers, what would you advise her to do? Why?

5. Compare Beneatha's ideas of her black heritage with George's. In your opinion, who has the more practical view? Explain.

6. Why did Lena buy a house in Clybourne Park, a place where no blacks yet lived? How did the rest of the family react to this? Do you think they were over-reacting? Explain.

7. What was your reaction to Lindner's offer on behalf of the Clybourne Park Improvement Association? Do you think the Association was right in their fear of having a black family move in? Could such an offer be made today? Explain.

8. How did Walter plan to make up for the loss of the money? What did the others think of his plan? What did you think of it? In your opinion, what made him change his mind?

9. Why does the old plant mean so much to Lena?

10. At the end of the story, Lena says quietly to Ruth about Walter: "He finally come into his manhood today..." What did she mean? Do you agree with her? Explain.

47-3. *PROJECTS AND ACTIVITIES TO CONSIDER FOR
A RAISIN IN THE SUN*

1. Write a descriptive sketch of each character. Include their desires and conflicts.

2. Work with your group and reflect on Walter's personality. Imagine he had been able to buy a liquor store. Would he have been successful as its owner? Discuss that question and come to a consensus. Have your recorder report your conclusions and reasons to the members of other groups.

3. Pick a scene that you found especially dramatic or moving. With classmates assuming the various roles, act the scene out. Perhaps you can videotape the scene.

4. Write a new act to the play, showing the Younger family moving into their house in Clybourne Park. With the help of classmates, act out this new material.

5. The book version of the play opens with a poem by Langston Hughes. Read other poems of Hughes. Which ones did you like the best? Why? Share your impressions with the members of your group.

6. View the movie version of *A Raisin in the Sun* and compare it to the play that you read. Which one, in your opinion, has greater impact? Why? Write a review that compares the two versions.

7. Organize a panel discussion on abortion. Should women have the unimpeded right to abortion? Or should abortion be limited or perhaps even banned? Panel members should research the topic to gain a solid command of the facts to balance against their opinions.

Curriculum Connections:

1. Trace the political gains made by blacks since the end of the Civil War. Create a time line that marks the most significant dates. Present your findings to the class in an oral report. (SS or A)

2. One of Walter's complaints in the play was his lack of a good job. Blacks, historically, have labored in lower paying jobs than whites in the U.S. Research the topic of blacks in the workforce and compare the occupations held by blacks to the occupations held by whites. Also compare the typical salaries. Write a report of your findings. Include graphs (bar graphs are good choices) comparing the jobs and salaries of blacks to whites. (SS or A)

48. <u>*Watership Down*</u> *by Richard Adams*
(Macmillan Publishing Company, 1972)

Synopsis

Hazel, Fiver, and Bigwig are three wild rabbits living securely in a comfortable but somewhat autocratic warren. Fiver, gifted with second sight, foresees the warren's destruction and persuades his brother Hazel, Bigwig, and several others to find a new home. After exhausting travels, they come to Watership Down and settle there. Later, two of the rabbits who stayed behind at the old warren find them and tell them that the warren was indeed destroyed by men. When the new dwellers, with Hazel as their leader, realize they have no females to breed with, they raid a nearby farm and collect three hutch rabbits, but they are unsure of their ability to breed and adapt to life in the wild. They travel many miles to Efrafa, a military-style warren run by the ruthless General Woundwort. Bigwig infiltrates their ranks and escapes with eight females, but Woundwort organizes a posse and attacks Hazel's warren. During the siege, Hazel and two other rabbits slip out to the farm and gnaw loose the rope that leashes a large dog. The dog pursues them back to the warren, and Woundwort's followers are caught above ground and destroyed. Hazel's leadership and willingness to risk his life continuously for his friends earn him the title of Chief Rabbit, and the Watership Down warren prospers.

Ideas and Concepts to Highlight

1. *Watership Down*, with its wide sweep and rich characterization, can be considered a modern epic. Discuss the novel as an epic, noting the major epic elements such as heroism, myth, oral tradition, predictions, fate versus free will, dramatic irony, and quest.

2. Discuss *Watership Down* as an allegory as well, and how it functions as an extended metaphor in which objects and characters symbolize or represent meanings beneath their visible surface. Metaphors may include such diverse areas as birth of civilization, triumph of good over evil, divine intercession, or actual historic events such as wars and politics.

3. Encourage scientific discussion about so-called "second sight."

4. Note the author's use of personification in the characterizing of the animals.

Writing Connection: "A Critic's Reaction"

Watership Down is a vast, sweeping work that people seem either to love or hate. For this assignment ask your students to assume that they are literary critics and that they have been asked to share their opinions about Adams's epic. Completing Worksheet 48-1 will help them to examine their thoughts.

48-1. A CRITIC'S REACTION

Directions: Assume that you are a literary critic and that you have been asked to comment about *Watership Down.* What would you say? Answer the questions below and then write about your reaction to the novel.

1. In a sentence, tell what the novel is about: _____

_____

_____

_____

2. What was Adams's purpose in writing this story?_____

_____

_____

_____

3. Would you consider this story an epic? _____ Why or why not?_____

_____

_____

_____

4. On another sheet, analyze the following:

    * the characterization

    * the author's style

    * the author's use of techniques such as foreshadowing, symbolism, similes, metaphors, and personification

5. On a scale of 1 to 5 with 5 being highest, how would you rate this book?_____ Why?

_____

_____

_____

48-2. QUESTIONS TO CONSIDER FOR
WATERSHIP DOWN

1. The rabbits seem to have trouble understanding concepts we humans take for granted such as numbers, floating objects, and shapes. Write down a few other such things that you believe the characters would have difficulty with, then write a dialogue in which one of the rabbits explains the concepts.

2. Recount the elements of foreshadowing in *Watership Down*. How do they enhance the story? Decide if any of the foreshadowing events could have led to some other occurrence and explain why you feel that way.

3. When do you think Hazel becomes Chief Rabbit? When does Hazel feel he is Chief Rabbit? What characteristics make him a good leader, and when does he exhibit them? Explain.

4. Most of the survivors of the Sandleford warren have a special talent or significance that they contribute to the new tribe. List each character and his contribution.

5. Explain Cowslip's hesitation in answering any question beginning with "Where?"

6. When they arrive at Watership Down, the rabbits number 12. What significance do you think the author attaches to that?

7. Note the author's technique of opening chapters with poems. Why does he do this? What is the effect? Select two or three of your favorites and explain why you like them.

8. Symbolism abounds in the book. What do you think the following represent? The Efrafan warren, Blackavar, Kehaar, the down itself, Fiver, the Black Rabbit of Inle, El-ahrairah, and the wires.

9. What sort of creature do you suppose King Darzin was? Support your answer with examples from the story.

10. In Chapter 43, Hazel-rah approaches Woundwort with reasonable terms for peace before hostilities erupt, and for a moment the general entertains the idea. Why did he turn the terms down and fight? What does his action tell you about his leadership? Explain.

48-3. PROJECTS AND ACTIVITIES TO CONSIDER FOR WATERSHIP DOWN

1. Discuss precognition with your group. Consult references and try to reach a consensus on whether precognition is possible. Appoint a recorder to write down your conclusions and share them with the members of other groups.

2. Find a parable in the Bible, or a story in another religious book, that is similar to one of the legends told by the rabbits to explain their creation. Share the parable or story with the members of your group.

3. Why do you suppose Adams chose rabbits to be the focus of his epic? What other animals could be subjects for this kind of wide-sweeping story? Work with a partner and create an outline for another saga, selecting a different animal as the lead characters. Include an opening, body, rising and falling action, and conclusion. Write a few scenes of your story.

4. Find out the meaning of "Dea ex Machina," Chapter 48's title. What do you think the author's meaning was?

5. Name the events that each of the rabbits' myths explains. Then concoct another legend featuring El-ahrairah that the rabbits might utilize to explain a natural occurrence or attribute of themselves.

6. Write a poem from Fiver's point of view about any major event in the story.

7. Working with your group, identify and list what you feel are the major events of the book. Next, decide why each of the events you selected is significant to the story and how it adds to the story's epic nature. Share your results with other groups.

Curriculum Connections:

1. Draw a floor plan for the Honeycomb and the rest of the Watership Down warren. (A)

2. Consult references about rabbits and write a short report about the phenomenon of female rabbits reabsorbing young into their bodies. Find out if any other creatures can do this. What other such attributes are more or less unique to rabbits? (Sci)

49. A Little Love by Virginia Hamilton
(Philomel Books, 1984)

Synopsis

Sheema, a 17-year-old high school student who was raised by her Granmom and Granpop, desperately wants to find the father she has never met. She has never met her mother either, because she died while giving birth to Sheema. Aside from her grandparents, the only other person who loves Sheema is Forrest, her boyfriend. Forrest understands Sheema's hurt and wants to take care of her. That's why when she tells him that she has to find her father he is willing to help her. Although Sheema has tried in the past to get her grandparents to tell her about Cruzey, her father, who is a sign-painter, until she decides to find him they won't tell her much. Finally, Granmom explains to Sheema that Cruzey was never able to accept Sheema's mother's death during childbirth. Incapable of coping with it, he left and never returned. That he kept sending a monthly check to her grandparents to help them in raising her makes Sheema feel that he loves her. Although he has many misgivings, Forrest agrees to take her in search of her father. Granmom is able to give them some clues where they might find Cruzey, but she doesn't have his address. Taking all the cash they have, and following one lead after another, Forrest and Sheema drive from Ohio through Kentucky and Tennessee, finally winding up in Georgia where Sheema meets her father. The meeting is not what she expects. Her father has remarried and it is clear that there is no place in his life for her. At first deeply hurt, Sheema is able to draw strength from the experience and pass from youth to adulthood.

Ideas and Concepts to Highlight

1. Discuss Sheema's powerful motivation for wanting to find her father.

2. Note the setting of the story, which takes place near Dayton, Ohio and moves through Kentucky, Tennessee, and Georgia.

3. Discuss the relationship between Sheema and her grandparents, and Sheema and Forrest. How did she draw support from each of them?

Writing Connection: "Love Is..."

Sheema was supported by the love of her grandparents and Forrest. However, she was also driven by the need for her father's love to find him, and was hurt when she did. Love, unquestionably, is a powerful force in anyone's life.

For this assignment, ask your students to reflect on love. Why do we need it? Or, do we really need it? Instruct them to complete Worksheet 49-1 and write about their opinions about love either in a story or essay.

NAME _____ DATE _____ SECTION

49-1. LOVE IS...

Directions: Love is one of the strongest of human emotions. It can drive us, sustain us, or make us miserable. Answer the questions below and then write a story or essay about what you think love is.

1. In your opinion, what is love?_____
_____
_____
_____

2. How can love motivate, or drive, a person to do something? _____
_____
_____
_____

3. How can love sustain, or support, a person? _____
_____
_____
_____

4. How can love hurt, or make a person miserable? _____
_____
_____
_____

5. Can a person live a full, satisfying life without love? _____ Why or why not?
_____
_____
_____
_____

49-2. QUESTIONS TO CONSIDER FOR
A LITTLE LOVE

1. Describe the joint. What type of students go there? How does Sheema feel about it?

2. Describe Sheema. How does she feel about herself?

3. Describe the relationship between Sheema and Forrest. What bound them to each other? Compare Sheema to Forrest. Who, in your opinion, was the more realistic of the two? Explain, using examples from the story.

4. Why did Sheema feel that she needed to find her father? How did Forrest feel about helping her? Why did he?

5. What did Sheema learn about her father from the album her grandmother gave her? Why do you think her grandparents didn't tell her the truth about her father and mother before? How did Sheema react to Granmom's telling her about her father?

6. After Granmom told Sheema about her father, she said: "Don't make a move, nothin ever even start to change. Movin is livin. Changin is life!" What did she mean? Do you agree with her? Explain.

7. When Sheema and Forrest left to search for her father, did you think they had a reasonable chance of finding him? Why or why not?

8. Describe the trip searching for Sheema's father. What problems did Sheema and Forrest encounter? How did they solve them?

9. Did finding her father turn out the way Sheema expected it would? Explain. How did the meeting change her?

10. What is your opinion of Cruzey?

© 1994 by The Center for Applied Research in Education

49-3. PROJECTS AND ACTIVITIES TO CONSIDER FOR A LITTLE LOVE

1. Imagine that you are Sheema and you are planning a menu for your school cafeteria. What would your menu be? Keep in mind that it should be nutritious, varied, and tasty.

2. This story takes place before the ending of the Cold War and Sheema is concerned about "the bomb." Interview a parent, older brother or sister, or relative about the Cold War and worries about a nuclear war. Prepare a list of questions ahead of time so that your interview runs smoothly. (You might wish to do some background reading first.) After your interview, write an article based on your interview.

3. Discuss Cruzey with your group. Why did he leave Sheema? Can his action of leaving her be justified? Did his monthly checks for her welfare make up for his absence? What is your opinion of his action? Have a recorder keep notes of the discussion and then share your ideas with other groups.

4. Write a scene showing Forrest telling his father that he and Sheema plan to get married.

5. Predict what will happen to Sheema and Forrest in the future. Will they get married? Will they be happy together? In a short essay write what you think the future holds for them.

6. Plan a trip to a destination in another state or country. Where would you go? Why would you go there? What would you take with you? How far away is your destination? How would you get there? How long will the trip take? About how much money would you need for the trip? Write a short piece about your trip.

Curriculum Connections:

1. Create a sign advertising Sam's Garage, as you think Cruzey would do it. (A)

2. Using a map and referring to the story, trace the trip Sheema and Forrest made in search of her father. What cities and major towns did they pass? How many miles did they travel? Consult references and write brief descriptions of the states they drove through. (SS)

3. Work with a partner and write a song or lyric poem about Sheema's search for her father. Share it with other members of your class. (If you write a song, try setting it to music and performing it for the class.) (A)

50. *Dune* by Frank Herbert
(Chilton Book Company, 1965)

Synopsis

When Duke Leto Atreides is ordered to Arrakis, a dry, barren planet known as Dune, he knows that there will be trouble. Taking his entire House, which includes his consort Jessica, his son, Paul, and his advisors and troops, Leto assumes control with military efficiency. Jessica is a Bene Gesserit, a woman who has undergone ancient mental and physical training. Often referred to as a witch because of her special powers, Jessica has trained Paul in her wisdom, bestowing on him great powers that will one day serve him well. Leto takes various precautions in securing his position on Dune, because his rival, the Baron Harkonnen and his followers, have had control of Dune and are unwilling to give it up. Dune is the only place where melange, a spice prized for its geriatric qualities, is produced. Control of the spice trade is worth a fortune. Because of its great worth, all of the major Houses, including the Emperor, have a stake in its control, and the plot of this story is filled with intrigue, betrayal, and expedient political alliances. When Leto dies because of a Harkonnen plot that also destroys virtually all of House Atredides, Jessica and Paul escape to the desert where they are accepted into a band of Fremen, fierce desert dwellers who hate the Harkonnens. Awed by Paul, who they suspect is the Kwisatz Haderach, a male Bene Gesserit who has the ability to see the future, they become followers. Paul eventually becomes the leader of all the Fremen, whom he molds into an unstoppable force. In the final battle, Paul defeats the Harkonnens and the forces of the Emperor, clearing the way for an Atreides to gain the throne.

Ideas and Concepts to Highlight

1. Discuss the scope and breadth of this science fiction story. Herbert has created a world, Dune, populated it with a wide assortment of believable characters, and given it a history, religion, social and military order. He even includes appendices and a glossary.

2. Discuss the plot and the many conflicts, noting the many individuals vying for power and how they try to achieve it.

3. Discuss the possibility of a future for humankind as Herbert depicts it in the story. Will people ever colonize the stars? Will we meet other lifeforms?

4. Note the similarities between Dune and Earth's deserts.

Writing Connection: "Out Among the Stars"

In Frank Herbert's *Dune,* set far in the future, humankind has traveled to the stars and populated the galaxy. Discuss the possibility of interplanetary and interstellar travel in the future with your students. Ask them to speculate on what the future might be. Is it likely or unlikely that we will find other forms of life? What are the chances?

For this assignment, instruct your students to consider what the future of humankind will be. Will we go to the stars just like the explorers and colonists of the past came to the New World? Completing Worksheet 50-1 will help them to generate ideas. Suggest that students consult references if necessary.

50-1. OUT AMONG THE STARS

Directions: Speculate on what humankind's far future will be. Will we reach and colonize the stars? What will life be like then? Answer the questions below and then write an essay of what you think our future will be.

1. Will people explore the planets of our solar system? _____ Why or why not? _____

   _____

   _____

   _____

   _____

2. Given the great distances to the stars, will people ever explore other star systems? _____
   Why or why not? _____

   _____

   _____

   _____

   _____

3. Will humans ever encounter other forms of life? _____ Why or why not? _____

   _____

   _____

   _____

   _____

4. Describe what you think the distant future of humans will be. _____

   _____

   _____

   _____

   _____

   _____

50-2. QUESTIONS TO CONSIDER FOR
DUNE

1. Why did the Atreides go to Dune? What was so important about the planet? Why did Baron Harkonnen plan to destroy the Atreides?

2. How did Duke Leto react when he was informed that the Harkonnens intended to use the Lady Jessica against him?

3. Why did Dr. Yueh betray the Duke? Why wasn't he suspected of being a possible traitor?

4. After the Duke's death, what happened to Jessica and Paul? What happened to the Atreides' guards and supporters?

5. What changes occurred in Paul soon after his father's death? What do you think brought about the changes? Why do you think he was unable to grieve?

6. After he destroyed the Atreides, what was Baron Harkonnen's plan for Dune?

7. Why was the spice, melange, so valuable?

8. Why were the Fremen willing to accept Paul and Jessica? How did Paul win the respect and support of the Fremen?

9. After Paul passed the test of becoming a sandrider, many of the Fremen wanted him to challenge Stilgar for leadership. Why did Paul refuse? How did he manage to keep the loyalty of the Fremen?

10. What was the Kwisatz Haderach? How did Paul become the Kwisatz Haderach?

11. How did Paul plan to defeat the Baron and the Emperor in the final battle on Dune? Why was he so sure that he would be successful?

12. Describe the changes Paul underwent throughout the story, from being a 15-year-old boy to the leader of an entire planet with a claim to the Emperor's throne.

© 1994 by The Center for Applied Research in Education

50-3. *PROJECTS AND ACTIVITIES TO CONSIDER FOR DUNE*

1. Who was your favorite character in the story? Write a short character sketch and then write a new scene in which your character plays a major role.

2. Read one or more of the other books in the Dune Chronicles (all written by Frank Herbert): *Dune Messiah, Children of Dune, God Emperor of Dune,* and *Chapterhouse Dune.* Write a short review of the one you like the best.

3. Watch the movie version of *Dune* (1984) and compare it to the novel. Which one do you like better? Why? Write an essay comparing the two versions of the story.

4. Imagine that you are Princess Irulan. Write a short biography of Paul-Muad'Dib.

5. Work with your group and discuss the characters of the story. Which of them, if any, was truly noble? Give reasons for your answers and share your conclusions with the members of other groups.

Curriculum Connections:

1. In the glossary of the book, Dune, Arrakis, is described as the third planet of Canopus. Consult a reference on stars and determine how far Canopus is from Earth. How many light-years? How many miles? Research the possibility of interstellar travel. What developments in spacecraft would be necessary before a trip like that could be attempted? (Sci or M)

2. Sketch a stillsuit, and label its various parts. (A)

3. Compose a lyric poem or song about Dune, as Gurney Halleck might have sung it. (A)

4. Research one of Earth's deserts and compare it to Dune. Describe the plant and animal life of the Earth desert. How do plants and animals adapt to an environment in which water is scarce? Write a brief report. (Sci)

5. Create a chart showing the House of Atreides with its supporters and allies. (A)

51. *Gone with the Wind* by Margaret Mitchell
(Macmillan Publishing Company, 1936)

Synopsis

Scarlett O'Hara is the daughter of a wealthy planter in the South just before the Civil War. Scarlett is pretty, spoiled, and ruthless in her desires. When she can't have Ashley Wilkes for a husband because he marries Melanie Hamilton, Scarlett marries Charles Hamilton, Melly's brother. The war breaks out, and Charles dies of pneumonia. As the war continues and worsens, the South that Scarlett grew up in is destroyed. Many of the young men she knew are killed, her mother dies of typhoid, and her father loses his mind to grief. Although she manages to save Tara, her home, Scarlett comes to know hunger, fear, and bitterness. Throughout her ordeal, she continues to love Ashley, even though Rhett Butler, a dashing, arrogant gambler and blockade runner, has fallen in love with her. After the war, Scarlett struggles during Reconstruction. Unable to pay the taxes on Tara, she marries Frank Kennedy. Eventually, with the help of money borrowed from Rhett, Scarlett becomes a successful businesswomen. She still loves Ashley, but after Frank's death she gives in to Rhett's proposal of marriage. Although Rhett, who is wealthy because of his shrewd business dealings during the war, can give her everything, she doesn't recognize his love. Only later, after much tragedy that destroys their marriage, does Scarlett finally come to realize that she has truly loved Rhett all along. But it is too late.

Ideas and Concepts to Highlight

1. Discuss the pre-Civil War South and the causes of the war. Slavery, the dispute over state's rights, and economic factors all helped contribute to the war.

2. Note the effects of the war on the South, as well as the characters. Emphasize that the war resulted in the end of an entire way of life.

3. Discuss the strong characters in the story, and their conflicts.

4. Note that while the story takes place during the Civil War, its focus is on the relationships of the people and the effects of the war on them.

Writing Connection: "Scarlett and Rhett"

Margaret Mitchell created two of literature's most memorable characters in *Gone with the Wind*—Scarlett O'Hara and Rhett Butler. Both were complex individuals, finely detailed, who were in conflict with their world, their contemporaries, and each other. At times they were heroes, while at other times they were downright scoundrels. Fascinating in their own right, it is their love and hate of each other that supplies the flame of the story.

For this assignment, ask your students to analyze Scarlett and Rhett. Completing worksheet 51-1 will help them to organize their ideas.

51-1. SCARLETT AND RHETT

Directions: Scarlett O'Hara and Rhett Butler are two of literature's most memorable characters. Their love and conflict is at the heart of *Gone with the Wind.* Answer the questions below and then write an analysis of these two complex people.

1. Describe Scarlett's personality. What are her strongest traits? What are her weakest? _____

   _____

   _____

   _____

   _____

   _____

   _____

2. Describe Rhett's personality. What are his strongest and weakest traits? _____

   _____

   _____

   _____

   _____

3. Which one do you believe is the stronger character? _____ Why?_____

   _____

   _____

   _____

4. Would the story have been as powerful if they had been changed in some way? Explain.

   _____

   _____

   _____

   _____

51-2. *QUESTIONS TO CONSIDER FOR*
GONE WITH THE WIND

1. Describe Scarlett at the beginning of the story. What is your opinion of her? Explain.

2. Why do you think that Scarlett can't accept Ashley's marrying Melanie? Why did Scarlett then marry Charles?

3. Gerald says to Scarlett: "Land is the only thing in the world that amounts to anything, for tis the only thing in this world that lasts..." What does he mean? Do you agree or disagree? Why?

4. Describe Rhett. What was Scarlett's first impression of him? What was your first impression of Rhett? Did your opinion of him change?

5. Describe how the war affected life in the South. What were some of the reasons the North eventually won?

6. Describe the relationship between Scarlett and Melanie. What was Scarlett's opinion of Melanie? What was Melanie's opinion of Scarlett? Of the two, which one did you like better? Why?

7. Why did Scarlett return to Tara? What did she find there? How had her father changed? How had Scarlett changed during the war?

8. Compare Tara before the war and after the war. What were some of the problems Scarlett faced at Tara? How did she solve them? Do you approve of her methods? Why or why not?

9. What was Rhett's opinion of Ashley? Do you agree with him? Why or why not?

10. Why do you think Rhett proposed marriage to Scarlett? Why did she accept? Given their personalities, what did you think their chances were for a successful marriage? Why? What eventually came between them?

11. At the end of the story, Scarlett is convinced that she has loved Rhett all along. Do you think she really did? Explain.

© 1994 by The Center for Applied Research in Education

51-3. PROJECTS AND ACTIVITIES TO CONSIDER FOR
GONE WITH THE WIND

1. One of the most interesting aspects of *Gone with the Wind* is the relationship between Scarlett and Rhett. There are many examples of irony in it, especially their dialogue. Working with a partner, go through the story and find several examples of irony. Share your findings with other members of your group.

2. Working with your group, discuss the characters of Scarlett and Rhett and how each was a rebel against their society. Use examples from the story to support your opinions. Appoint a recorder to write down your conclusions and share them with other groups.

3. Why do you think Margaret Mitchell chose *Gone with the Wind* for the title of her book? Write a short essay sharing your ideas.

4. There were many powerful scenes in the story. Choose your favorite and in an essay tell why you liked it.

Curriculum Connections:

1. Create a time line of the major events of the Civil War. (A or SS)

2. The Civil War was a defining point in American history. Work with your group and research the causes and results of the war. Organize a panel discussion on the war's effects on the United States. Seek to answer the question of how the war changed America. (SS)

3. Create a map of the Civil War South. Mark the states, major cities, and important battles. Be sure to include a legend. (SS or A)

4. Research the period of Reconstruction and the Carpetbaggers. Who were they? Why were they so hated by the former Confederates? Present your findings orally to your group or class. (SS)

5. Consult reference books and compare the economic differences between the North and South prior to and during the Civil War. Which side had more industrial capacity? Which had the greater population? In your opinion, how much of a factor was economic might in the winning of the war? Write a short report. (SS)

© 1994 by The Center for Applied Research in Education

52. <u>Native Son</u> by Richard Wright
(Harper and Row, 1940)

Synopsis

Bigger Thomas is a young African-American man living in Chicago in the 1930s. Because of the white society, which Bigger feels is biased and hostile to blacks, he is filled with hatred, bitterness, and frustration. He has few values and shows his brutality by mercilessly beating his friend Gus. Offered a job as a chauffeur for the Daltons, a wealthy white family, Bigger reluctantly accepts. The Daltons proudly donate money to help blacks, but at the same time they own much of the ghetto in which blacks, including Bigger, live. The first day on his job, Bigger is supposed to drive Mary, the Daltons' daughter, to school, but instead she has Bigger pick up Jan Erlone, a Communist. Mary, a headstrong, rebellious girl, is also a Communist, and she and Jan speak to Bigger about wishing to be his friend. Jan gives him some material about Communism to read, and they insist that he join them while they eat at a black diner. Despite their apparent friendliness, Bigger remains suspicious of them. They wind up drinking and by the time Bigger drives Mary home, she is drunk. He helps her inside and to her room—a dangerous act for a black man at that time. When her mother (who is blind) comes to check on her, Bigger becomes frightened that Mary will say something. Trying to keep her quiet, he accidentally kills her. He disposes of Mary's body by burning it in the furnace, and then invents a story that diverts suspicion of Mary's disappearance to Jan. Hoping to trick the Daltons into thinking that Mary was kidnapped by Communists in an effort to raise money for their cause, Bigger sends a ransom note, but his plan abruptly ends when Mary's bones are discovered in the furnace. Desperate to escape, Bigger winds up killing his girlfriend, Bessie, but he is caught. Although Bigger still must undergo a trial, he knows that he will be found guilty and executed.

Ideas and Concepts to Highlight

1. Discuss the differences between the worlds of blacks and whites of 1930 Chicago. Talk about what changes, if any, have occurred in the relations between blacks and whites since then.

2. Note that one of the major motifs of the novel is fear. Bigger hates the white world, but he is also afraid of it. This prevailing fear is woven throughout the story.

3. Explain that the Daltons symbolize white society that feels it helps blacks, yet in fact profits from the very system that makes it difficult for blacks to get ahead.

4. Discuss Bigger's character. Given his personality and the conditions he lived in, did he have a fair chance in life?

Writing Connection: "Race in America"

One of Richard Wright's messages in *Native Son* is that white society is largely responsible for the conditions and plight of blacks. Discuss this view with your students. Is Wright accurate in his assessment? Is he being fair?

For this assignment, instruct your students to write an essay or short story showing what they believe is the condition of race relations between blacks and whites today. Completing Worksheet 52-1 will help students to generate ideas.

NAME _____ DATE _____ SECTION _____

52-1. RACE IN AMERICA

Directions: Race has always been a major issue in American society. Either through an essay or short story, express your views about race in the United States today. Answer the questions below before writing.

1. Describe Richard Wright's views of the relations between blacks and whites, as depicted in *Native Son.* _____

_____

_____

_____

_____

2. Would he feel the same way today?_____ Why or why not?_____

_____

_____

_____

_____

3. Name some books, movies, or TV shows that fit your own view of race relations today, and explain how they support your views. _____

_____

_____

_____

_____

4. How can the relations between blacks and whites be improved?_____

_____

_____

_____

_____

1. Describe Bigger Thomas. Why is he so bitter? How is he different from his brother, Buddy? Why do you think they look at their world differently?

2. Some people would consider Mr. and Mrs. Dalton to be hypocrites for donating money to help blacks, but at the same time owning much of the ghetto in which blacks live. What is a hypocrite? Do you agree that they are hypocrites? Explain.

3. Describe how fear is a major motif of the novel.

4. When they were talking about robbing Blum's store, Bigger called Gus yellow for hesitating, but Gus claimed that Bigger was yellow, too. What was his reason for saying this? Do you think he was right? Why or why not?

5. What was Bigger's impression of the Daltons when he first met them? Do you believe he viewed the job as chauffeur as an opportunity? Explain.

6. What was Bigger's impression of Mary Dalton and Jan Erlone? Why was he unable to trust them?

7. Why did Bigger kill Mary? How did he feel about it? How did the murder change Bigger's opinion of himself?

8. How did Bigger plan his story so that he would not be a suspect in Mary's disappearance? Why did he involve Bessie with his plan? Why did he kill Bessie?

9. Throughout his trial, did Bigger show any remorse? Did he show any feelings for Mary? For Bessie? Explain.

10. Why do you think Wright chose *Native Son* for the title of this book? What significance does the title have?

11. Do you feel that Bigger is a tragic character? Explain.

© 1994 by The Center for Applied Research in Education

52-3. *PROJECTS AND ACTIVITIES TO CONSIDER FOR*
<u>*NATIVE SON*</u>

1. Read Richard Wright's autobiography *Black Boy* (New York: Harper and Row, 1945). Compare it to *Native Son*. Do any of the same ideas and themes appear in both books? Explain.

2. Watch the movie version of *Native Son* (1986), and compare it to the novel. How are the two versions of the story alike? How are they different? Write about your impressions.

3. Working with a partner, compare the newspaper accounts in the book of the disappearance and murder of Mary Dalton with similar types of articles found in today's newspapers. (You might wish to consult the library for articles on file.) Based on your research, do you think that a modern-day Bigger would have been convicted of the same crime? Do you think he would have gotten the same sentence? Share your conclusions with others.

4. The author seems to be making the point that Bigger and his violence are a product of white society. Because of the conditions and circumstances of his life, which was forced upon him by white America, Bigger was doomed to do what he did. Discuss this idea with the members of your group, and then, working alone, write an essay expressing your feelings and opinions. Use examples from the story to support your views.

Curriculum Connections:

1. Research and trace black migration from the South to the North. Answer these questions: Why did blacks migrate? About how many blacks moved northward? Where did they eventually settle? What were the results of the migration? Write a report of your findings, and include a map or graphs to highlight your information. (SS or A)

2. Race and ethnic origin have always been factors in American society. Research the races and major ethnic groups in the United States today. Create a table and pie graph to illustrate the diversity of America's population. Find studies that project the numbers into the future. What will be the percentages of race and major ethnic groups then? Based on your results, what changes do you anticipate in American society in the future? Share your ideas in a brief report. (SS, M, or A)

3. Research the Communist Party in the United States. When was it founded? How many people belong to it? What does the party advocate? Why has it never become a major force in American politics? Write a report sharing your findings. (SS)

53. *Jane Eyre* by Charlotte Brontë

Synopsis

Jane Eyre is a 10-year-old orphan living with relatives, the Reeds—Mrs. Reed and her children, Eliza, Georgiana, and John. Jane is treated badly and is glad to be sent away to Lowool School. Although her adjustment at Lowood is hard, during the next several years she comes to love the school. It is here that she grows up. After eight years, Jane begins to realize that she would like to know more of the world. She leaves Lowood and becomes the teacher of a young girl, Adele, at Thornfield Hall. The little girl does well under Jane's tutelage, but Jane still feels something is missing, until the master of the house, Mr. Rochester, returns home. An abrupt, changeable man, Jane learns that he is sullen over past experiences, although she is unable to find out more. Despite his moods, Jane sees good, strong qualities in Mr. Rochester and falls in love with him. There is much mystery in Thornfield Hall, however. One of the servants is Grace Poole, a strange woman, who keeps to herself and whose duties remain obscure. Moreover, there are screams in the night and on one occasion a guest suffers a serious knife wound. None of these incidents are satisfactorily explained to Jane. When Jane learns that Mr. Rochester is planning to marry Blanche Ingram, a pretty but shallow woman, she is dejected. She sadly continues with her duties until she is summoned by the Reeds because Mrs. Reed is dying. Dutifully, Jane returns. On her deathbed Mrs. Reed tells Jane that her (Jane's) uncle had wanted to adopt her but that she (Mrs. Reed) wrote to him and told him that Jane was dead. Jane forgives her and helps settle Mrs. Reed's daughters after her death. Returning to Thornfield Hall, Mr. Rochester tells Jane that he is not going to marry Blanche and proposes to Jane. She is thrilled. When the wedding day comes, however, the marriage is stopped because it is revealed that Mr. Rochester already has a wife—a mad woman who is taken care of by Grace Poole. When asked by Mr. Rochester to marry him anyhow, Jane reluctantly declines. She leaves and stays with the Rivers' family. It is while she lives with the Rivers' that Jane receives an inheritance from her uncle. Although Jane receives a proposal of marriage from Mr. Rivers, she feels she must return to Thornfield Hall. When she does, she finds the house burnt down. Mr. Rochester's mad wife caused the fire that took her life. Mr. Rochester, himself, was severely injured, losing a hand and an eye. Jane goes to him immediately and finds that their love for each other is still strong.

Charlotte Brontë

Ideas and Concepts to Highlight

1. Note that the story is told by Jane as an adult. The years of her childhood are told in retrospect, and from an adult's viewpoint.

2. Point out Brontë's descriptive settings.

3. Note the symbolism, especially when Rochester proposes to Jane amid the gathering storm. The storm symbolizes the power and turmoil of their emotions.

4. Discuss Brontë's use of foreshadowing, especially her use of dreams.

Writing Connection: "The Brontës"

The Brontës—Charlotte, Branwell, Emily, and Anne—were a unique literary family. Although they lived relatively short and tragic lives, books by Charlotte and Emily became known and read around the world.

For this writing assignment, instruct your students to research and write about the Brontës. Worksheet 53-1 will help them gather information for a thorough report.

53-1. THE BRONTËS

Directions: Research and write a report about the Brontës. Answering the questions below will get you started in your research. Include footnotes and a bibliography.

1. Who were the Brontës? _____

   _____

2. Where were they born? _____

Where did they grow up? _____

Who were their parents? _____

How did their parents influence their future accomplishments? _____

   _____

   _____

   _____

3. How did their background and childhood experiences affect their writing? _____

   _____

   _____

   _____

4. Of the Brontës, who, in your opinion, became the most accomplished author? _____

   _____ Why? _____

   _____

5. What was some of the critical reaction to the published works of the Brontës?_____

   _____

6. What is your opinion of their works? _____

   _____

   _____

© 1994 by The Center for Applied Research in Education

53-2. QUESTIONS TO CONSIDER FOR
JANE EYRE

1. Describe Jane's life with the Reed family. Cite examples from the story to support your answer. Why was she staying with them?

2. Describe Jane's experience at Lowood School during the eight years she stayed there. Use examples from the story to support your answer.

3. Why did Jane go to Thornfield Hall. Was she helpful to Adele? Explain. Was Jane happy at Thornfield? Explain. What did she feel was missing in her life?

4. What was Jane's initial opinion of Mr. Rochester? What was your opinion of him? How did Jane's opinion of him change? Did your opinion of him change? Explain.

5. How did Jane view Lady Blanche Ingram? Having fallen in love with Mr. Rochester, do you think Jane could be objective in her appraisal of Blanche? Explain.

6. Why did Jane return to Gateshead? What did she find there? How had Jane changed since she had left there eight years before? What did Mrs. Reed confess to Jane? What was Jane's reaction? What would your reaction be in a similar situation?

7. When Mr. Rochester proposed to Jane in the orchard, she doesn't believe him at first. Why not? What do you think Brontë was telling the reader, if anything, through the lightning splitting the horse-chestnut tree in two?

8. After the wedding was stopped, why do you think Jane didn't go with Mr. Rochester to his villa in France? Do you think her explanation was reasonable? Explain.

9. How did Jane react to St. John's proposal of marriage? Do you think she did the right thing? Why or why not?

10. What had happened to Thornfield Hall during Jane's absence? What did she do when she learned of Mr. Rochester's condition?

© 1994 by The Center for Applied Research in Education

53-3. PROJECTS AND ACTIVITIES TO CONSIDER FOR *JANE EYRE*

1. In Chapter 12, Jane feels that women have a right to a full life, the same as men do. She seems to be calling for equal rights for women. Working with a partner, research the status of women's rights during the 1840s, which was about the time the novel was written. Compare women's rights then to women's rights today. Present an oral report of your findings.

2. Working with your group, identify instances of foreshadowing. Decide what coming action each pointed to. Discuss how Brontë's use of foreshadowing made her plot more believable. Share your findings with the members of other groups.

3. Brontë used excellent descriptive writing in the story. Pick one of your favorite scenes and write your own description of it.

4. Read *Wuthering Heights* by Emily Brontë. Heathcliff in that story and Mr. Rochester in *Jane Eyre* have much in common. Write an essay analyzing these two characters.

5. Sickness, especially tuberculosis, played a large role in Charlotte Brontë's life. How does this come out in the novel?

Curriculum Connections:

1. Draw or sketch a portrait of Jane, as you think Jane herself would do it. (A)

2. In the story, Georgiana Reed becomes a nun. Research the Catholic and Anglican Churches. At one time, they were the same. When did the split come? Why? How different are the two churches in outlook and beliefs? Have there been any attempts to reconcile? Write about your findings in a report. (SS)

3. The Brontës grew up in Yorkshire, England. What was Yorkshire like in the early 1800s? Describe its climate, economy, and population. How might have their upbringing in Yorkshire affected the stories the Brontës wrote? Write a short report. (SS)

54. <u>Dinner at the Homesick Restaurant</u> by Anne Tyler
(Ballantine Books, 1982)

Synopsis

Pearl Tull is dying. She is an old woman who had spent the best years of her life raising her three children—Cody, Ezra, and Jenny—after her husband, Beck Tull, left. Told from multiple viewpoints, the story examines the effects of Beck's abandonment. Pearl, working as a cashier at a small store and struggling to support her family, often takes her frustration and anger out on her children. Cody becomes a successful, hard-driving business consultant, Ezra comes to own a restaurant, and Jenny, on her third marriage by the time the story ends, becomes a pediatrician. The family seems unable to love. Cody steals Ezra's fiancee away from him, eventually marrying her more to spite his brother than out of love; Ezra is never able to form another loving relationship; and Jenny selects men more out of whim and convenience than emotion. Except for Ezra, who remains living at home with Pearl, Cody and Jenny have a strained relationship with their mother. This is especially true of Cody, who slips out of touch for long periods, blaming his work. The family's underlying conflicts are aptly shown through repeated scenes in Ezra's restaurant. Whenever there is a gathering and they sit down to a meal, someone always gets angry and they are never able to finish it. Only at the gathering after Pearl's funeral, with their father attending, does the family resolve to finish the meal.

Ideas and Concepts to Highlight

1. Note that the viewpoint characters change throughout the story. This gives readers the chance to see the family from various perspectives.

2. Point out that many parts of the story are told in flashbacks.

3. Discuss the relationships and conflicts of the family members, and how they cope with them.

Writing Connection: "Trouble in the Family"

In recent years much has been written about the American family being in trouble. In many ways the Tulls are a good example—the father abandons the family, the mother is forced to raise the children alone, and the children grow up into adults scarred by their childhood. In turn, each of the children, as an adult, has trouble building a stable family of his or her own.

Discuss the issue of the disintegrating American family and ask your students to write an essay detailing their views. Encourage them to base their essay on the story, other readings, and their own experiences. Completing Worksheet 54-1 will help them to uncover their thoughts and feelings about this difficult topic.

© 1994 by The Center for Applied Research in Education

NAME _____ **DATE** _____ **SECTION** _____

54-1. TROUBLE IN THE FAMILY

Directions: According to many social observers, the American family is under assault these days. Some go so far as to say that the traditional family of a father, mother, and children is no longer the norm. Consider the issue of the breakdown of the American family, answer the questions below, and write an essay detailing your opinions.

1. Do all families fit the model of the traditional family?_____ Why or why not? _____

_____

_____

2. Give some examples of non-traditional families. _____

_____

_____

3. Can non-traditional families provide a loving, nurturing atmosphere for family members?
_____ Why or why not? _____

_____

_____

4. Why do some families break down? _____

_____

_____

5. What are some results of broken families? _____

_____

_____

6. What, if anything, should be done to save the traditional family?_____

_____

_____

_____

54-2. QUESTIONS TO CONSIDER FOR
DINNER AT THE HOMESICK RESTAURANT

1. How did Pearl react when Beck left her? Why do you think she acted like that? Do you think her reaction is common when a husband or wife leaves his or her family? Explain.

2. How did each of the children react to his or her father's abandonment? Cite examples from the story to support your answer.

3. Pearl hoped that she could lean on Cody for support after Beck left. Was Cody helpful to her? Explain.

4. How did Pearl react to the news that Ezra had become a partner in Scarlatti's restaurant? Pearl says, "I've never been the type to meddle." Do you agree? Explain.

5. Why did Jenny marry Harley? Did she really know him? How did her opinion of him change after they were married? How was Harley's treatment of Jenny similar to Pearl's treatment of Jenny?

6. Describe Ezra's relationship with Mrs. Scarlatti. Why do you think he liked working with her? Do you think that in some ways Mrs. Scarlatti took the place of Pearl? Explain.

7. What changes did Ezra make to the restaurant when Mrs. Scarlatti was sick in the hospital? Why did he make the changes? Do you think he was right to make them? Just before she died, Mrs. Scarlatti said to her nurse: "Tell Ezra to change the sign...it isn't Scarlatti's restaurant anymore." What did she mean?

8. Why did Cody steal Ruth away from Ezra? What is your opinion of his actions?

9. Describe Jenny's life with Joe and the children. Do you think they provided a nurturing environment in which children could grow up? Explain.

10. What is your opinion of Beck Tull? What was his reason for leaving his family? Do you feel he was justified in leaving, or was he simply being irresponsible? Explain.

54-3. PROJECTS AND ACTIVITIES TO CONSIDER FOR DINNER AT THE HOMESICK RESTAURANT

1. Would you describe Pearl and her children as a loving, caring family? Write down your opinion and then share it with the members of your group. Group members should then discuss the various opinions and arrive at a consensus that their recorder can share with other groups.

2. How do you think Pearl's death will affect the members of her family? Finish the final scene at the Homesick Restaurant.

3. Write a skit that the Tulls might play, your own version of "The Mortgage Overdue." With classmates assuming the various roles, act the skit out for the rest of the class.

4. Anne Tyler reveals much about each character through the eyes of other characters. Work with a partner, review the story, and find at least three examples where she does this. Share your examples with other members of your group and discuss whether or not this is an effective way to characterize. What other ways did she reveal character?

5. Imagine that you are Jenny. Instead of Harley writing a letter of proposal to her, you are to write one to him. How would Jenny have worded such a letter?

6. Design a menu for the Homesick Restaurant as Ezra might have made one.

7. Which of Pearl's children—Cody, Ezra, or Jenny— do you feel you have the most in common with? Write a short essay explaining why.

Curriculum Connections:

1. At one point in the story, Pearl starts to mention that Becky, Jenny's daughter, suffers from anorexia nervosa. Research this condition and write a report on its causes, symptoms, and treatments. (Sci)

2. Research the city of Baltimore, the setting of the story. Compare the Baltimore of the 1940s (when the story began) to the Baltimore of today. Include facts about its population, ethnic and racial make-up, economy, and climate. Undoubtedly, you will find many changes have occurred to Baltimore over the years. What has caused these changes? Write a report of your findings. (SS)

55. *Slaughterhouse-Five* by Kurt Vonnegut, Jr.
(Dell Publishing Company, 1972)

Synopsis

Slaughterhouse-Five is an account of a fictitious war "hero," Billy Pilgrim, who, through escapism and fantasy, travels through time and space. In an attempt to "make sense" of his past, he hallucinates being kidnapped to the planet Tralfamadore as a specimen from Earth. While there he tries to come to terms with what he perceives as the absurdity of life. His time and space travels arise out of his deeply buried war experiences. During World War II he was a valet to a chaplain, was captured by the Germans, and survived the firebombing of Dresden which killed nearly twice as many people as the atomic bomb dropped on Hiroshima. As a POW he experienced many labor camps, including living in an abandoned slaughterhouse, until the Allies liberated him. After the war, he marries a rich woman, is set up as an optometrist in upstate New York, and has two children. Vonnegut's story is told in a roundabout, jumping style with no linear plot. Billy, as taught by the Tralfamadorians, is "unstuck in time," and his experiences are related in small segments that often do not connect right away.

Ideas and Concepts to Highlight

1. Note that Billy lives as much in reality as he does fantasy. His time and space travels arise from his need to understand the absurdity of war.

2. Encourage the class to identify imagery throughout the book, and discuss symbolism as a literary technique.

3. Note how Vonnegut uses names to suggest ideas. Pilgrim, for instance, suggests a person who seeks enlightenment or understanding. Roland Weary parallels Roland, one of Charlemagne's generals, in the *Song of Roland*. After battling the Saracens in Spain, Roland was given the charge of guarding the rear of the main army as it returned to France. When attacked by the Saracens, Roland, wanting to defeat the enemy himself, refused to call for reinforcements. His entire company was killed. Ilium, Billy Pilgrim's hometown, is the classical name for the ancient city of Troy.

4. Discuss Vonnegut's rambling, non-linear style, and how the novel itself is "unstuck in time." Is this an effective way to tell this story?

5. Encourage the class to share thoughts on Vonnegut's purpose for writing the book, and what this unusual novel achieves. Is this, in fact, an anti-war novel?

Writing Connection: "An Anti-War Novel?"

There are many themes in Kurt Vonnegut's *Slaughterhouse-Five,* three of the most important being good versus evil, war and its effects, and nationalism. As these themes recur throughout the novel, the reader must ask him- or herself why Vonnegut emphasizes them so much. Was his purpose in writing this story primarily to show the terrible effects of war, or was his purpose an indictment of the absurdity of war?

For this assignment, ask your students to consider the extent to which *Slaughterhouse-Five* is an anti-war novel. Instruct students to complete Worksheet 55-1, and write about their thoughts in the form of an essay. Having students then return to their groups to discuss their impressions before writing can help broaden their perspectives.

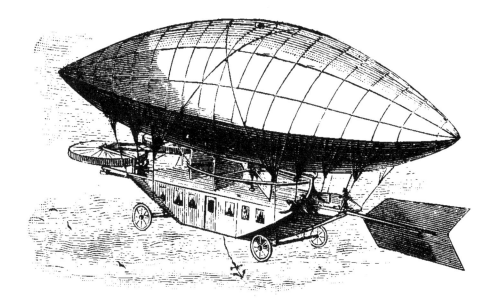

55-1. AN ANTI-WAR NOVEL?

Directions: Three of the most important themes in Kurt Vonnegut's *Slaughterhouse-Five* are good versus evil, war and its effects, and nationalism. Was he using these as a vehicle to protest the absurdity of war? Answer the questions below and then write an essay explaining your thoughts.

1. Give some examples of how Vonnegut brings out the theme of good versus evil. _____

_____

_____

_____

_____

2. List some ways that Vonnegut supports his theme of nationalism. _____

_____

_____

_____

_____

3. List some ways that Vonnegut shows the effects of war. _____

_____

_____

_____

_____

4. Do these themes support the opinion that the story is an anti-war novel? _____

Why or why not? _____

_____

_____

_____

_____

_____

55-2. *QUESTIONS TO CONSIDER FOR SLAUGHTERHOUSE-FIVE*

1. Discuss the author's continuous use of "So it goes." What was his purpose? Why the repetition?

2. Define your understanding of Vonnegut's term "unstuck in time." Describe how Billy was "unstuck in time." Use examples from the story to support your answer.

3. What is the significance of the name "Billy Pilgrim"? Why do you suppose the author placed him in Ilium, New York?

4. In Chapter 2, the author writes that Billy's mother, "like so many Americans, was trying to construct a life that made sense from things she found in gift shops." What do you think this means? When you answer, be sure to take into account the kind of person Billy turned out to be.

5. In Chapter 4, what is the significance of Billy being able to see the war movie in reverse?

6. Record Vonnegut's many digressions and tangents in *Slaughterhouse-Five,* many of which end in death of some sort and the phrase "So it goes." What is the purpose of such tangents? What do they accomplish? Are they disruptive or essential? Support your answer with examples from the story.

7. Billy is portrayed as abnormally detached from reality. Why is he like this? Why does Vonnegut accentuate it so? Explain.

8. Describe Billy's stay on Tralfamadore. What provides the substance for Billy's fantasy life? Why do you think Billy needs this fantasy life? What is he really trying to find on Tralfamadore?

9. Decide whether Billy Pilgrim represents Everyman, the author himself, or somebody else. Support your conclusions with specific examples.

10. What is the "moral," or message, of *Slaughterhouse-Five?*

55-3. PROJECTS AND ACTIVITIES TO CONSIDER FOR SLAUGHTERHOUSE-FIVE

1. Research other stories about people who say they were kidnapped by outer-space creatures. Share the stories with the members of your group or the whole class, and select the most believable. What makes some more believable than others? With your group, discuss the possibility of some of these stories actually being true.

2. Strong symbolism abounds in *Slaughterhouse-Five*. Working with your group, select several examples of symbolism. Discuss what each represents, then share your conclusions with the members of other groups.

3. The novel contains strong religious imagery. Work with a partner and find as many religious images and references as you can. Define them, and explain their use in context. Share your findings with the members of your group.

4. Create a plot for a Kilgore Trout novel.

Curriculum Connections:

1. Draw or sketch a representation of Billy's habitat on Tralfamadore. (A)

2. Consult the necessary references and write a report on the destruction of Dresden during World War II, highlighting the most significant events. In addition, try to answer these questions: Why was the attack ordered? How much destruction was caused? How many lives were lost? Were the military objectives gained? In your opinion, was the attack justified? Include a map detailing the attacks or the areas of heaviest damage. (SS)

3. Conduct research to find possible reasons why the Germans did not slaughter American captives the way they did Jews and other prisoners. Present an oral report to your group or class about your findings. (SS)

4. Research the concept of time. What is time? Is time travel a theoretical possibility? Write a short report. (Sci)

© 1994 by The Center for Applied Research in Education

56. *One Flew Over the Cuckoo's Nest* by Ken Kesey
(Viking Penguin, 1962)

Synopsis

To escape work on a prison farm, con man Randle P. McMurphy has himself committed to a mental hospital. The story is told by the Chief, a patient who hasn't spoken in years and is believed to be deaf and dumb. Once committed, McMurphy tries to change the routines of the hospital to suit himself. This puts him in conflict with Nurse Ratched, the Big Nurse, a former army nurse who maintains order through manipulations and fear. McMurphy, who symbolizes individuality (the Big Nurse represents society's need for conformity), quickly becomes a hero to the other patients. They draw strength from him and start to get better. Even the Chief begins speaking again. The Big Nurse, however, is unwilling to let her authority slip away and she is determined to "break" McMurphy. After fighting with an orderly, McMurphy is given shock treatment, but he still challenges the Big Nurse. Bribing the night attendant, McMurphy stages a party, inviting prostitutes he knows, one of the purposes being to help Billy, another patient, lose his virginity. The next morning, the Big Nurse is furious. Berating Billy, she threatens to tell his mother, a prospect that Billy can't face. Left alone for a few minutes, Billy takes a razor and kills himself. Now McMurphy is furious. He attacks the Big Nurse and tries to strangle her. McMurphy is stopped and taken away from the ward. When he returns, he has been lobotomized and is merely a vegetable. The Chief, unwilling to let the Big Nurse have the final victory, smothers McMurphy in the night. Having gained strength and courage from McMurphy, he is able to escape.

Ideas and Concepts to Highlight

1. Discuss how Kesey uses the mental hospital to represent society.

2. Note that by using a patient as the narrator, Kesey allows the reader to glimpse the hospital from the inside out. This sometimes gives the impression that the "inside" is saner than the outside world. Also point out that since the Chief is insane, his observations are thus tainted by his condition. Is he always objective?

3. Note that the conflict between McMurphy and Nurse Ratched symbolizes the battle between good and evil, and the individual against the authority of society that demands conformity.

4. Discuss the religious imagery throughout the story, particularly McMurphy being portrayed symbolically as Christ.

5. Note the strong conflict of male versus female. Many consider this novel to be misogynistic.

Writing Connection: "The Individual Versus Society"

In the story, Kesey uses the mental hospital as a setting for a showdown between the individual (McMurphy) and his need for "being what he is" and society (the Big Nurse) that demands conformity. Discuss the needs of individuals and the needs of society. Are they mutually exclusive? Or are there times they are convergent?

For this writing assignment, ask your students to write an essay or story that shares their feelings on the topic. Completing Worksheet 56-1 will help them to organize their thoughts.

56-1. THE INDIVIDUAL VERSUS SOCIETY

Directions: One of the themes of *One Flew Over the Cuckoo's Nest* is the conflict between individuals and their quest for freedom, and society, which often demands conformity. Answer the questions below and then write an essay or story that reflects your feelings about the topic.

1. List the major needs of individuals: _____

_____

_____

_____

_____

2. List what society expects of individuals: _____

_____

_____

_____

_____

3. List needs of the individual that might be in conflict with the needs of society: _____

_____

_____

_____

_____

4. What might happen when needs are in conflict? _____

_____

_____

_____

_____

56-2. QUESTIONS TO CONSIDER FOR
ONE FLEW OVER THE CUCKOO'S NEST

1. How did McMurphy come to be admitted to the mental hospital? How did he treat the other patients? How did they react to him?

2. What is the conflict between McMurphy and the Big Nurse?

3. Describe a typical group meeting. What was the purpose of these meetings? Do you think they were helpful to the patients? Why or why not? What do you think the Big Nurse was really trying to do at the meetings?

4. Why do the patients think of themselves as rabbits? Does McMurphy feel that way? Explain.

5. Why did the Big Nurse argue against sending McMurphy to Disturbed? What do you think her real reason was?

6. After McMurphy realizes that he can be discharged only after the hospital staff, including Nurse Ratched, believes him to be ready to re-enter society, he stops challenging Nurse Ratched. How do the other patients react to his change in behavior? Why did Cheswick commit suicide? How does his death affect McMurphy?

7. How do the patients gain strength from McMurphy? What does McMurphy help the Chief to realize?

8. After the fishing trip, how does the Big Nurse get the others to turn against McMurphy? What do you think were her motives?

9. Why was McMurphy given the shock treatments? What did the Big Nurse hope to gain?

10. After Billy's suicide, why did McMurphy attack the Big Nurse? What happened to McMurphy because of this?

11. Why did the Chief kill McMurphy? Was he wrong or right to do this? Explain.

56-3. PROJECTS AND ACTIVITIES TO CONSIDER FOR ONE FLEW OVER THE CUCKOO'S NEST

1. Work with your group and discuss the characters of McMurphy and the Big Nurse. What drove them? Why, from the beginning of the story, was it inevitable that they would come into conflict? Why couldn't McMurphy back down? Why did Nurse Ratched force him to conform? In the end, was she successful? Answer the above questions during your discussion and then share your conclusions with the members of other groups.

2. Write a story showing the Chief's first days outside the hospital. Is he able to adapt to the outside world?

3. Kesey uses much religious imagery throughout the novel, especially in the final parts, and implies that McMurphy is like Christ in the mental hospital. Working with a partner, review the story and identify examples of religious imagery. Then, write an essay discussing the parallels between McMurphy and Christ. Is the parallel justified? Why or why not?

4. Who is your favorite character in the story? Write a new scene for the story in which your character plays a central part.

5. At the end of the novel, some readers feel that the Chief represents the "Noble Savage," a term often used in literature and the social sciences. Research the term and apply it to the Chief. Is he truly a "Noble Savage"?

Curriculum Connections:

1. The Chief is described as being a paranoid-schizophrenic. Research this condition. What are its causes, symptoms, and treatments? Is the condition curable, or at least controllable? Write a report. (Sci)

2. Along with their mental illness, Sefelt and Fredricks suffer from epilepsy. Research this disorder and write a report on its causes, symptoms, and treatments. (Sci)

3. This story was copywritten in 1962. Has the treatment of the mentally ill changed much since then? Consult the necessary references and present an oral report to your class about the treatment of mental illness today. Include some of the common conditions and treatments. Also include the ways patients receive treatment, for example, through institutionalization, out-patient clinics, or personal physicians. (SS or Sci)

57. *The House on Mango Street* by *Sandra Cisneros* *(Vintage Contemporaries, 1991)*

Synopsis

Esperanza Cordero is growing up in a house on Mango Street in the Hispanic section of Chicago. Through a series of vignettes, she shares with the reader her feelings and thoughts about the oppressive street where hopelessness and hardship are staples. The reader learns about Esperanza's family, friends, and neighbors, their routines, sorrows, and joys. Throughout the book Esperanza's desire to one day leave Mango Street is unshakable. She draws her strength from this, even as she sees her neighbors and friends submit to the desolation of their reality. This short book is told with a simple, yet compelling prose that carries the reader from one vignette to another without the slightest pause.

Ideas and Concepts to Highlight

1. Note that the story is told in a series of vignettes. Although the vignettes may not at first seem to be related, they build to a whole that gives a detailed description of Mango Street and its effect on the people who live there.

2. Discuss the setting of Mango Street.

3. Discuss Esperanza's character as it is slowly revealed through the vignettes.

Writing Connection: "Esperanza and Me"

Esperanza has many of the same basic values and ambitions as other young people. For this writing assignment, ask your students to compare their goals and values to those of Esperanza. Completing Worksheet 57-1 will help your students to organize their thoughts.

NAME _____ **DATE** _____ **SECTION** _____

57-1. ESPERANZA AND ME

Directions: How much do you have in common with Esperanza Cordero? Answer the questions below and then write an essay comparing yourself to Esperanza.

1. Complete the charts.

My Goals	Esperanza's Goals

My Values	Esperanza's Values

2. Ways Esperanza and I are alike:_____

_____

_____

_____

_____

3. Ways Esperanza and I are different: _____

_____

_____

_____

57-2. QUESTIONS TO CONSIDER FOR
THE HOUSE ON MANGO STREET

1. Is the house on Mango Street the kind of house Esperanza always wanted? What kind of house does she want? Explain.

2. Describe Esperanza's neighborhood. Would you like to live there? Explain.

3. In "Those Who Don't," Esperanza says of her neighborhood, "All brown all around, we are safe." What does she mean? How does she feel about going into a neighborhood of another color?

4. Esperanza introduces the reader to many different characters on Mango Street. Do they have any common bonds? If yes, what are they? If no, why not?

5. Why are the Four Skinny Trees important to Esperanza?

6. In "Beautiful and Cruel" Esperanza says, "I have begun my own quiet war." What does she mean?

7. Of the three sisters, what did the sister with the marble hands mean when she told Esperanza that she (Esperanza) must remember to come back for the others? What does the circle refer to?

8. Throughout the story, Esperanza clings to her desire to leave Mango Street. Keeping her character in mind, do you think that one day she will leave? Explain.

9. Describe Esperanza. Do you believe her to be a keen observer of her world? Explain, using examples from the story.

10. In English, "Esperanza" means Hope. Does Esperanza's name fit her character? Explain.

11. This book has a distinct narrative structure. What effect did this structure have on you? Did it enhance or detract from the book? Explain.

57-3. PROJECTS AND ACTIVITIES TO CONSIDER FOR
THE HOUSE ON MANGO STREET

1. What do you predict for Esperanza's future? Write a short story showing what you think her future holds.

2. Read *Woman Hollering Creek* by Sandra Cisneros (Random House, 1991), which is a collection of short stories. Compare the stories to *The House on Mango Street* and note similarities and differences in the ideas and writing style. Write an essay comparing the two works.

3. Discuss with your group Cisneros's telling of her story in a series of vignettes. Was this format effective? Could she have told the story another way that might have improved it? Work toward a consensus and then have your recorder share your conclusions with the members of other groups.

4. Write a poem about Mango Street, as Esperanza might write one.

5. In "Bums in the Attic," Esperanza states that once she owns her own house, she will not forget where she came from, and that when passing bums ask if they can come in, she will offer them the attic and ask them to stay. Will she really do this? Or once she has a nice house away from Mango Street will she forget her past? Discuss these questions with your group. When you are done, your recorder should share your conclusions.

6. *The House on Mango Street* is unusual in its format. Imagine that you were telling a friend about this book. What would you say? Write down your impressions.

Curriculum Connections:

1. Hispanics—Americans of Spanish or Latin American descent—comprise a major ethnic group in the United States. Research this group. From what countries do they come? In which areas of the U.S. are Hispanic populations concentrated? How well are they able to enter the mainstream? Write a report of your findings. (SS)

2. American culture incorporates the customs and traditions of many of the large ethnic groups that have settled here. It has always been this way. Find out how the cultures of people from Spanish and Latin American descent have found a place in the overall culture of the United States. Consider things like food, language, and specific events. Create a chart that shows your findings. (SS or A)

58. *Fallen Angels* by Walter Dean Myers
(Scholastic Inc., 1988)

Synopsis

Richie Perry is a fresh-faced, African-American teenager from Harlem who enlists in the army because he is not sure what to do after high school. Sent to Vietnam in the late 1960s just prior to the Tet offensive, he and a small squad of men experience war for the first time almost immediately. These young men—Peewee, Brunner, Johnson, Lobel, Monaco and Walowick—become friends and comrades as they fight the Viet Cong and the North Vietnamese army village by village, through rice paddies, ambushes, and exploding children. Although many come from rough-and-tumble city life, they still have childlike fears and anguish. Richie is wounded in a firefight but heals well enough to return to combat. He is wounded more gravely a second time after finding his way back to his comrades when he and Peewee are lost. Also wounded, Peewee joins Richie on a plane back to the United States. Both are changed forever, redefining their values and their views about God, death and relationships.

Ideas and Concepts to Highlight

1. Discuss the Vietnam War and how it was different from any previous conflict involving Americans. Talk about things such as public opinion, the treatment of returning veterans, political posturing and propaganda, and fighting in the jungle.

2. Discuss the military experience, including boot camp, machismo, tensions between blacks and whites, death and dying, camaraderie, assignments (orders), and relationships with family.

3. Discuss the state of Communism today. Encourage the class to discuss what they think the Vietnam War accomplished, and if today's situations were affected by it.

4. Note Richie's coming of age, and the major events in his life that influence the man he will become. Have the class talk about these events in a group setting.

Writing Connection: "The Impact of the War on Richie Perry"

We all experience defining moments that can redirect the course of our lives. War, like other great events, unquestionably changes people.

For this writing assignment, ask your students to consider how the war changed Richie Perry. Ask them to compare the Richie before the war to the one after the war. How was he changed? Will the changes affect him throughout the rest of his life? Instruct your students to answer the questions on Worksheet 58-1 and then write an essay detailing their opinions.

NAME _____ **DATE** _____ **SECTION** _____

58-1. THE IMPACT OF THE WAR ON RICHIE PERRY

Directions: Without doubt, the war changed Richie Perry. Answer the questions below, and then in an essay write your opinions about how the war did in fact change him.

1.   Describe Richie Perry in the boxes below.

Before the War	**After the War**

2.   What was the biggest change in him? _____

_____

_____ What caused this change? _____

_____

_____

3.   Will his war experiences affect him for the rest of his life? _____ Why or why not?

_____

_____

_____

_____

58-2. *QUESTIONS TO CONSIDER FOR FALLEN ANGELS*

1. Richie describes himself as a "middle-of-the-road kind of guy." Do you agree with this assessment? Explain, using examples from the story to support your answer.

2. Did white soldiers have different war experiences than black soldiers? Using examples from the book, write about what you think were the differences, if any. What caused the differences?

3. What was a "pacification mission"? During a "pacification mission," Richie insists to Lobel, "I am not a killer." Why did he say this? What did he mean?

4. Describe the terrain that Richie fought in. What was difficult about fighting there?

5. Describe the enemy. Was it always clear who the enemy was? Explain. How did this affect the Americans?

6. Why did Richie feel so strongly about his younger brother? What character traits and experience did Richie have that intensified his emotions regarding his brother?

7. Why did Richie's mother write to Peewee? Write a diary entry for Mabel on the day she wrote the letter.

8. During a mission, Richie says to himself, "Would God think I was a hypocrite, praying every time I was scared?" What is your opinion?

9. Describe Captain Stewart. What effect did he have on the men under his command?

10. Write a short epilogue to the book, using Richie's first-person point of view.

11. What part of the book had the greatest impact for you? Explain.

58-3. PROJECTS AND ACTIVITIES TO CONSIDER FOR
FALLEN ANGELS

1. Richie wrote to Lt. Carroll's wife about his death, and mentioned his bravery and leadership. Write a similar letter to Jenkins's mother, considering that he was a new private.

2. Describe, as Richie Perry did after Jenkins was caught in the trap, your first major experience with death.

3. Have a Vietnam War veteran speak to the class about his experiences. Then write an essay about your feelings before and after the presentation.

4. During most overseas conflicts that the United States has been involved in, it has been a popular custom for people to write to American soldiers whom they do not know. Write a letter to any of the characters in *Fallen Angels*.

5. Work with your group. From general reading, media proliferation, talking to others and the novel, what conclusions can you draw about the generation that fought (or did not fight) in the Vietnam War? How was it affected in the long run? What are its values? What is its legacy? What is its future?

Curriculum Connections:

1. What is the state of the U.S. armed forces today? Clip articles and photos and make a collage of news stories about them. Write about trends you find. How are the armed forces of today different from those of the Vietnam War? (SS or A)

2. Find articles and data from the Vietnam War era. Create a chart showing public opinion about American intervention in the conflict. Break out your data across age, region and ethnic lines. Contrast sentiment from the late 1960s with that near the end of the war. (SS or A)

3. Work with a partner and compare the Vietnam War with Desert Storm. Consult the necessary references and try to answer the following questions: What were the causes of each? How did the U.S. public react? How did public sentiment affect the war effort? What were the results of each war? Why were the results so different? Present your findings in the form of an oral report. Feel free to use charts and graphs to support your presentation. (SS)

59. *Hamlet* by William Shakespeare

Synopsis

A ghost with the likeness of the dead king of Denmark appears to guards at Elsinore Castle. The guards tell Prince Hamlet, who concludes that the ghost, who looks like his dead father, is a sign of trouble. Hamlet is despondent over his father's recent death and his mother Gertrude's hasty marriage to his Uncle Claudius, now King. Hamlet meets the ghost, who tells him that it is indeed the spirit of his father, and that Hamlet must avenge his murder by Claudius. Feigning madness, Hamlet makes his plans. Soon, however, he comes to question the ghost, and worries that it is the spirit of a demon sent to trick him. Although Claudius handles Hamlet with apparent consideration, the King is concerned about what Hamlet might do with the people's support. Polonius, Claudius's councillor, offers to have his

William Shakespeare

daughter, Ophelia, meet with Hamlet while the King and he secretly listen to the conversation in an effort to observe Hamlet. After hearing Hamlet's bitter discourse, the King becomes more convinced that Hamlet is a potential threat. When Hamlet instructs actors who perform a play to do it in a manner that implies Claudius's role in King Hamlet's death, Claudius orders Polonius to find out what he can about Hamlet's supposed madness. Polonius hides behind a wall hanging in Gertrude's room; when Hamlet goes there to speak to his mother, Hamlet becomes aware that someone is listening and he kills Polonius with a sword thrust. Certain now that Hamlet is dangerous, Claudius orders two members of the Court to take Hamlet to England where he will be killed. But Hamlet thwarts the plan and returns to Denmark, where Ophelia has killed herself in despondency over Hamlet's murder of her father Polonius. As soon as Claudius hears of this, he engages Laertes, Polonius's son, to challenge Hamlet to a duel and through treachery kill him. It is decided that Laertes's rapier will not be blunted, and that Laertes will dip the tip in poison. Hamlet is challenged to a duel by Laertes. The duel takes place at Court, in front of Claudius and Gertrude. During the duel, Gertrude mistakenly drinks from a poisoned cup Claudius had meant for Hamlet (just in case Laertes didn't kill the Prince). In the meantime, Laertes wounds Hamlet with the poisoned rapier. The two scuffle and exchange rapiers, and Hamlet wounds Laertes. When his mother falls, she tells Hamlet that she has been poisoned and Hamlet kills Claudius. Laertes and Hamlet also die.

Ideas and Concepts to Highlight

1. Note the setting and time period. Explain that the play was written during the Renaissance, a time of revival in Europe during which the arts, literature, and learning flourished.

2. Discuss Hamlet's multifaceted character.

3. Emphasize the two major issues that lead to Hamlet's tragedy—Claudius murdering his father and then marrying his mother. Note how these issues underlie the conflict throughout the play.

4. Discuss the motif of revenge.

5. Discuss the difficulty Hamlet has in deciding what to do.

Writing Connection: "Prince Hamlet"

Hamlet is one of the most enigmatic characters in literature. Driven by his need for revenge, he decides to play the role of a madman, yet, after a while, the audience begins to wonder if in fact his grief and sorrow haven't truly made him insane. He lusts for revenge, but often wavers, not sure of what action to take. He is a tortured soul.

For this writing assignment, ask your students to consider what type of man Hamlet was, and then write an essay analyzing his character. Completing Worksheet 59-1 will help students to organize their thoughts.

NAME _____ DATE _____ SECTION _____

59-1. PRINCE HAMLET

Directions: In many ways Hamlet is one of the most puzzling and tragic characters in literature. Answer the questions below and then write an essay analyzing his character.

1.   List five facts about Hamlet's character. _____
    _____
    _____
    _____
    _____
    _____

2.   What was Hamlet's driving force in the play? _____
    _____
    _____
    _____

3.   Why didn't Hamlet kill Claudius at his first opportunity? _____
    _____
    _____
    _____

4.   Was Hamlet acting insane, or was he insane? _____ Explain. _____
    _____
    _____
    _____

5.   Given his character and his desire for revenge, was there any way for Hamlet to escape tragedy? _____
    _____
    _____

© 1994 by The Center for Applied Research in Education

59-2. *QUESTIONS TO CONSIDER FOR*
HAMLET

1. What troubles Hamlet at the opening of the play?

2. When Horatio tells Hamlet about the apparition, who does Hamlet think it might be? What does he decide to do? What type of omen does Hamlet think the apparition is?

3. Describe Hamlet's meeting with the ghost. Who is the ghost? Why has it appeared? What does the ghost tell Hamlet to do? What might be some other reasons for the ghost appearing?

4. Why does Hamlet act as if he were mad? What does Polonius think the reason for the madness is? Do you agree with him? Why or why not?

5. How does Claudius react to the performance of *The Murder of Gonzago?* Why? What does his reaction convince Hamlet of?

6. Describe Claudius and Gertrude. What does each think of Hamlet? How does each treat him? What does Hamlet think of them?

7. Why does Hamlet kill Polonius? How does Hamlet act after he finds out who he killed? What is your opinion of his actions?

8. How does Claudius feel about what he did to King Hamlet? As he is praying, Hamlet enters with his sword drawn. Why doesn't he kill Claudius?

9. Why does Claudius decide to send Hamlet to England? What does he plan for Hamlet upon Hamlet's arrival there? What happens instead?

10. How does Claudius hope to eliminate Hamlet during the Prince's duel with Laertes? Describe what happens during the duel.

11. Would you describe Hamlet as a tragic hero? Why or why not?

59-3. PROJECTS AND ACTIVITIES TO CONSIDER FOR
HAMLET

1. In Act III, Scene i, lines 56-89, Hamlet gives his famous soliloquy, "To be or not to be..." Interpret these lines and apply their meaning to our current era.

2. Imagine that Hamlet had followed his father to the throne instead of Claudius following King Hamlet. Would Hamlet have made a better king than Claudius? Which man had the better skills to be king? Write an essay.

3. Watch the movie version of *Hamlet* (1990) starring Mel Gibson. Compare it to the play. Does it follow the action of the play closely? Write an essay and discuss the film's realism. Do you think the producers created a realistic setting? Did the actors and actresses present believable characters? What was your overall impression of the film?

4. Select a favorite scene of the play and, with the help of classmates, act it out. Try to read the dialogue as realistically as possible to capture the flavor of the times.

5. Read another of Shakespeare's plays and compare the lead character to Hamlet. (*Macbeth* would be a good choice.) How are they similar? How are they different? Is there a possibility of either escaping destiny?

6. Claudius attains the Danish throne through deceit. Unlike some villains who clearly exhibit evil and have no redeeming qualities, Claudius is a man of various emotions. He is an intelligent and cautious man. At one point he even feels guilty for what he has done, but this doesn't stop him from plotting against Hamlet. Working with a partner, discuss Claudius's character and write a character sketch.

Curriculum Connections:

1. Research William Shakespeare. What kind of man was he? Include the major facts about his life. Did he really write all the plays attributed to him? Write a short biography. (SS)

2. Research the monarchies of Europe during the Renaissance. Concentrate on a few that interest you the most and answer the following questions in a report: Upon a king's death, how was succession decided? How did royal families retain power? What types of political alliances were formed and what were their purposes? What was meant by "divine right"? Did kings exercise absolute power during the Renaissance? (SS)

60. *Memory* by Margaret Mahy
(J.M. Dent & Sons Ltd., 1987)

Synopsis

Jonny Dart, 19 years old and haunted by his sister's accidental death, tries one evening to find her best friend, Bonny, in an effort to cope with some of the memories. But during his wanderings through the city that night, he meets Sophie, a sufferer of Alzheimer's disease, and follows her to her squalid house. Jonny, feeling like an outcast himself, takes refuge with her, partially to escape trouble he had gotten into while searching for Bonny but also to sort out his painful past. Over the course of a few days he begins to take care of the amnesiac Sophie, who believes him to be a relative to whom she had once been attracted. People from his past appear in coincidences and he is forced to face the parts of his life that he has chosen to bury. As Sophie's guardian and friend, however, he realizes that he has responsibility to others beside himself, and his life takes on new meaning. He ends his brooding and is able to make peace with some of the abuse and fear he had sustained as a youngster.

Ideas and Concepts to Highlight

1. Discuss Alzheimer's disease, amnesia, and senility, and note how memory and a person's past create his or her present conditions. Have the class speculate on how losing memory could rearrange their personal world.

2. Discuss Jonny's coming of age as a man, and how maturity is more often attained through experience rather than simply the passage of time or the reaching of a certain age.

3. Have the class reflect on the welfare of the aged, and how they often require as much care and comfort as children but are less likely to receive it.

4. Discuss people's feeling of responsibility to suffering strangers, and how helping them can bring good feelings to the provider.

Writing Connection: "Being Old"

Jonny's experience with Sophie helped him to understand some of the problems of growing old. Aging is a hard concept for young people to understand—when you're young you feel that youth lasts forever.

For this writing assignment, ask your students to think about an older person they know. This may be a grandparent, older relative, or even a neighbor. What type of relationship do they have with this person? Do they understand him or her? Does this person understand them? How might any gaps in understanding be bridged? Instruct them to answer the questions on Worksheet 60-1, and then write about their experiences.

60-1. BEING OLD

Directions: Through his relationship with Sophie, Jonny came to understand many of the problems of old people. Think about your relationship with a special grandparent, old relative or neighbor. Answer the questions below and then write about this relationship.

1. What is the name of this person, and his or her relationship to you? _____

_____

2. On what things do the two of you agree? _____

_____

_____

_____

3. On what things do you disagree?_____

_____

_____

_____

4. Why do you see some things differently? _____

_____

_____

5. What do you value, or cherish, most about this person? _____

_____

_____

6. Is there any way you would want to improve your relationship with this person? _____

If yes, how?_____

_____

_____

© 1994 by The Center for Applied Research in Education

60-2. QUESTIONS TO CONSIDER FOR
<u>MEMORY</u>

1. Why do you think that Jonny had a difficult time associating with people? Which of his character traits are responsible? What prejudices did people hold against him? Were those feelings about him valid? Explain.

2. When Jonny first met Sophie, he said, "I'm glad to meet you at last. You could be a big help to me." What do you think he meant?

3. How is Jonny affected by meeting Sophie? What changes occur in him?

4. What is the significance of Marribel Road to Jonny?

5. In Chapter 9, Jonny wonders "whether or not one was entitled to turn away from the wheel of fortune because its magical accidents offered something one didn't want to get mixed up with." What did he mean by this? Do you agree with him? Why or why not?

6. Discuss the function of the song lyrics interspersed throughout the novel.

7. Define your understanding of Jonny's term, "pythoness."

8. Compare the characters of Jonny and Bonny in terms of their treatment of Sophie.

9. Jonny often second-guesses himself, recalling situations where he might have acted differently or said something else. Recall situations where you have had this self-doubt. Why does Jonny do it? Does he do it less as his character evolves? Support your answer.

10. Try to find a specific moment in the story where Jonny makes peace with his sister's death. Support your answer.

60-3. PROJECTS AND ACTIVITIES TO CONSIDER FOR
MEMORY

1. Invite a person representing a support group for Alzheimer's caregivers to speak to the class. Write a report on the visit.

2. Work with your group and discuss this question: How do you think the story would have been different if Jonny had found Bonny Benedicta in the opening scene? After your discussion, work together to reorganize the story and then present it to the class in outline form.

3. Describe a situation in which you wanted to escape responsibility. What factors went into your decision? What were your feelings? Compare them to Jonny's.

4. Work with a partner and find out what social services are available through local government or non-profit organizations to people like Sophie. Make a chart, listing the pros and cons of the different services, then select one for Sophie. Explain your reasoning to your group.

5. In Chapter 14, Jonny imagines "what he might think if he were a social worker and someone like him turned up and told a strange tale of life with Sophie." Imagine that you are that social worker. What would you think if someone told you about Sophie and Jonny? Write about what your impressions would be.

Curriculum Connections:

1. Sketch Sophie's house, including the giant water tap jutting from its front. (A)

2. Research the Maori Land Treaty and the activism that Bonny's sister embraced. What is its current status? How do you feel about it? How does it compare with the Native American situation in North America? (SS)

3. *Memory* is set in New Zealand. Select another culture with which you are familiar. How would the story be different if set in that culture? Use examples from the culture's mores and norms. Consult the necessary references for accuracy, and write a brief report. (SS)

4. Sophie suffered from Alzheimer's disease. Research this disorder and find out its causes and treatments. As yet, there is no cure, but recent advances offer hope for limiting the disease's effects. What are these advances? Present your findings orally to the class. (Sci)